EASY PIANO

2ND EDITION

THE BEST CHILDREN'S SON

T0083302

ISBN 978-1-4950-6229-2

HAL•LEONARD®
CORPORATION

7777 W. BLUEMOUND RD. P.O. BOX 13819 MILWAUKEE, WI 53213

Visit Hal Leonard Online at
www.halleonard.com

ALOUETTE

Traditional

Moderately

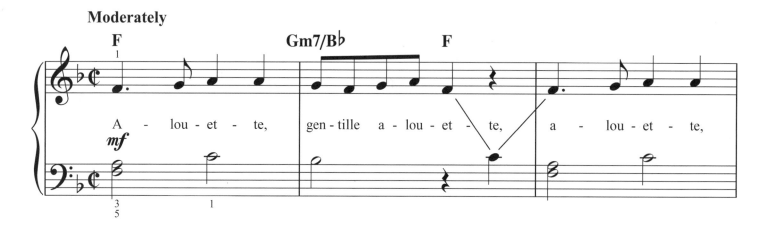

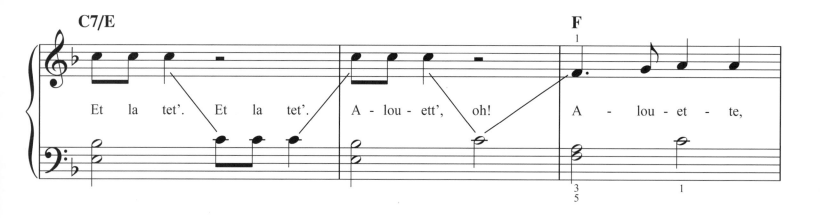

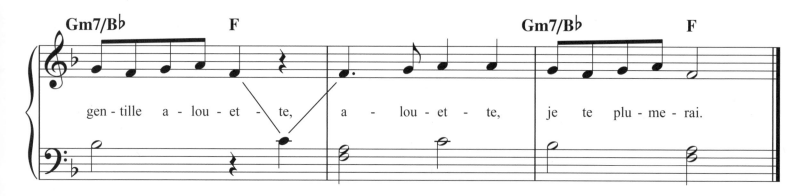

ALPHABET SONG

Traditional

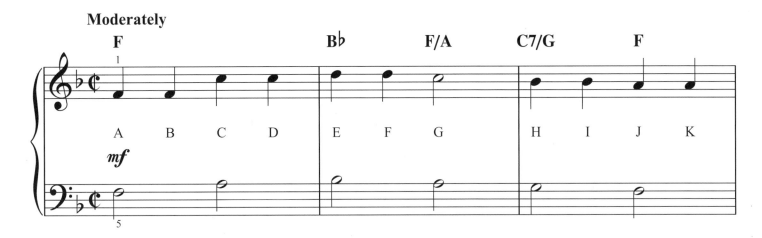

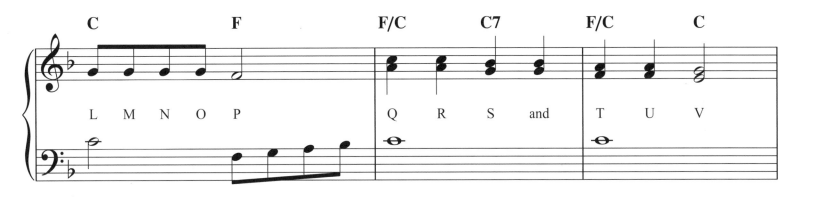

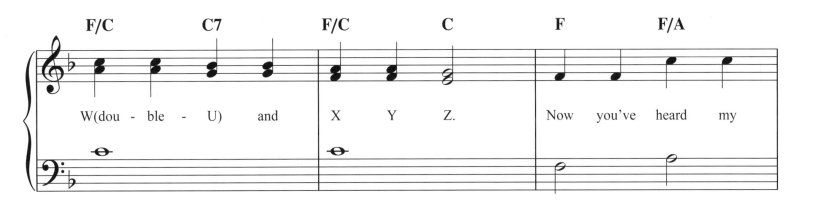

AMAZING GRACE

Words by JOHN NEWTON
Traditional American Melody

Slowly, with reverence

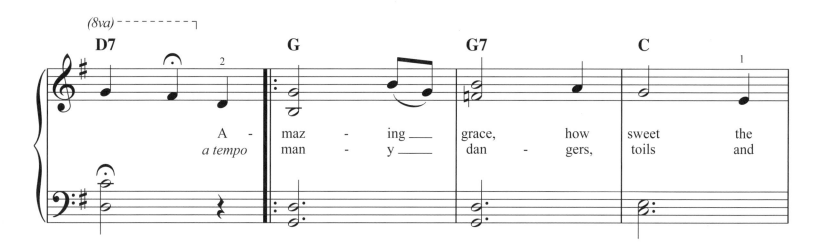

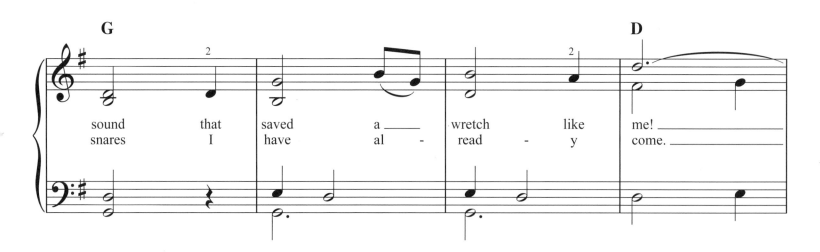

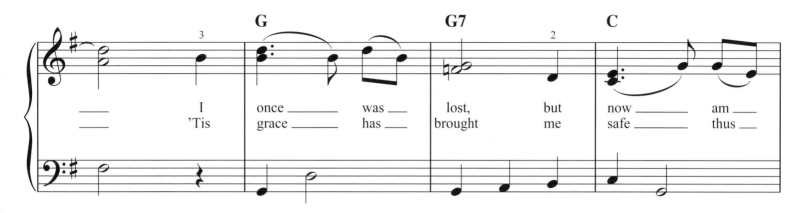

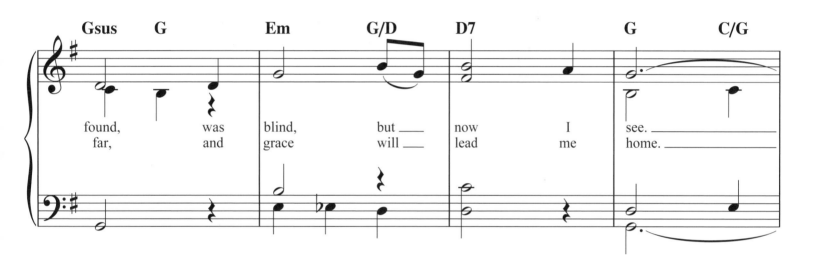

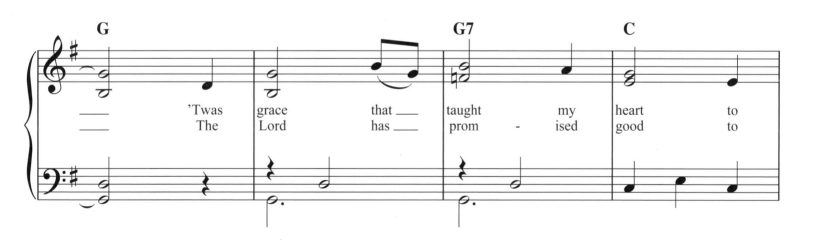

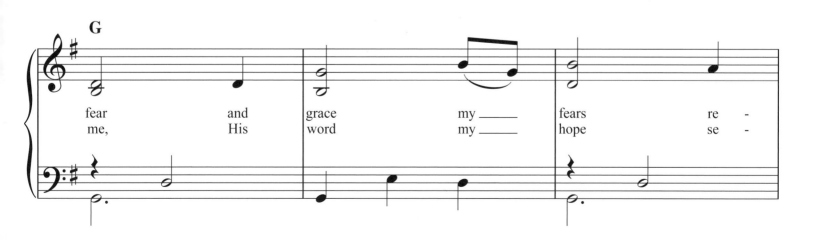

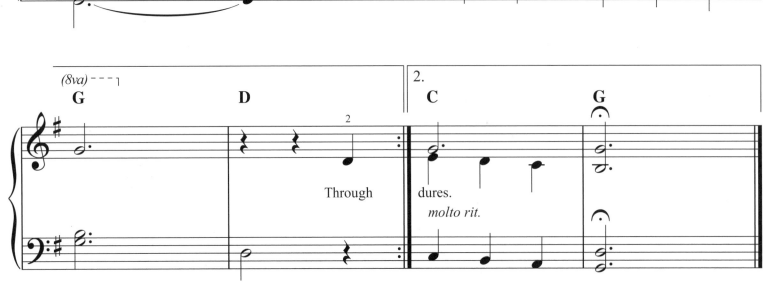

BE KIND TO YOUR PARENTS

from FANNY

Words and Music by
HAROLD ROME

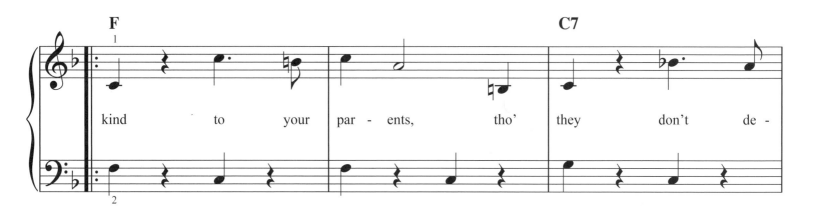

ner - vous and o - ver ex - ci - ted, con - fused from their

dai - ly storm and strife. _____ Just keep in mind, _____

_____ tho' it sounds odd, I know, _____ most par - ents once were

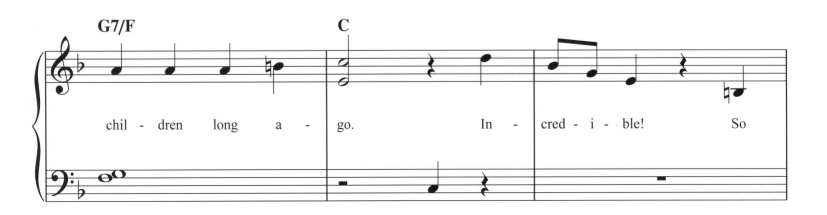

chil - dren long a - go. In - cred - i - ble! So

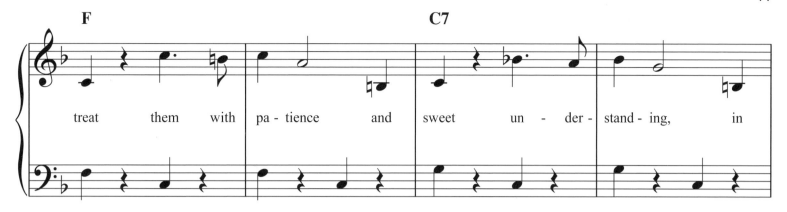

treat them with pa - tience and sweet un - der - stand - ing, in

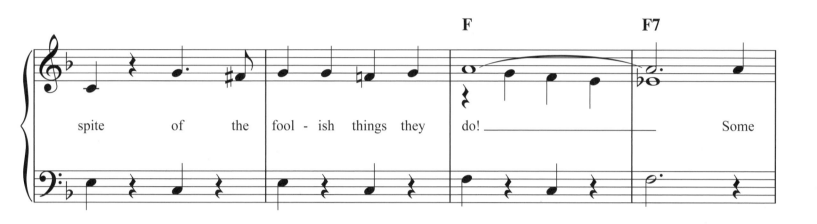

spite of the fool - ish things they do! _____ Some

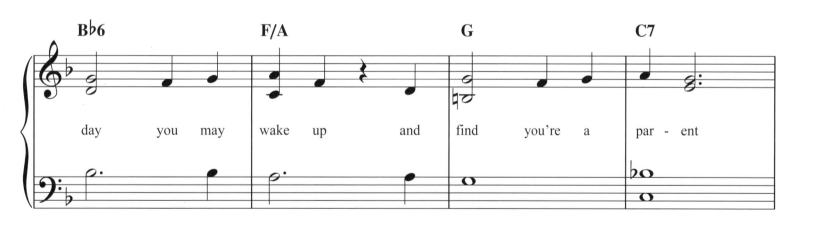

day you may wake up and find you're a par - ent

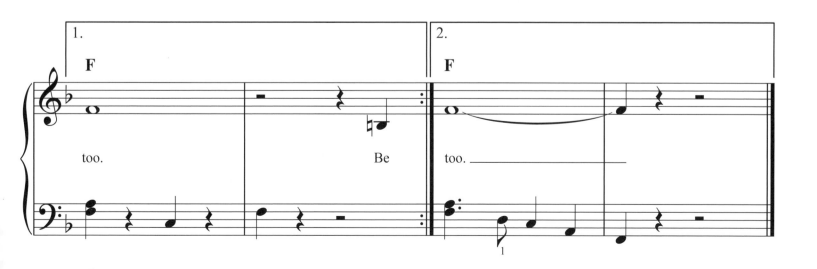

1.
too.   Be

2.
too. _____

ANY DREAM WILL DO

from JOSEPH AND THE AMAZING TECHNICOLOR® DREAMCOAT

Music by ANDREW LLOYD WEBBER
Lyrics by TIM RICE

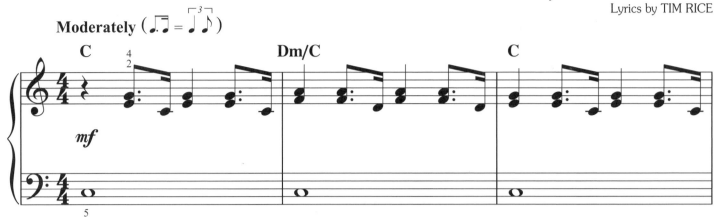

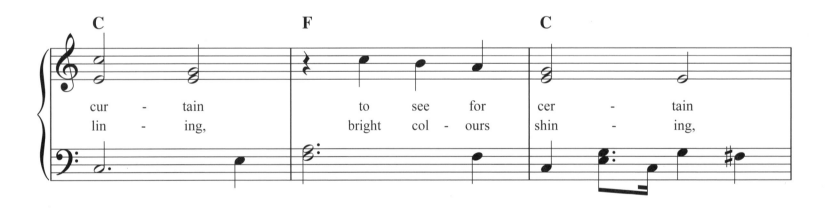

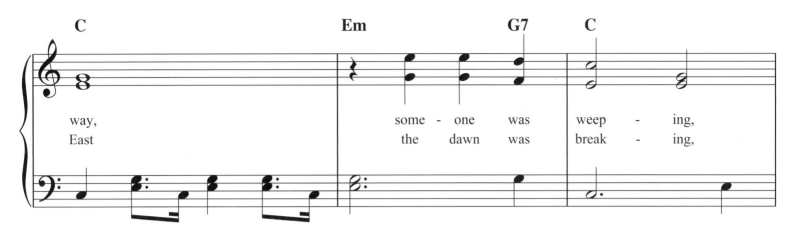

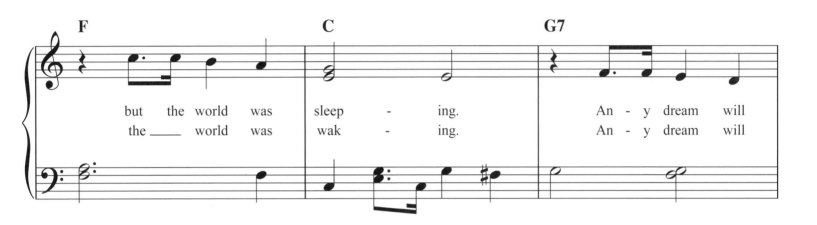

14

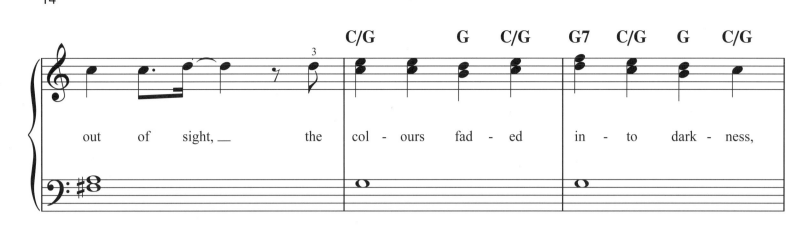

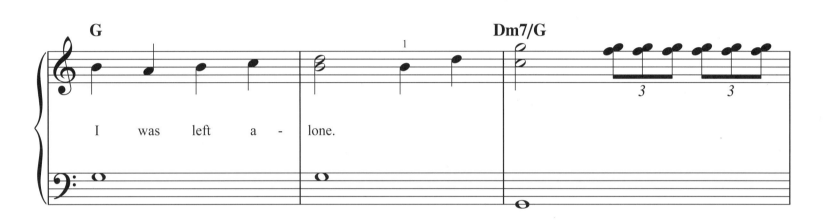

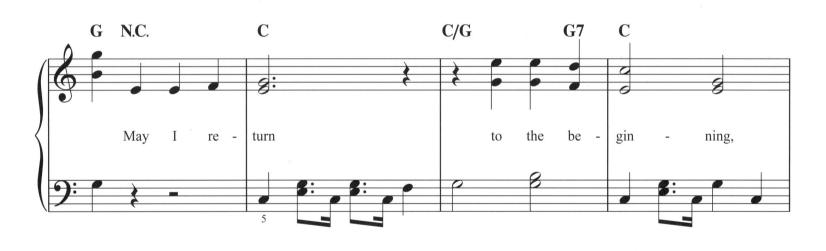

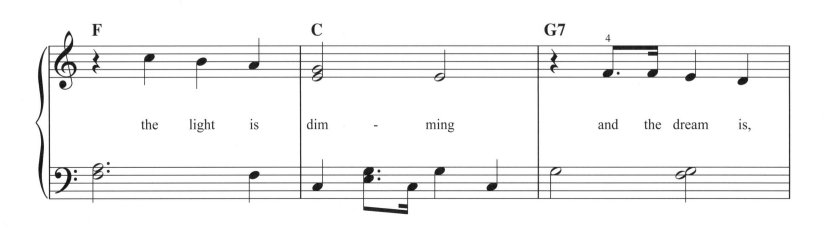

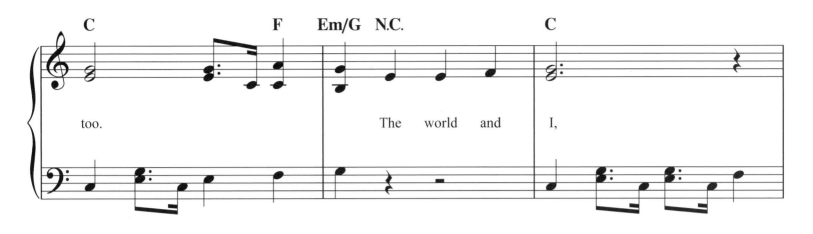

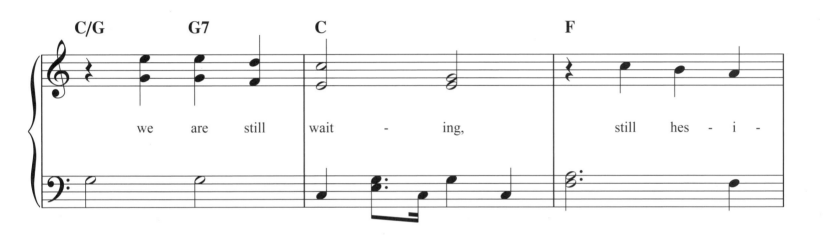

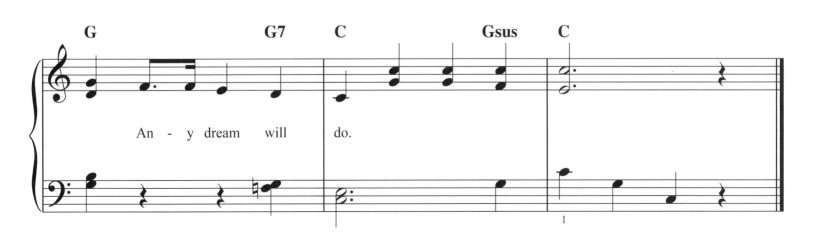

BABY MINE
from Walt Disney's DUMBO

Words by NED WASHINGTON
Music by FRANK CHURCHILL

Moderately slow

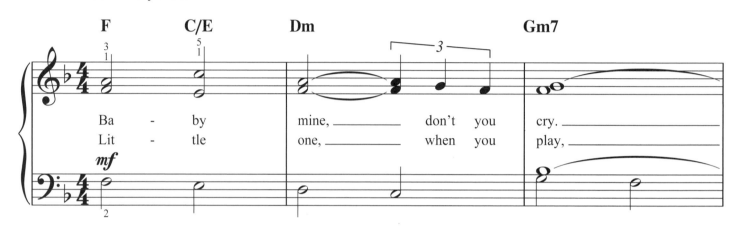

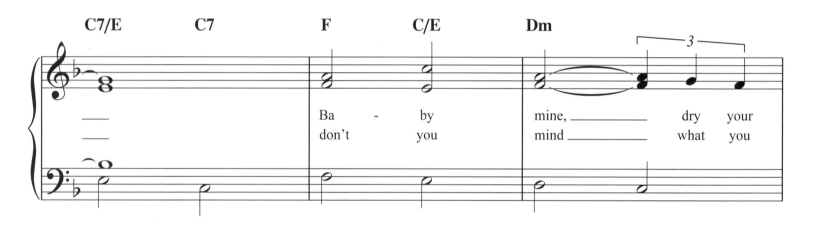

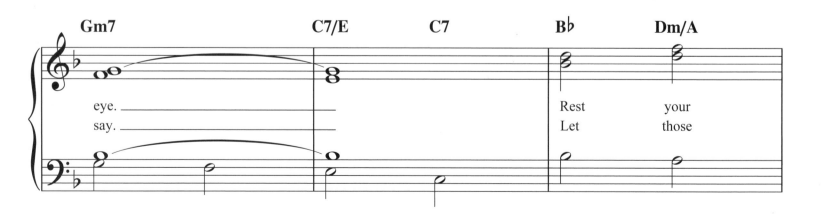

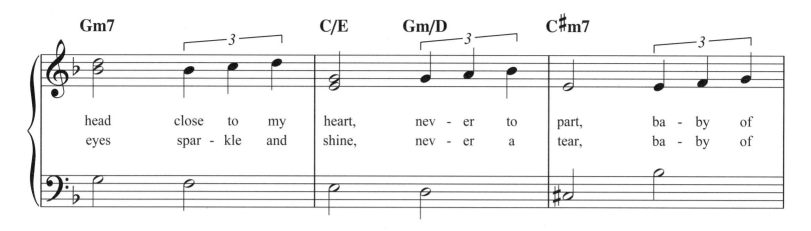

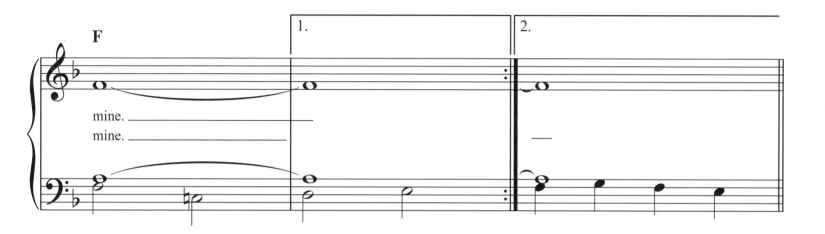

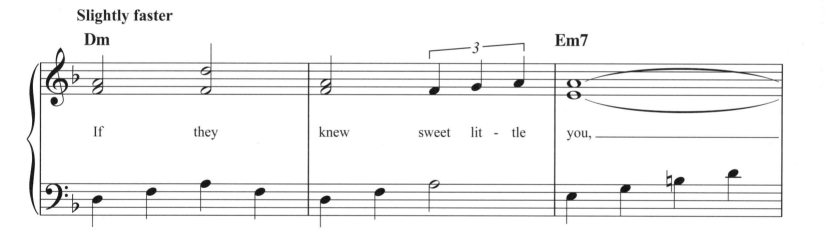

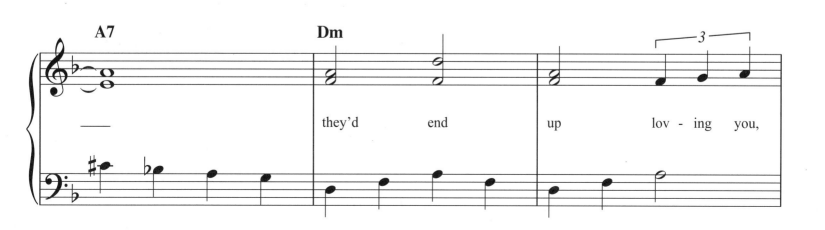

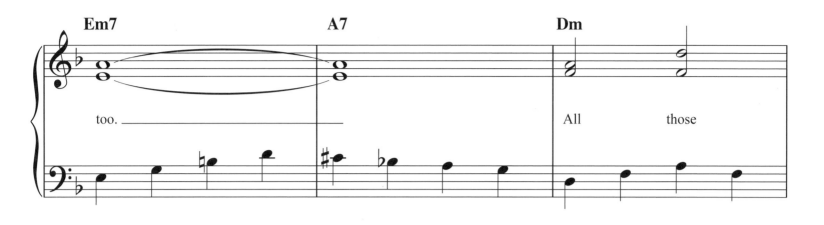

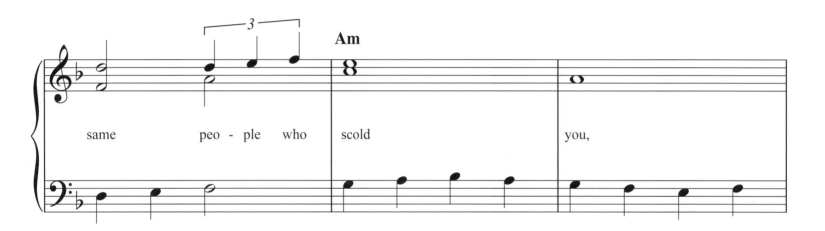

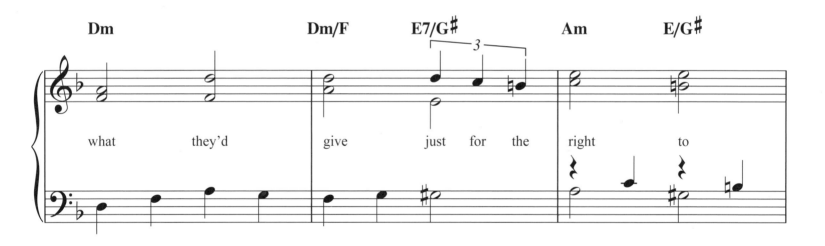

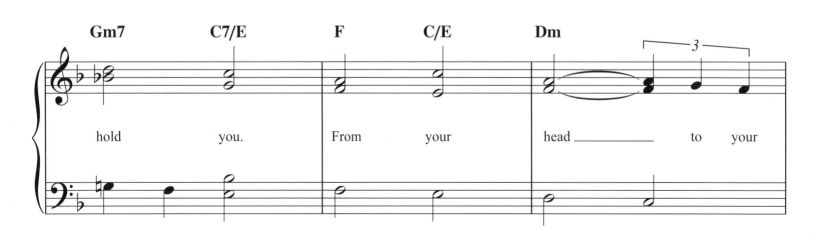

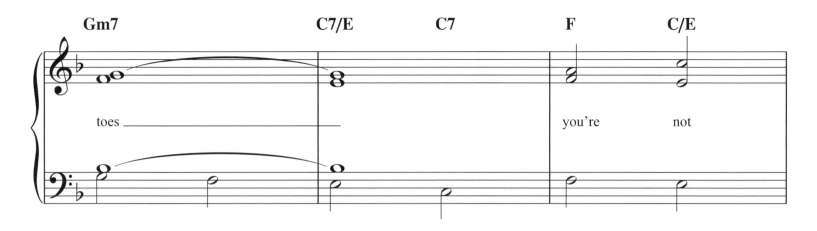

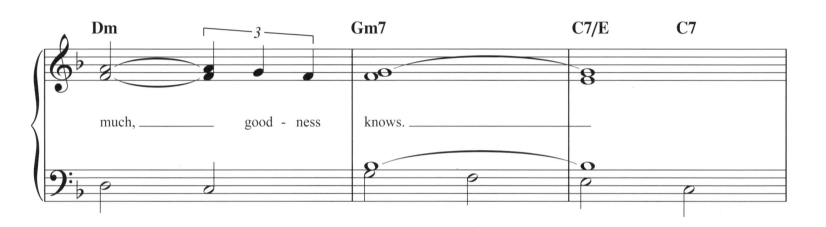

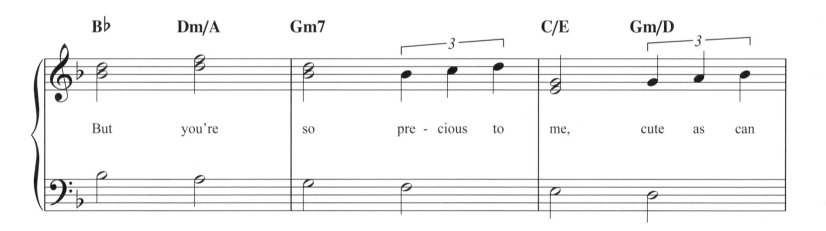

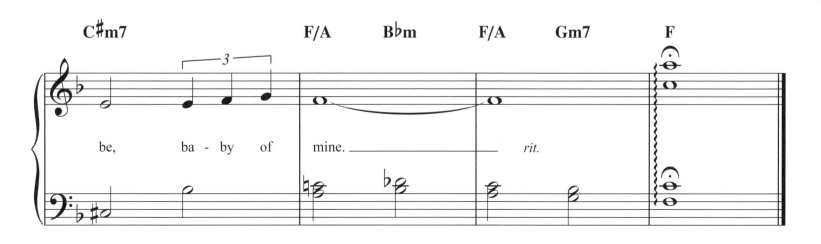

THE BALLAD OF DAVY CROCKETT

from Walt Disney's DAVY CROCKETT

Words by TOM BLACKBURN
Music by GEORGE BRUNS

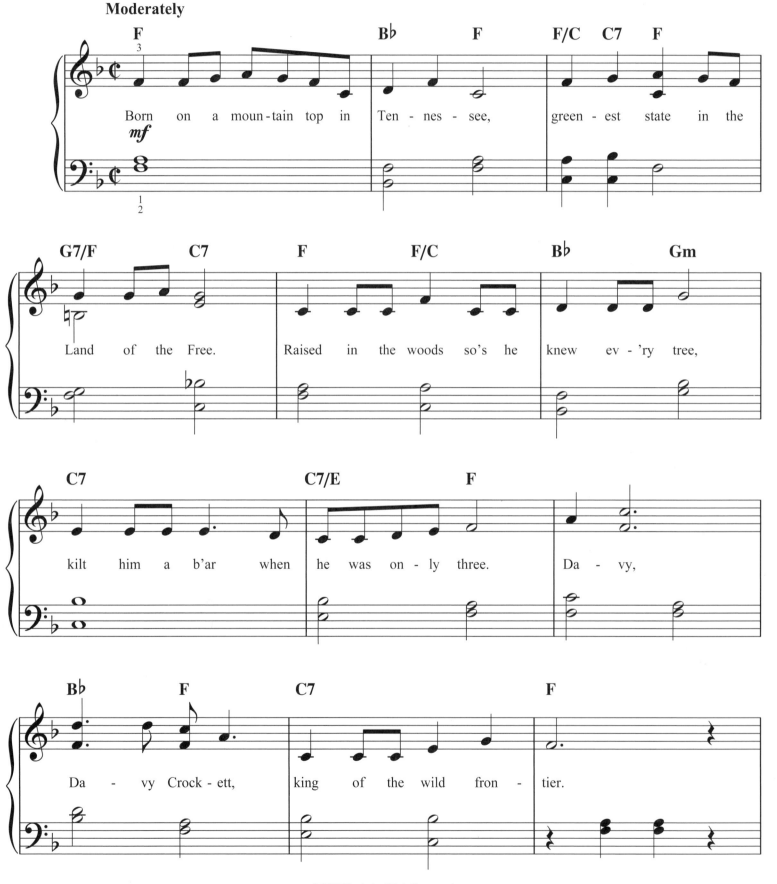

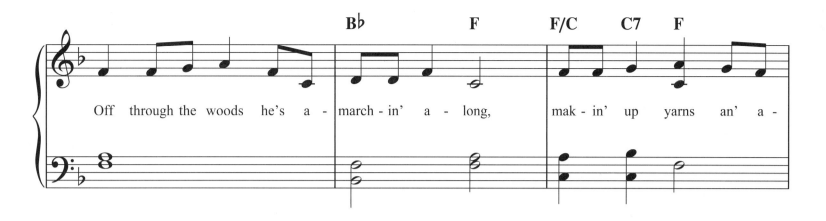

Off through the woods he's a - march-in' a - long, mak-in' up yarns an' a-

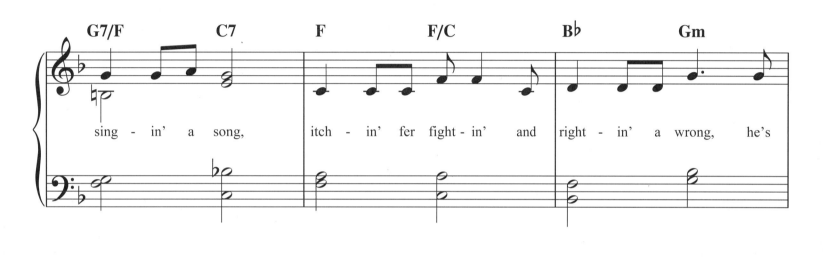

sing - in' a song, itch - in' fer fight-in' and right-in' a wrong, he's

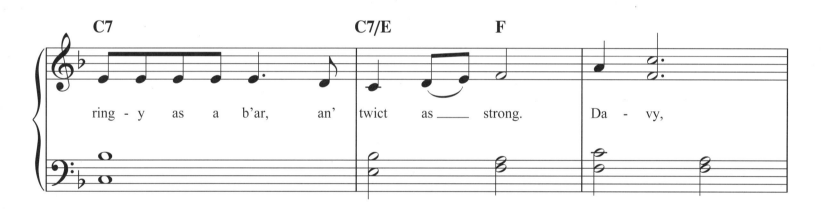

ring - y as a b'ar, an' twict as ___ strong. Da - vy,

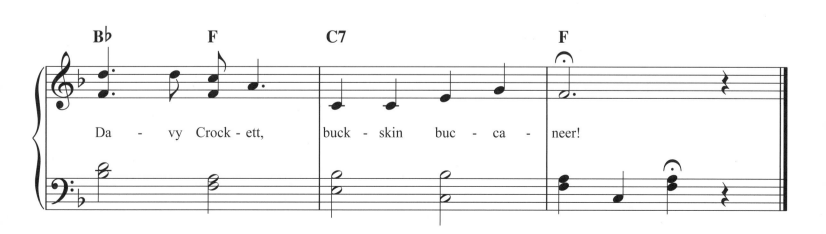

Da - vy Crock - ett, buck - skin buc - ca - neer!

THE BARE NECESSITIES

from Walt Disney's THE JUNGLE BOOK

Words and Music by
TERRY GILKYSON

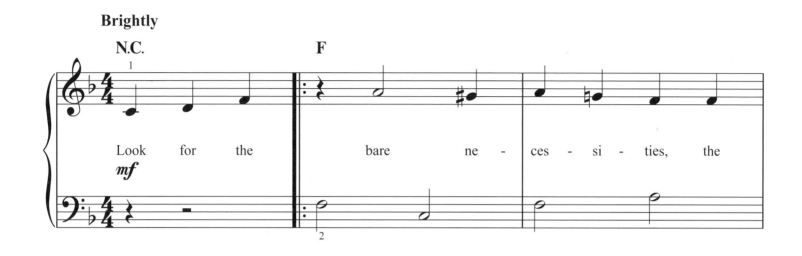

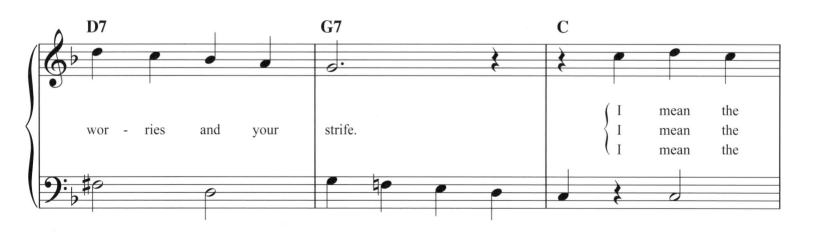

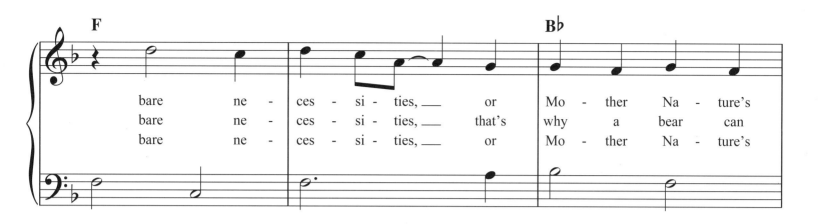

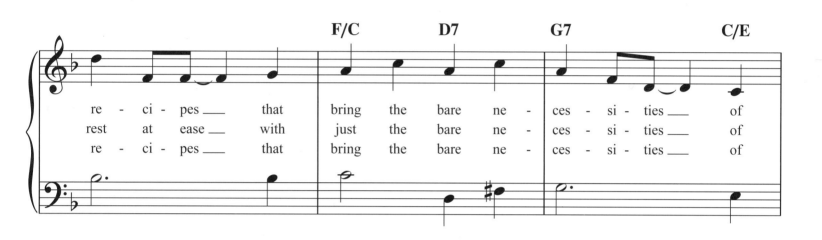

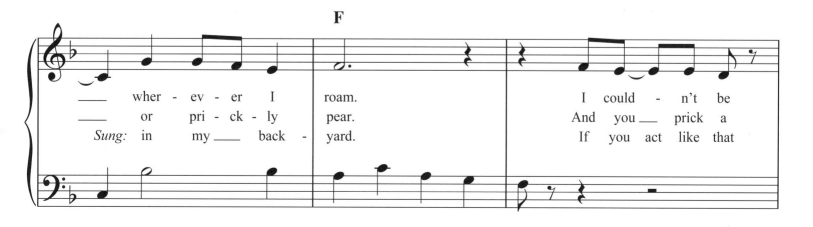

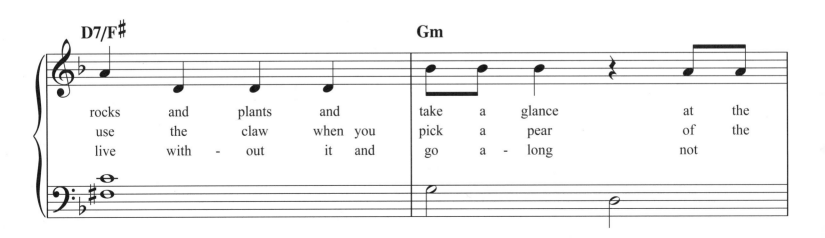

BEAUTY AND THE BEAST

from Walt Disney's BEAUTY AND THE BEAST

Music by ALAN MENKEN
Lyrics by HOWARD ASHMAN

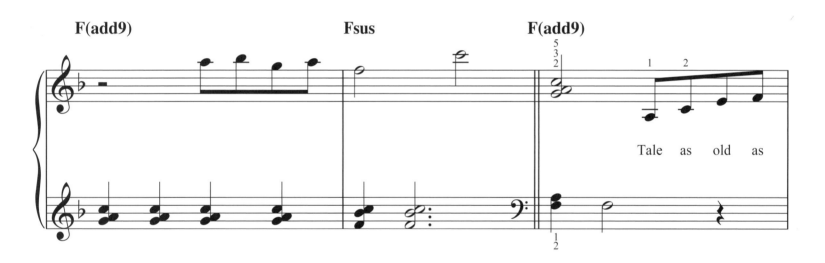

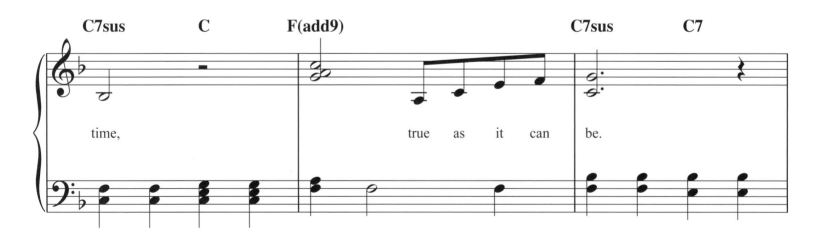

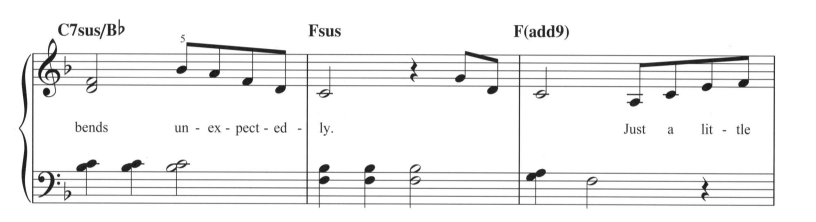

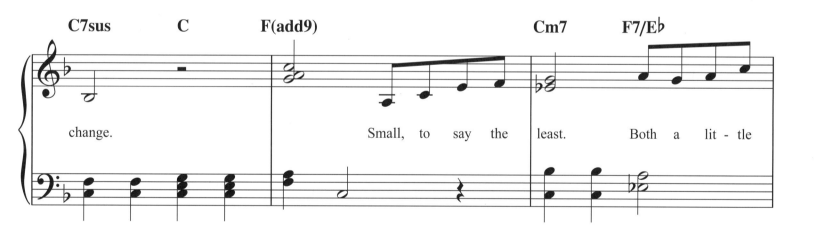

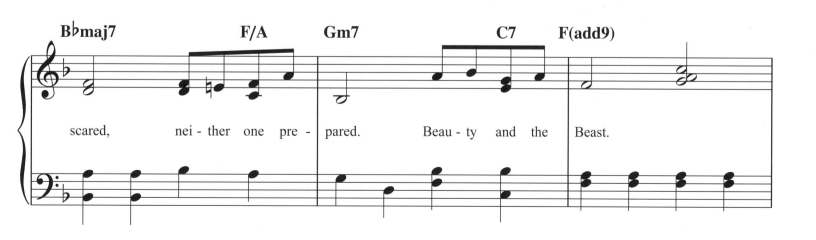

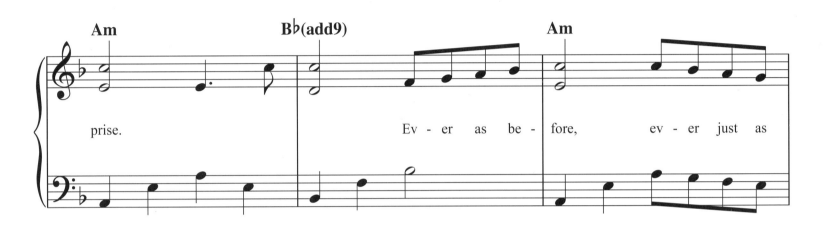

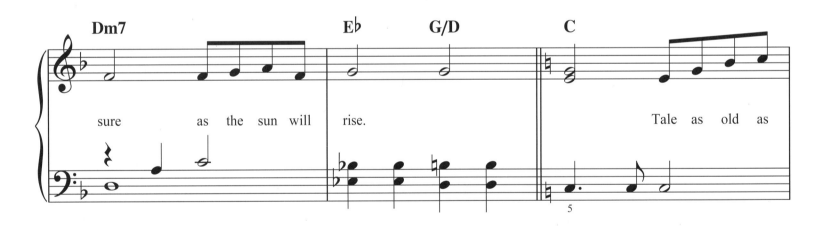

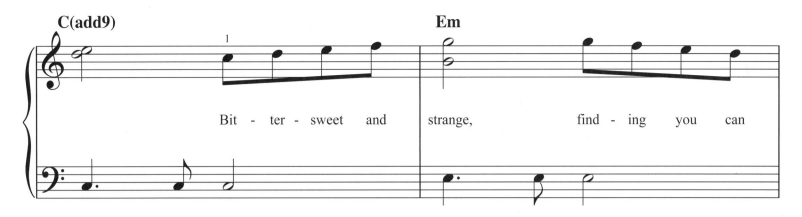

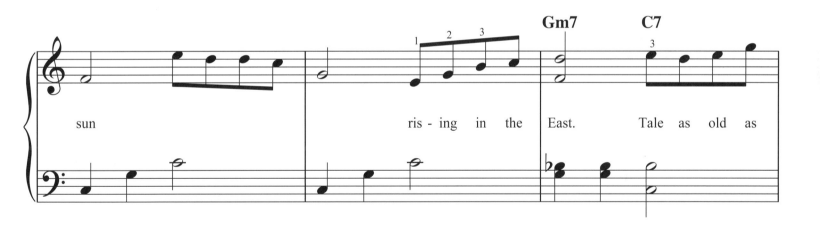

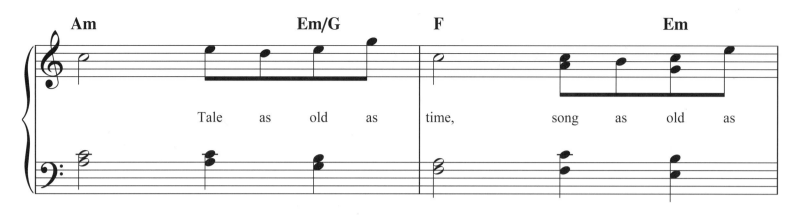

Tale as old as time, song as old as

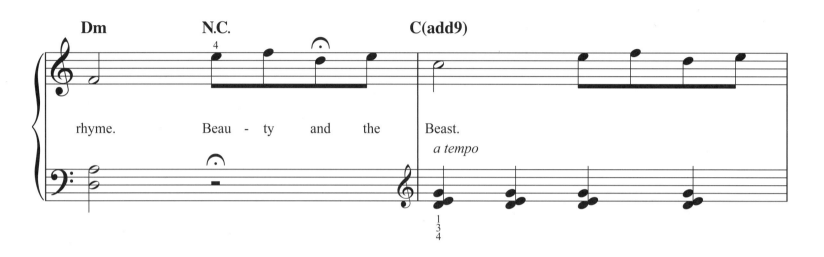

rhyme. Beau - ty and the Beast.

a tempo

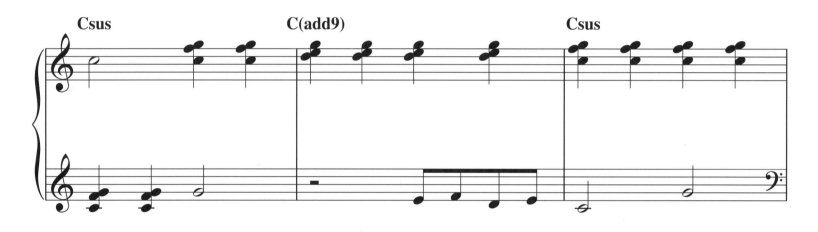

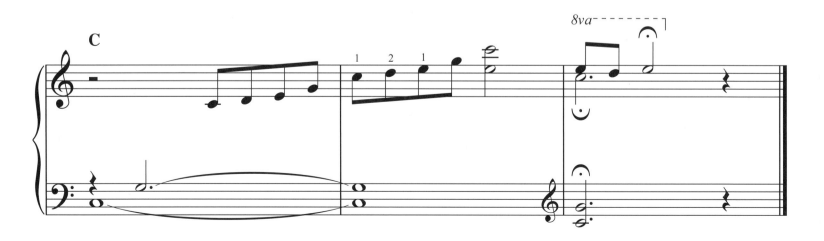

BIBBIDI-BOBBIDI-BOO
(The Magic Song)
from Walt Disney's CINDERELLA

Words by JERRY LIVINGSTON
Music by MACK DAVID and AL HOFFMAN

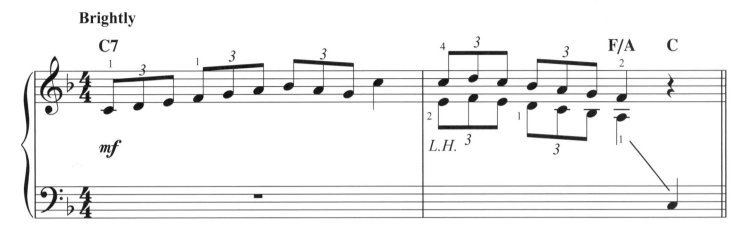

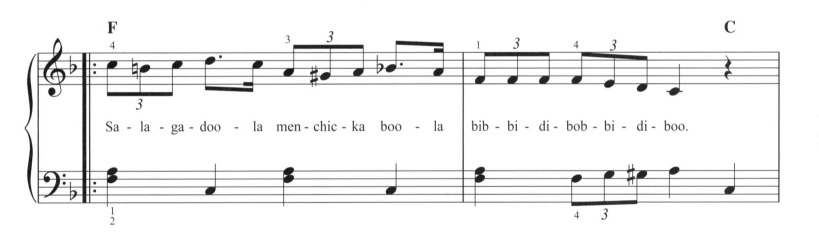

Sa - la - ga - doo - la men - chic - ka boo - la bib - bi - di - bob - bi - di - boo.

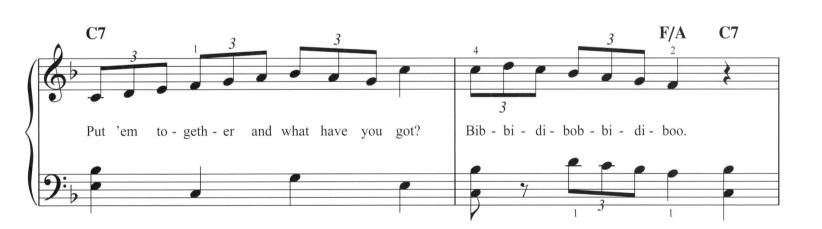

Put 'em to - geth - er and what have you got? Bib - bi - di - bob - bi - di - boo.

Sa - la - ga - doo - la men - chic - ka boo - la bib - bi - di - bob - bi - di - boo.

It - 'll do mag - ic, be - lieve it or not, bib - bi - di - bob - bi - di - boo.

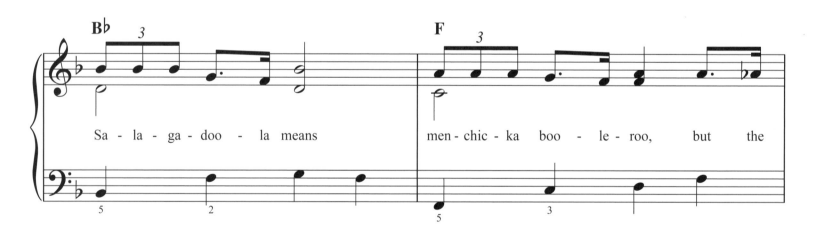

Sa - la - ga - doo - la means men - chic - ka boo - le - roo, but the

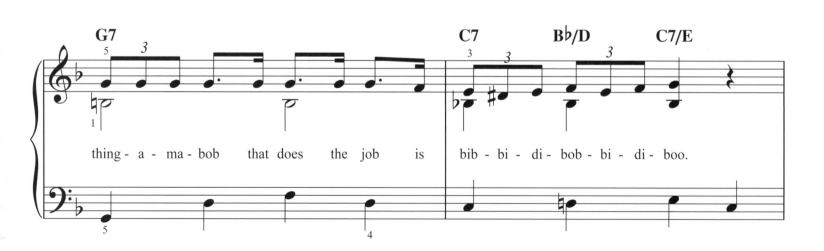

thing - a - ma - bob that does the job is bib - bi - di - bob - bi - di - boo.

THE BIBLE TELLS ME SO

Words and Music by
DALE EVANS

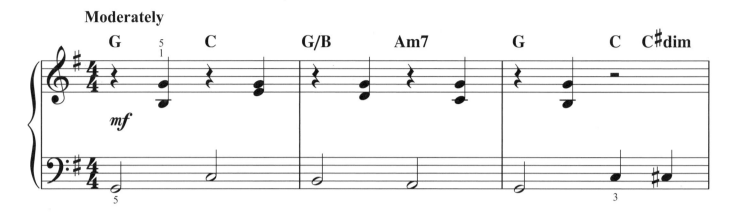

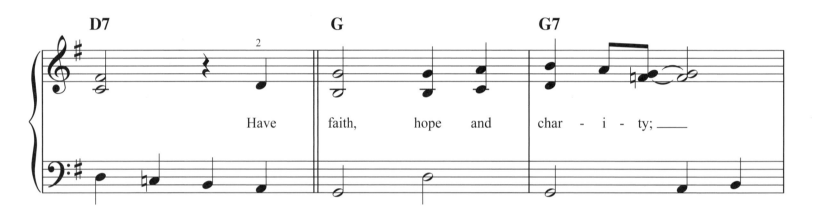

Have faith, hope and char - i - ty; ____

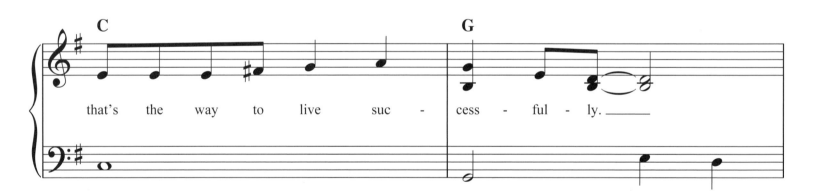

that's the way to live suc - cess - ful - ly. ____

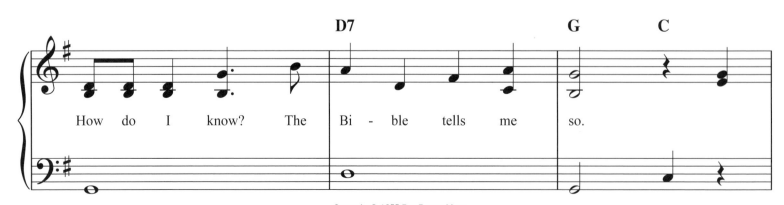

How do I know? The Bi - ble tells me so.

Do good to your en - e - mies, ___

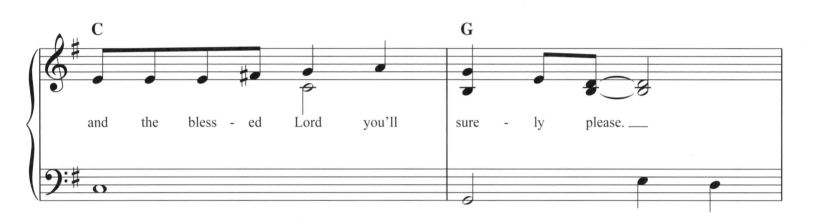

and the bless - ed Lord you'll sure - ly please. ___

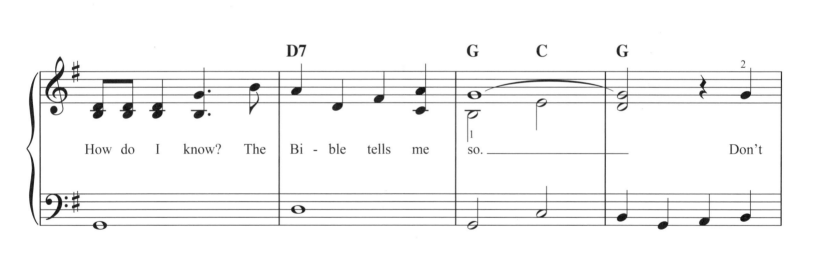

How do I know? The Bi - ble tells me so. ___ Don't

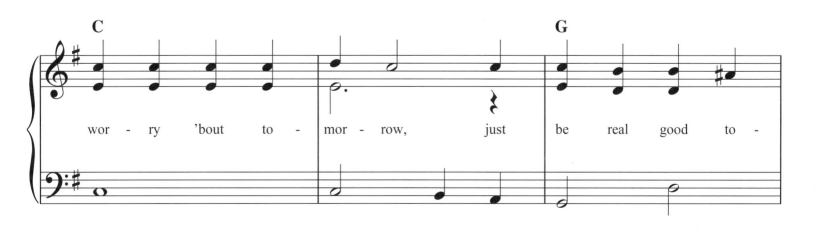

wor - ry 'bout to - mor - row, just be real good to -

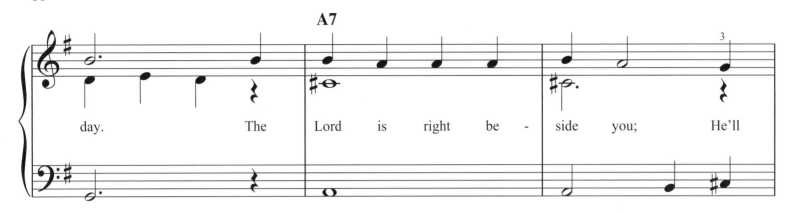

day.   The Lord is right be - side you;   He'll

guide you all the way.   Have faith, hope and   char - i - ty; ___

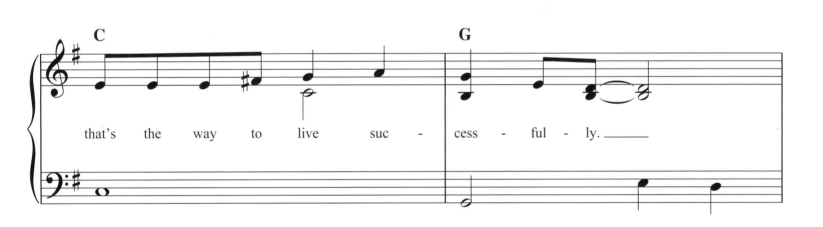

that's the way to live suc - cess - ful - ly. ___

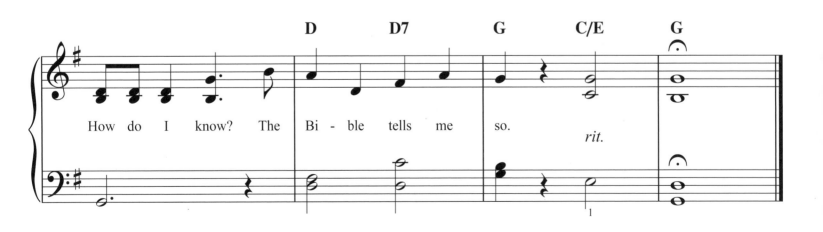

How do I know? The Bi - ble tells me so.

THE BLUE TAIL FLY
(Jimmy Crack Corn)

Words and Music by
DANIEL DECATUR EMMETT

Moderately

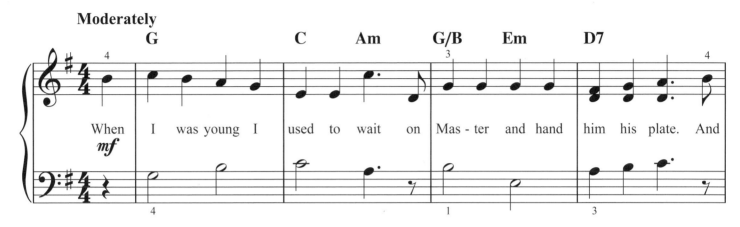

When I was young I used to wait on Mas-ter and hand him his plate. And

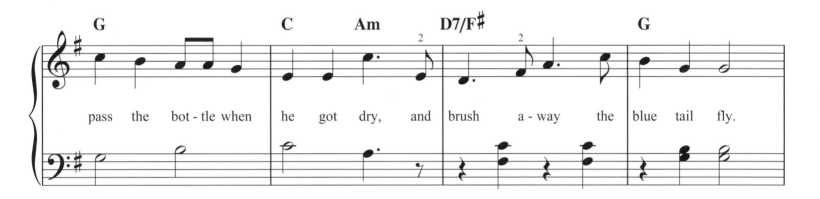

pass the bot-tle when he got dry, and brush a-way the blue tail fly.

Jim-my crack corn and I don't care, Jim-my crack corn and I don't care,

Jim-my crack corn and I don't care, my mas-ter's gone a-way.

"C" IS FOR COOKIE

from the Television Series SESAME STREET

Words and Music by
JOE RAPOSO

CASTLE ON A CLOUD
from LES MISÉRABLES

Music by CLAUDE-MICHEL SCHÖNBERG
Lyrics by ALAIN BOUBLIL, JEAN-MARC NATEL
and HERBERT KRETZMER

Very slowly

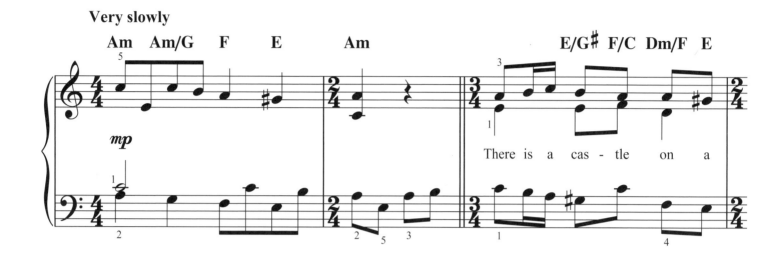

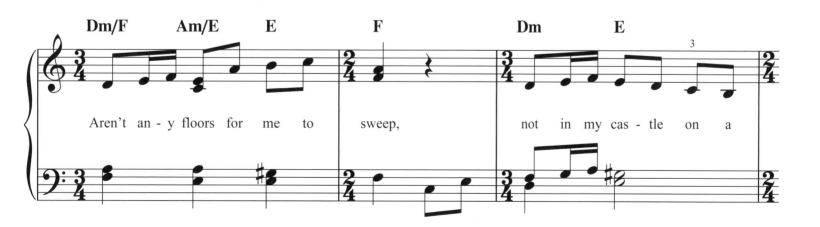

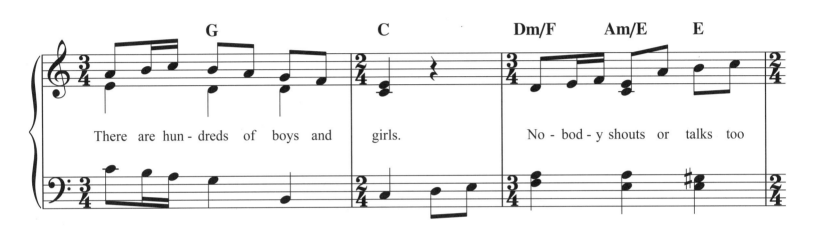

nice to see and she's soft to touch. She says, "Co - sette, I love you ver - y much."

rall.

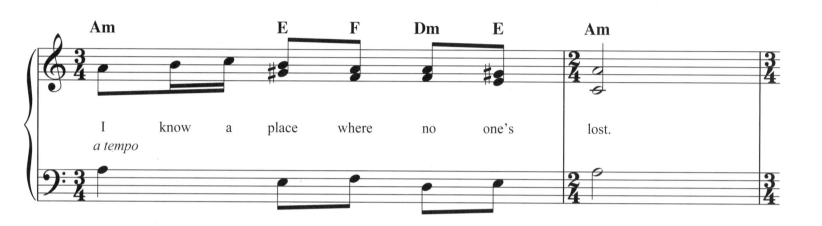

I know a place where no one's lost.

a tempo

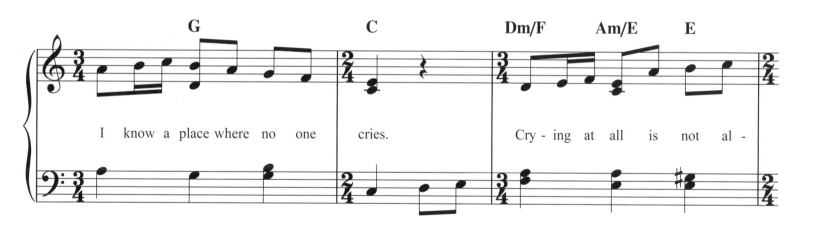

I know a place where no one cries. Cry - ing at all is not al -

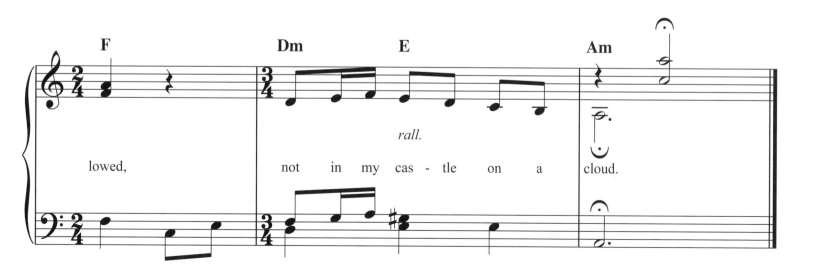

lowed, not in my cas - tle on a cloud.

rall.

THE CANDY MAN

from WILLY WONKA AND THE CHOCOLATE FACTORY

Words and Music by LESLIE BRICUSSE
and ANTHONY NEWLEY

Freely, but not too slowly

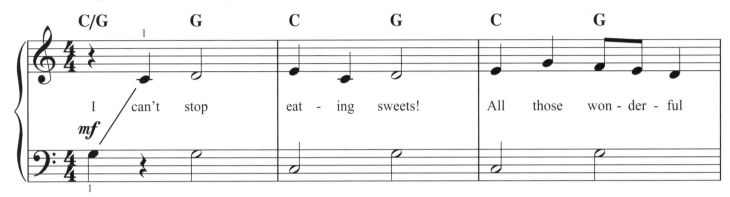

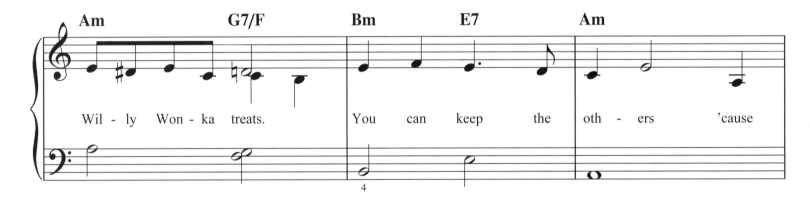

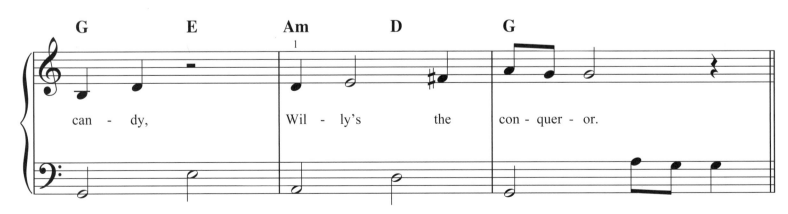

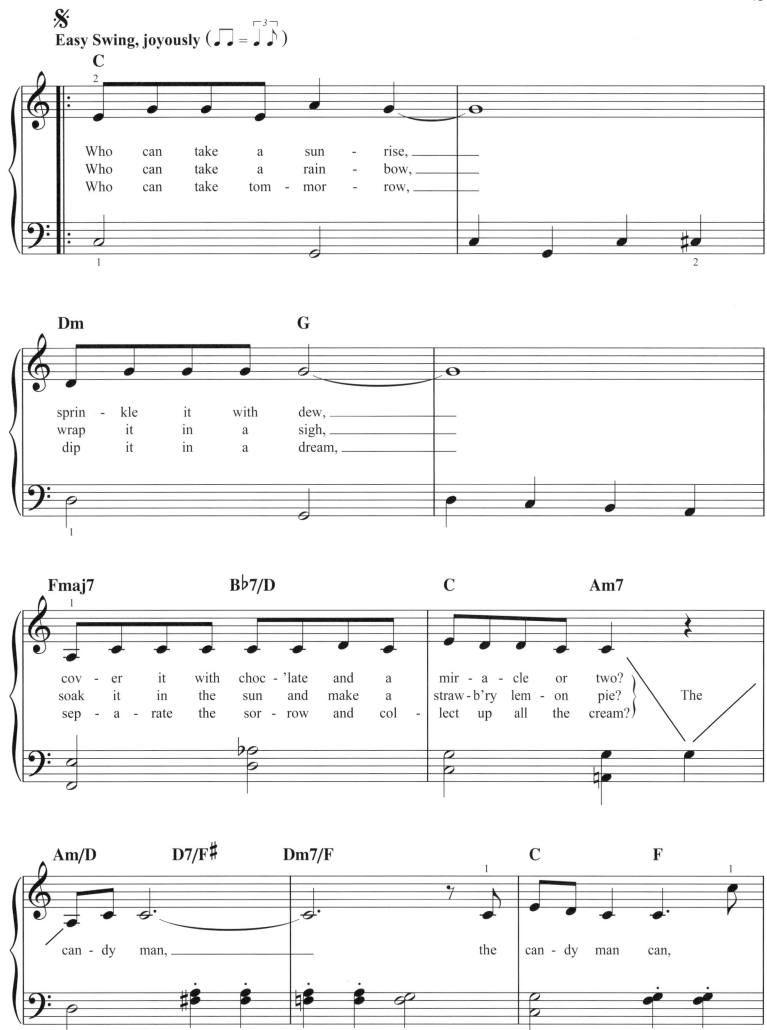

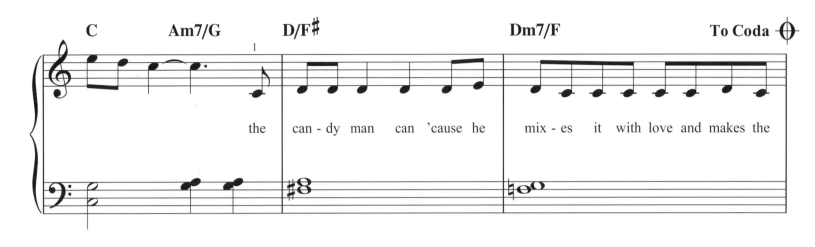

C **Am7/G** **D/F♯** **Dm7/F** **To Coda**

the can-dy man can 'cause he mix-es it with love and makes the

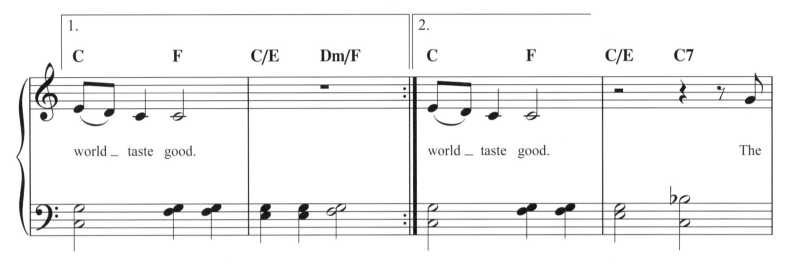

1.
C **F** **C/E** **Dm/F**

world — taste good.

2.
C **F** **C/E** **C7**

world — taste good. The

F **F♯dim7** **C/G** **C**

can-dy man makes ev-'ry-thing he bakes sat-is-fy-ing and de - li - cious.

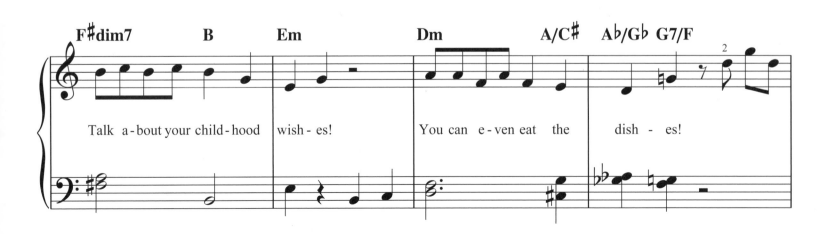

F♯dim7 **B** **Em** **Dm** **A/C♯** **A♭/G♭ G7/F**

Talk a-bout your child-hood wish-es! You can e-ven eat the dish - es!

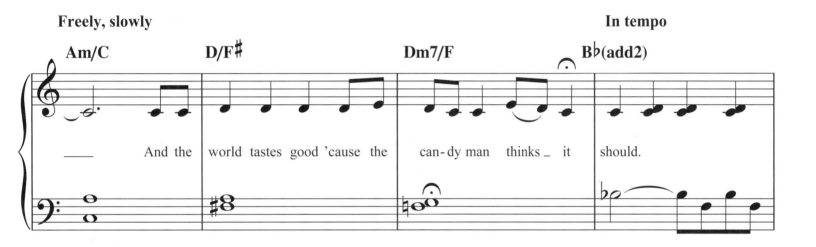

CHIM CHIM CHER-EE

from Walt Disney's MARY POPPINS

Words and Music by RICHARD M. SHERMAN
and ROBERT B. SHERMAN

Lightly, with gusto

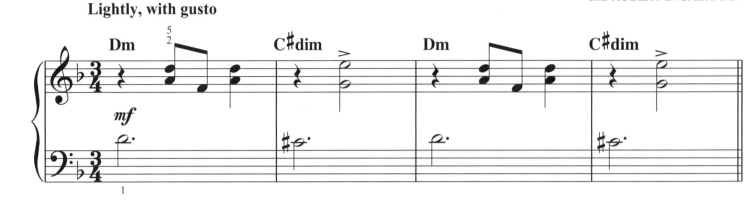

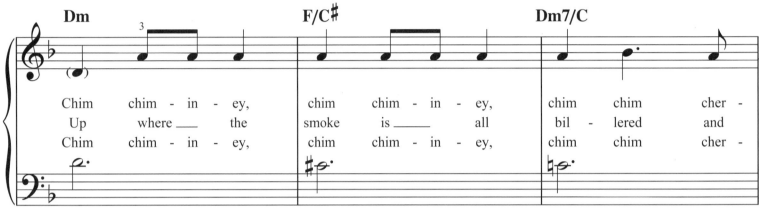

Chim chim-in-ey, chim chim-in-ey, chim chim cher-
Up where the smoke is all bil-lered and
Chim chim-in-ey, chim chim-in-ey, chim chim cher-

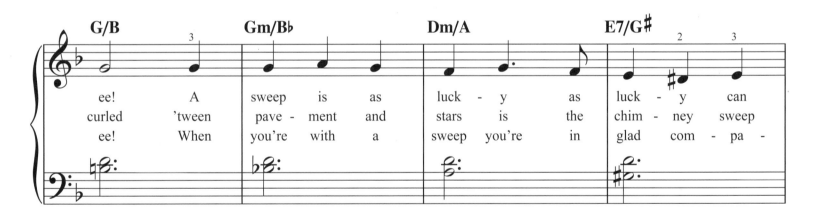

ee! A sweep is as luck-y as luck-y can
curled 'tween pave-ment and stars is as the chim-ney sweep
ee! When you're with a sweep you're in glad com-pa-

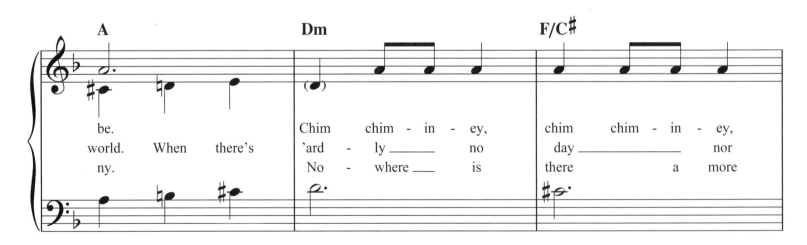

be. When there's Chim chim-in-ey, chim chim-in-ey,
world. 'ard-ly no day nor
ny. No-where is there a more

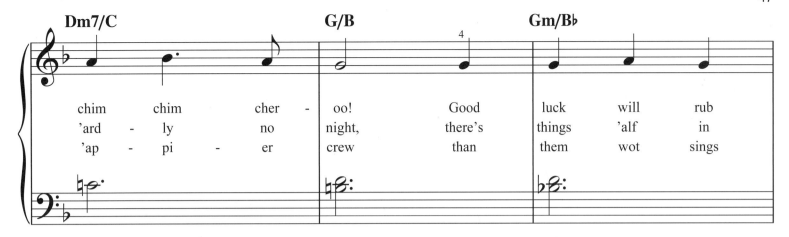

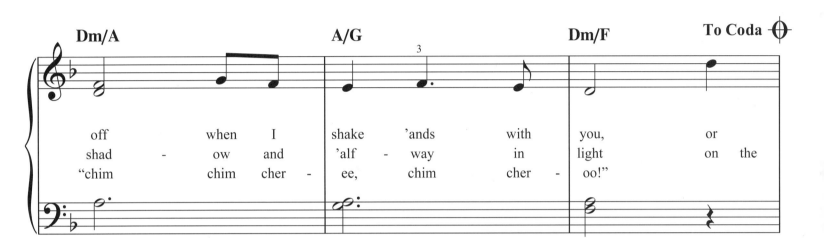

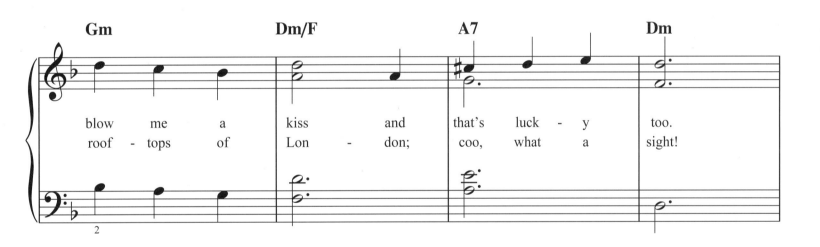

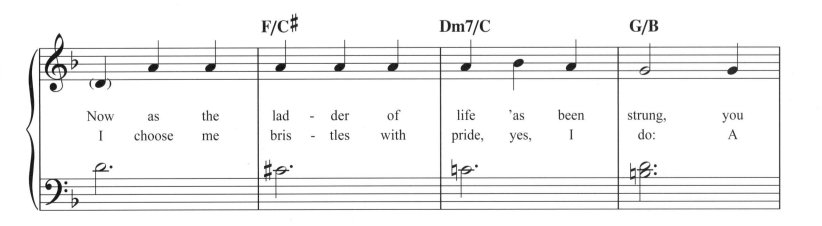

48

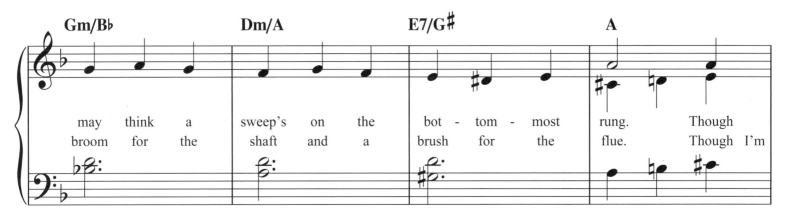

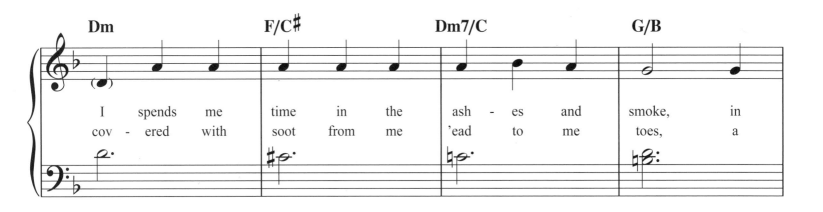

1st time: D.C.
2nd time: D.C. al Coda

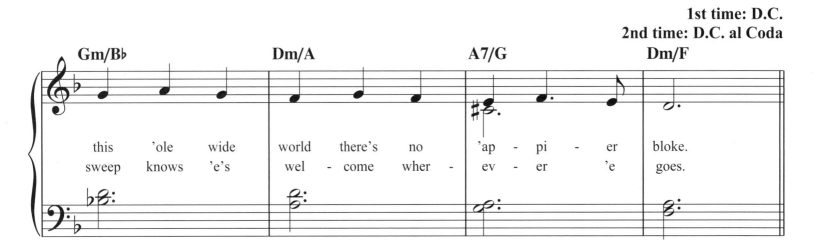

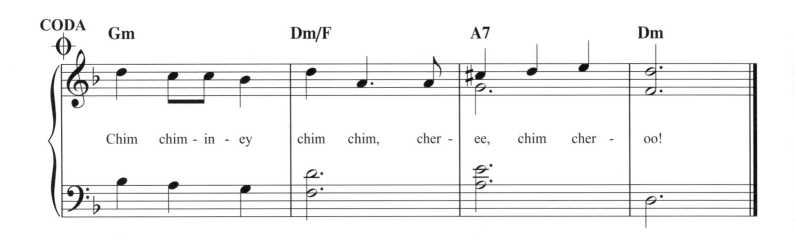

CHITTY CHITTY BANG BANG

Words and Music by RICHARD M. SHERMAN
and ROBERT B. SHERMAN

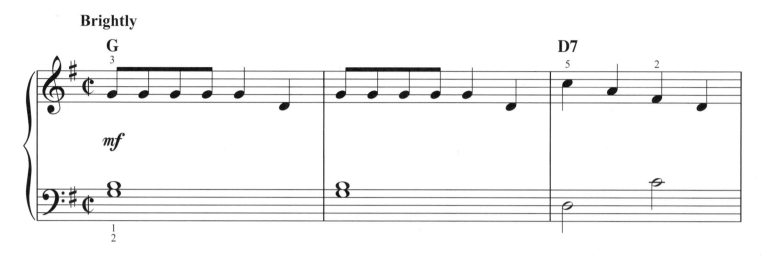

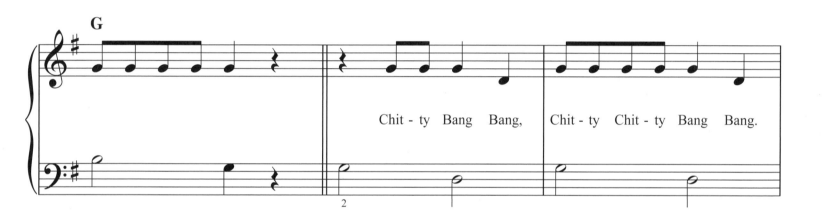

Chit - ty Bang Bang, Chit - ty Chit - ty Bang Bang.

Chit - ty Bang Bang, Chit - ty Chit - ty Bang Bang. Chit - ty Bang Bang,

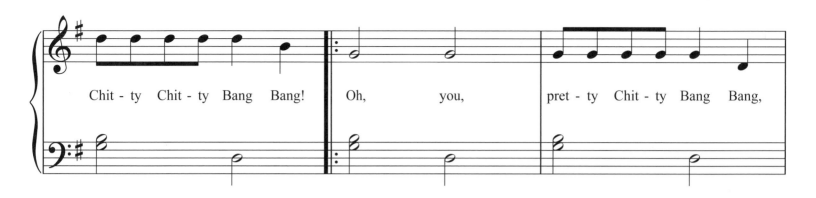

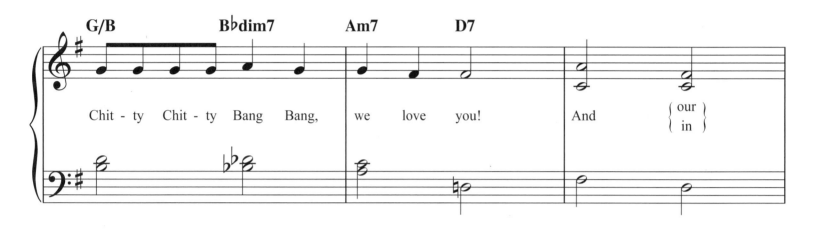

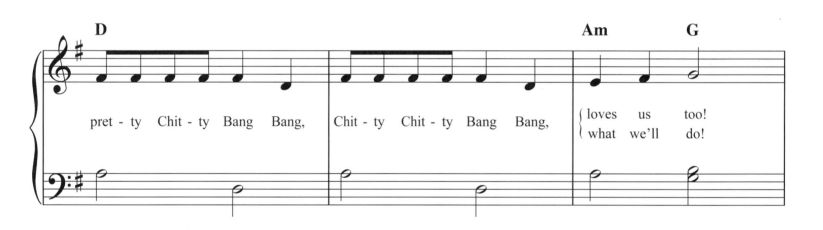

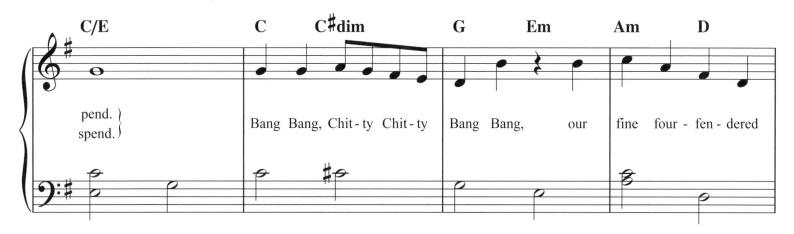

pend. / spend. Bang Bang, Chit-ty Chit-ty Bang Bang, our fine four-fen-dered

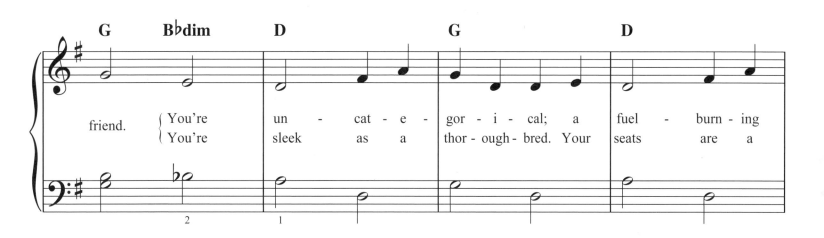

friend. You're / You're un- / sleek cat-e- / as gor-i- / a cal; a / thor-ough-bred. Your fuel- / seats burn-ing / are a

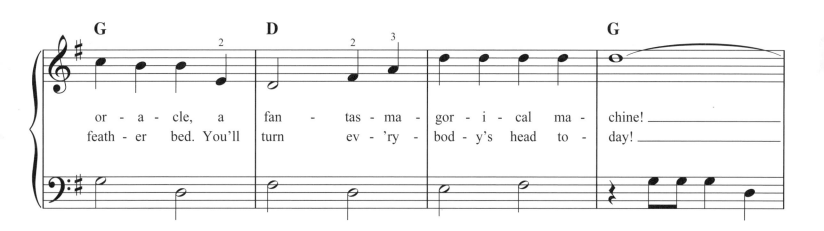

or-a-cle, a / feath-er bed. You'll fan- / turn tas-ma- / ev-'ry- gor-i- / bod-y's cal ma- / head to- chine! / day!

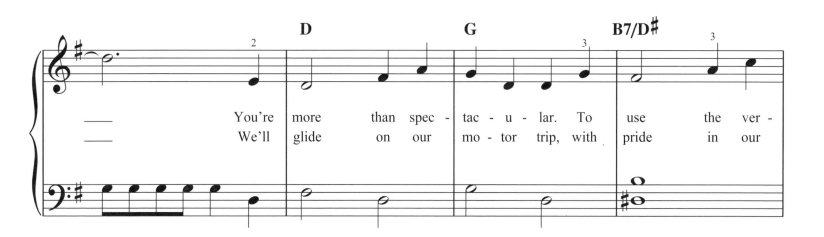

You're / We'll more / glide than / on spec- / our tac-u- / mo-tor lar. To / trip, with use / pride the / in ver- / our

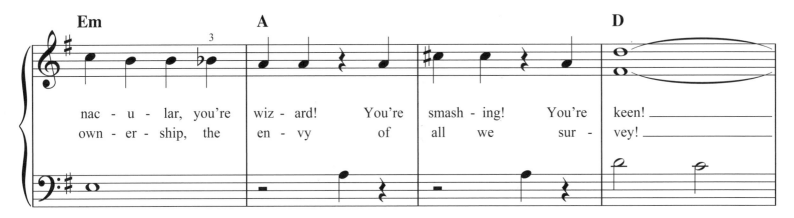

nac - u - lar, you're wiz - ard! You're smash - ing! You're keen! _____

own - er - ship, the en - vy of all we sur - vey! _____

Oh, Chit-ty, you, Chit-ty, pret-ty Chit-ty Bang Bang. Chit-ty Chit-ty Bang Bang,

we love you! And Chit-ty, {our/in} Chit-ty, pret-ty Chit-ty Bang Bang, Chit-ty Chit-ty Bang Bang,

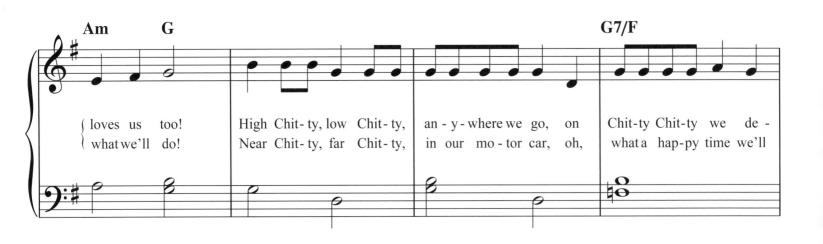

{loves us too!/what we'll do!} High Chit-ty, low Chit-ty, / Near Chit-ty, far Chit-ty, an-y-where we go, on / in our mo-tor car, oh, Chit-ty Chit-ty we de - / what a hap-py time we'll

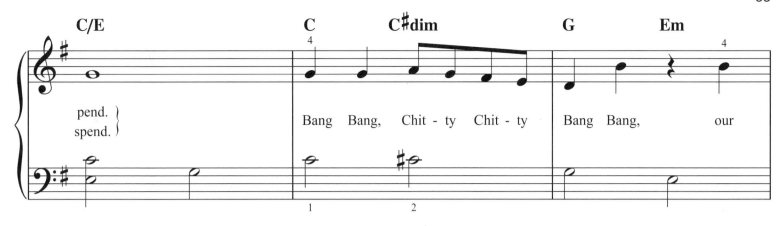

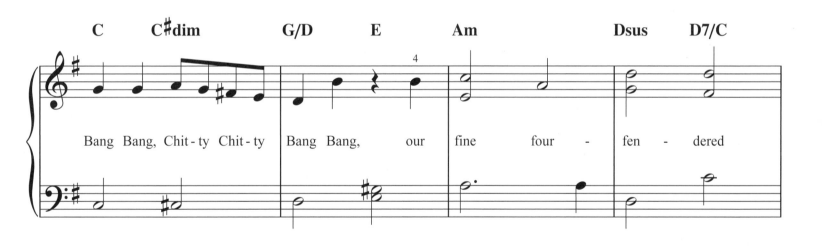

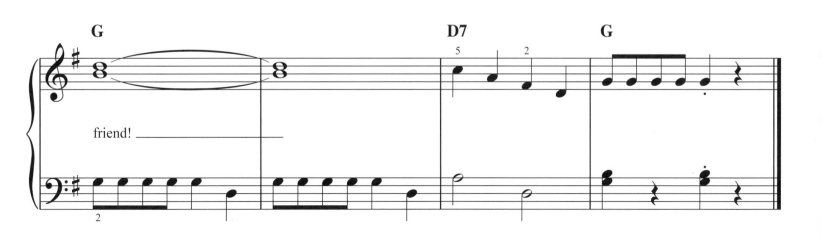

CHOPSTICKS

By ARTHUR DE LULLI

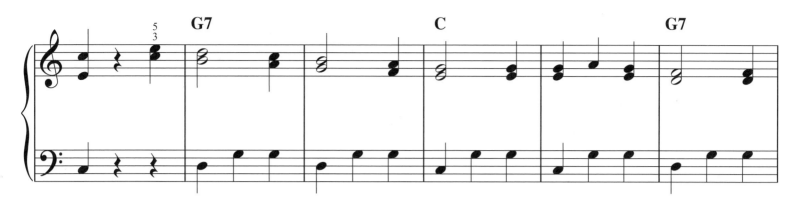

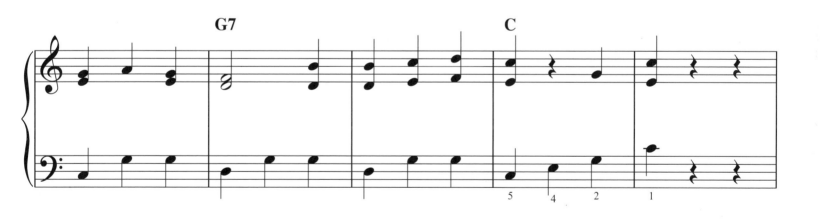

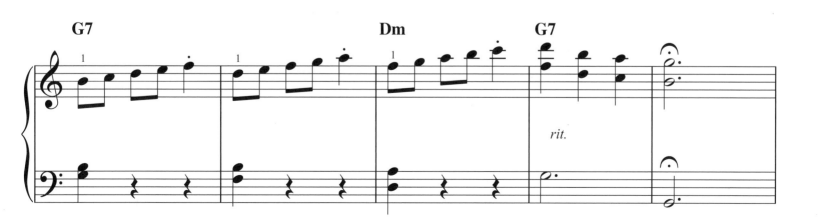

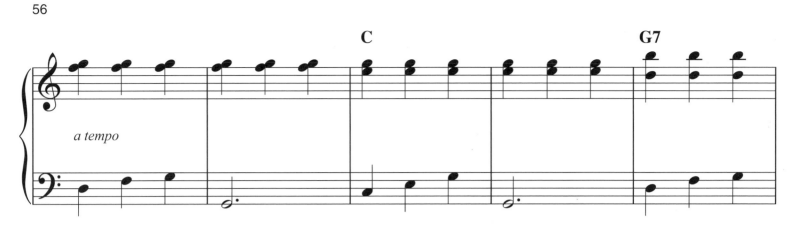

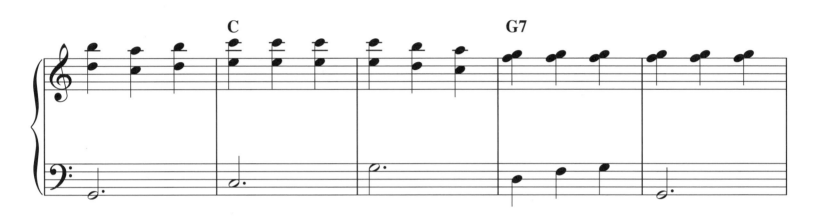

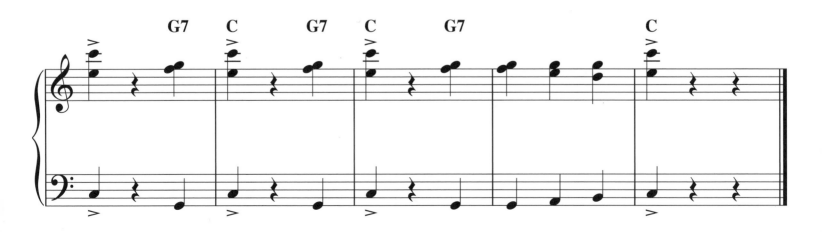

(Oh, My Darling)
CLEMENTINE

Words and Music by
PERCY MONTROSE

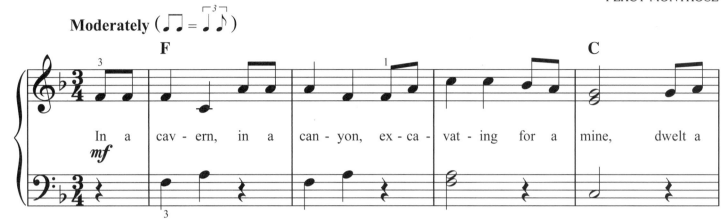

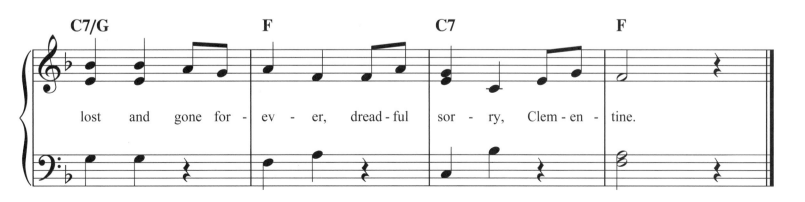

CONSIDER YOURSELF

from the Broadway Musical OLIVER!

Words and Music by
LIONEL BART

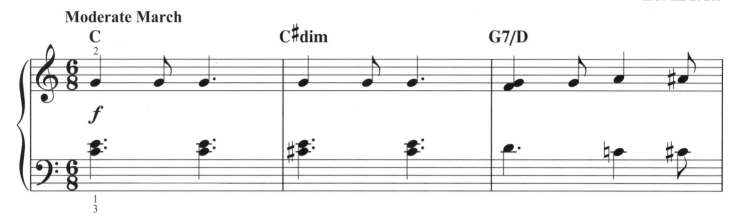

Moderate March

Con - sid - er your - self ___ at
sid - er your - self ___ well

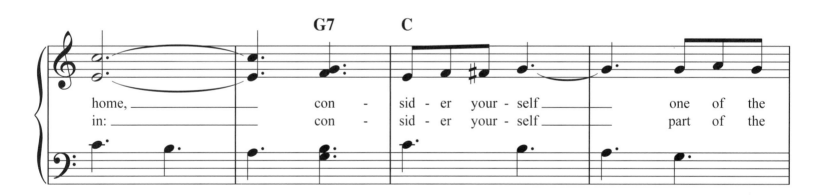

home, ___ con - sid - er your - self ___ one of the
in: ___ con - sid - er your - self ___ part of the

fam - i - ly. ___ I've tak - en to you ___ so
fur - ni - ture. ___ There is - n't a lot ___ to

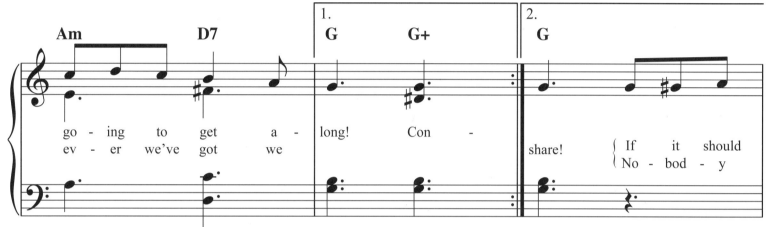

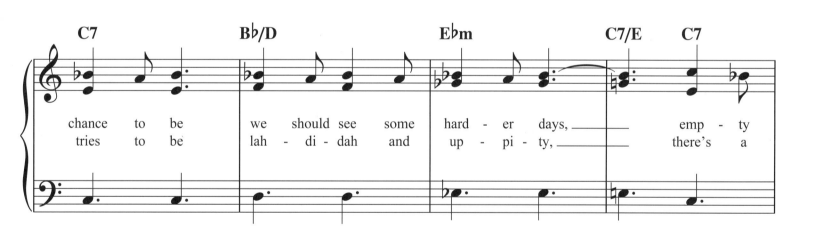

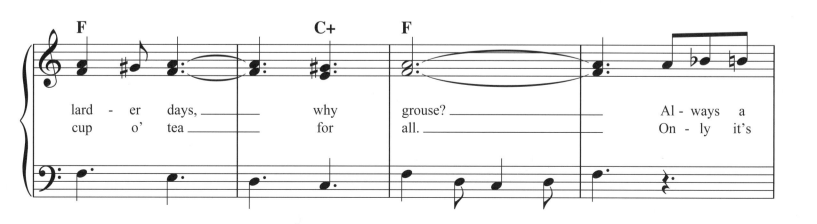

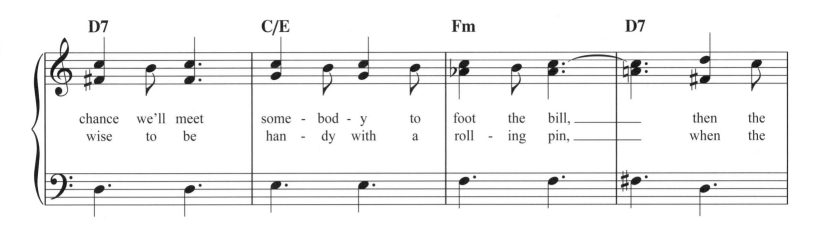

chance we'll meet / wise to be — **D7** — some·bod·y to / han·dy with a — **C/E** — foot the bill, / roll·ing pin, — **Fm** — then the / when the — **D7**

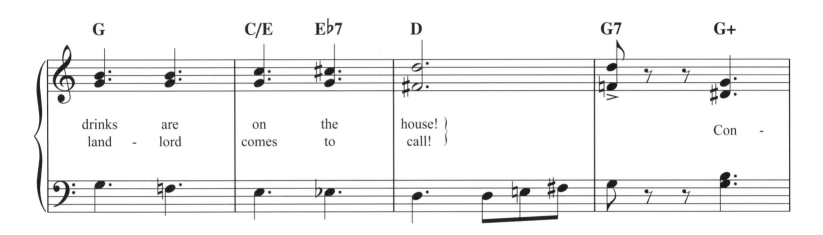

drinks are / land·lord — **G** — on the / comes to — **C/E** **E♭7** — house! / call! — **D** — **G7** **G+** — Con -

sid·er your·self — **C** — our — mate, — we — **A7/G**

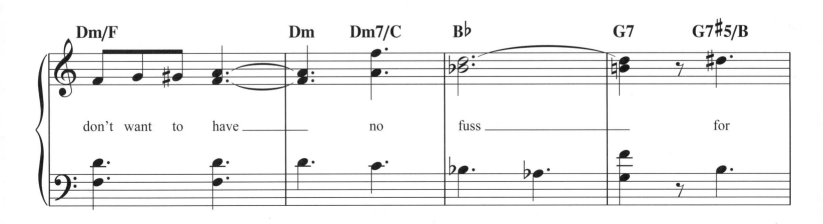

don't want to have — **Dm/F** — no — **Dm** **Dm7/C** — fuss — **B♭** — for — **G7** **G7♯5/B**

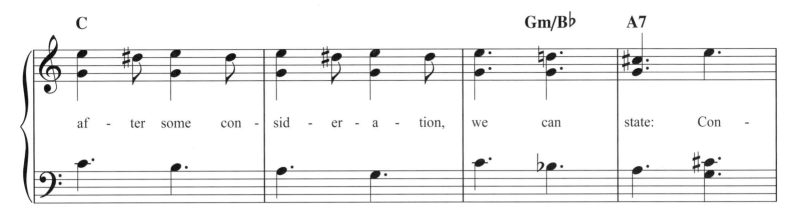

af - ter some con - sid - er - a - tion, we can state: Con -

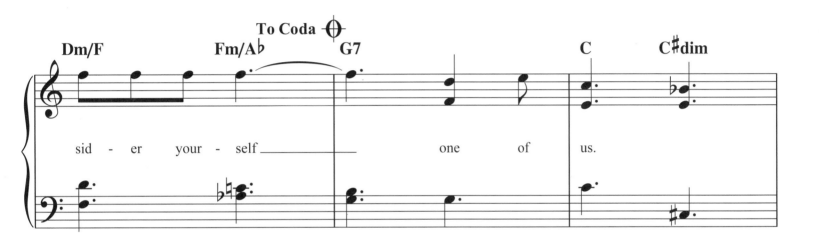

sid - er your - self _____ one of us.

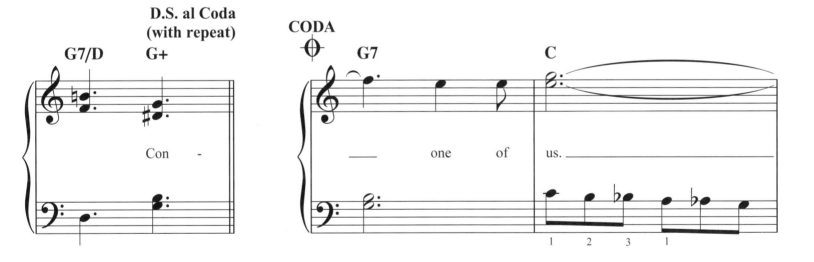

D.S. al Coda
(with repeat)

Con -

CODA

_____ one of us. _____

CRUELLA DE VIL
from Walt Disney's 101 DALMATIONS

Words and Music by
MEL LEVEN

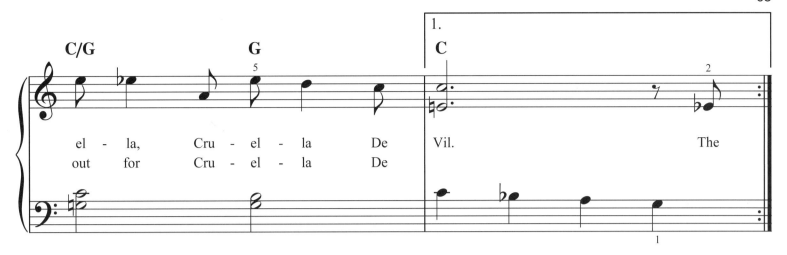

C/G   **G**   **1.**   **C**

el - la,   Cru - el - la   De   Vil.   The
out   for   Cru - el - la   De

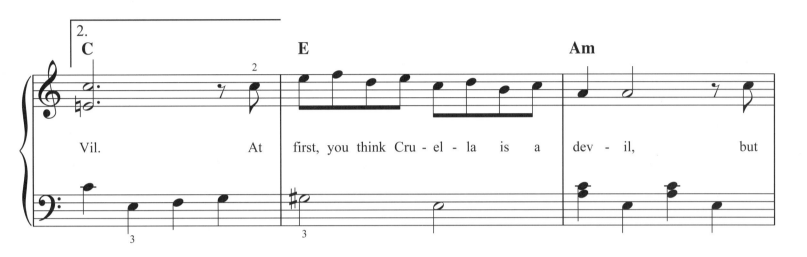

2.   **C**   **E**   **Am**

Vil.   At   first, you think Cru - el - la   is   a   dev - il,   but

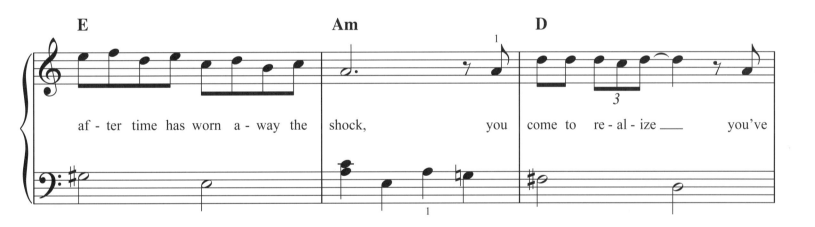

E   **Am**   **D**

af - ter time has worn a - way the   shock,   you   come to re - al - ize _____   you've

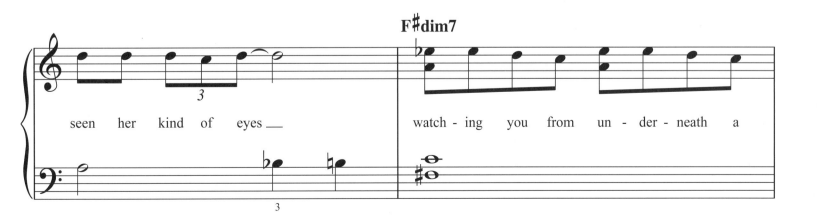

F#dim7

seen her kind of eyes _____   watch - ing   you   from   un - der - neath   a

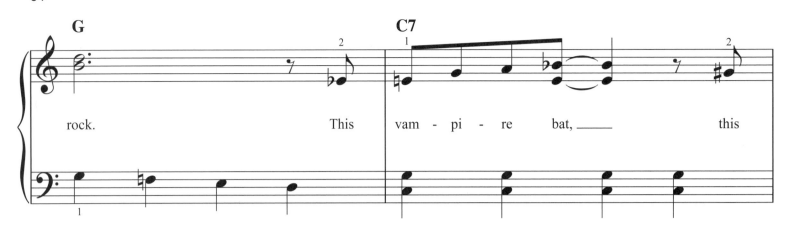

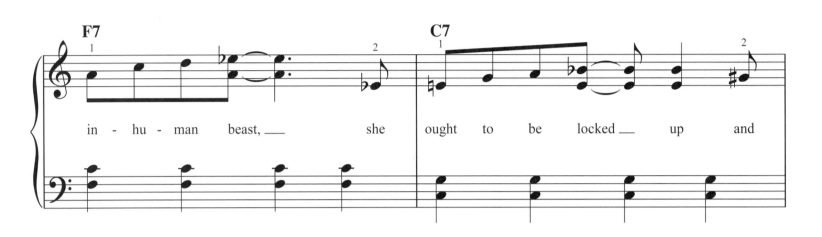

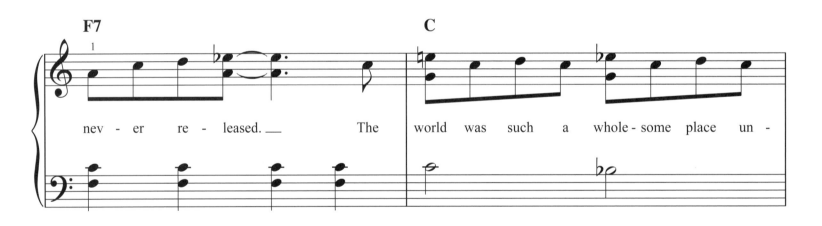

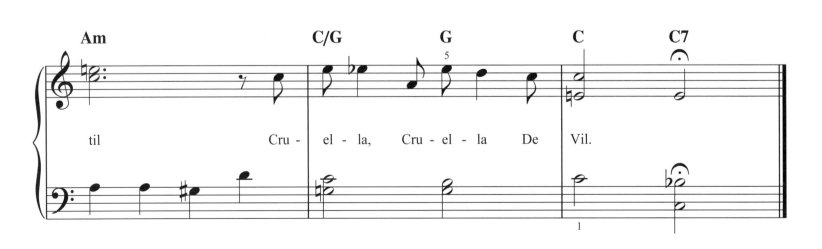

A DREAM IS A WISH YOUR HEART MAKES

from Walt Disney's CINDERELLA

Words and Music by MACK DAVID,
AL HOFFMAN and JERRY LIVINGSTON

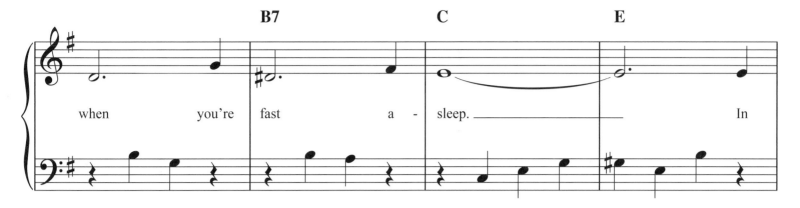

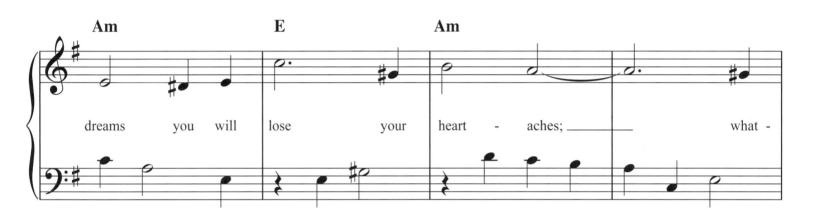

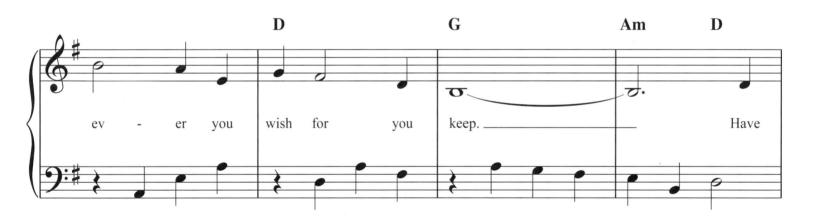

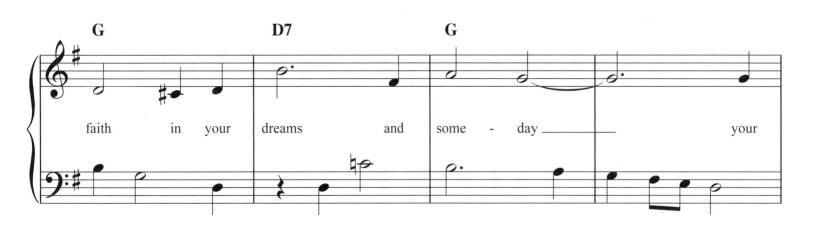

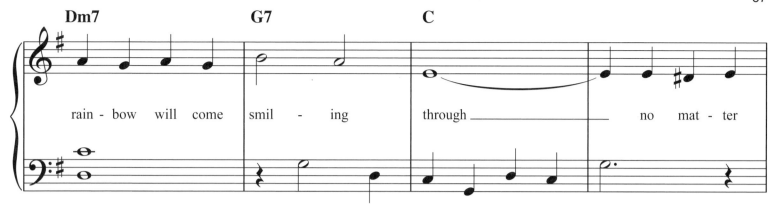

Dm7   G7   C

rain - bow will come smil - ing through _____ no mat - ter

F7/E♭   G/D

how your heart is griev - ing, if you keep on be -

A7   Am7   D7

liev - ing, the dream that you wish will come

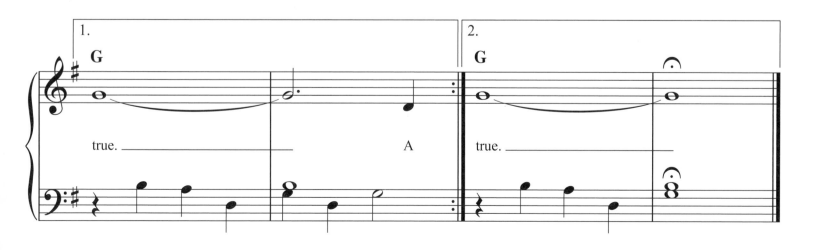

1.   G

true. _____ A

2.   G

true. _____

DITES-MOI
(Tell Me Why)
from SOUTH PACIFIC

Lyrics by OSCAR HAMMERSTEIN II
Music by RICHARD RODGERS

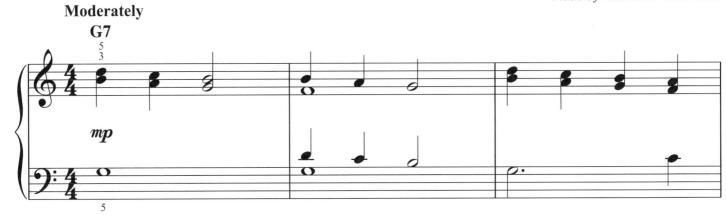

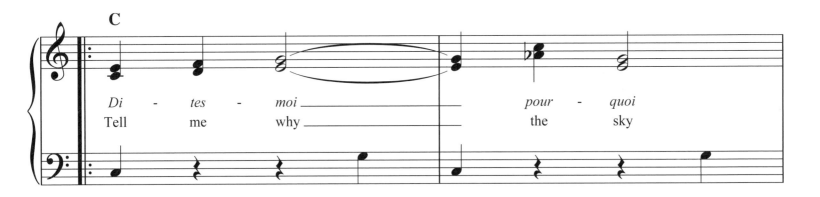

Di - tes - moi _____ pour - quoi
Tell me why _____ the sky

la vie est bel - le, di - tes - moi _____
is filled with mu - sic, tell me why _____

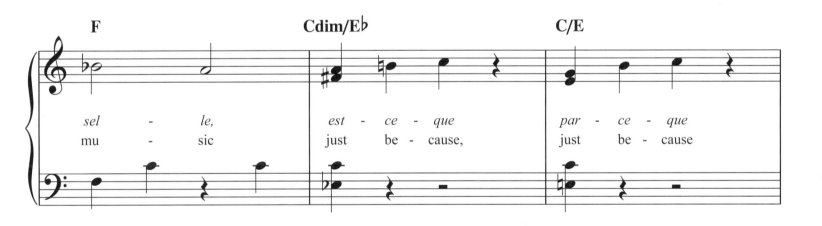

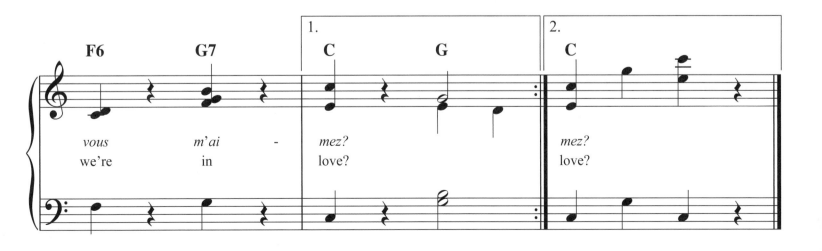

DO-RE-MI
from THE SOUND OF MUSIC

Lyrics by OSCAR HAMMERSTEIN II
Music by RICHARD RODGERS

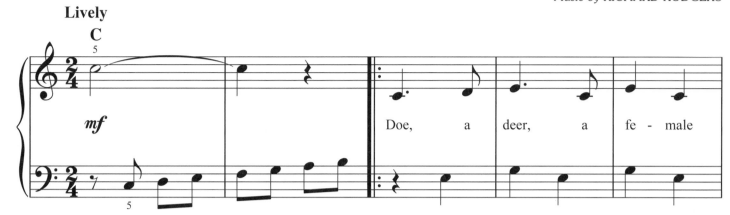

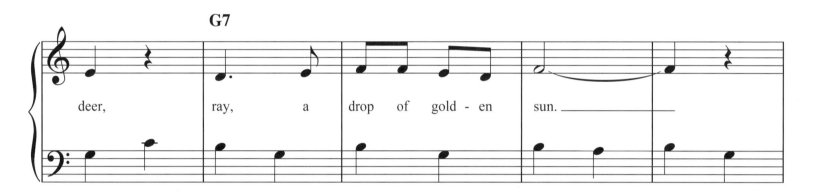

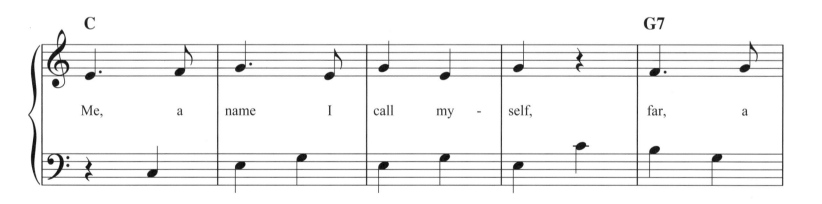

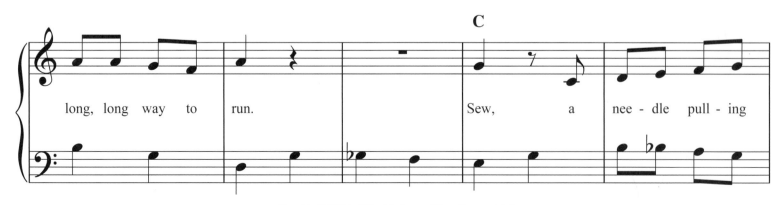

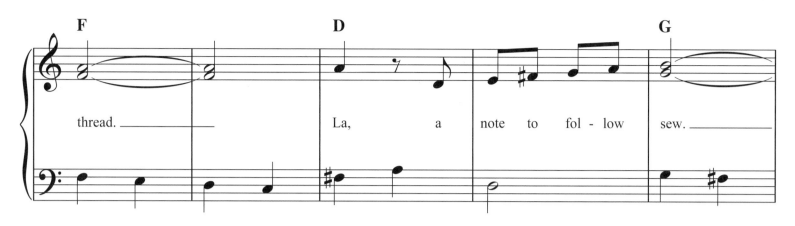

thread. _____ La, a note to fol - low sew. _____

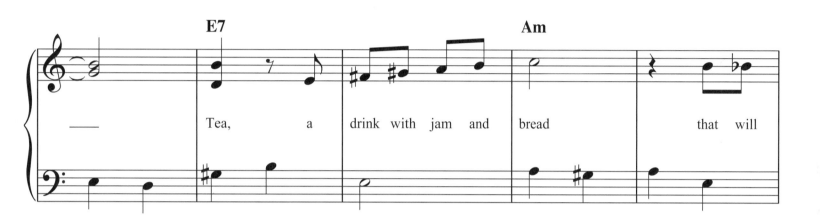

_____ Tea, a drink with jam and bread that will

bring us back to do.

do ti la sol fa mi re do.

DOWN BY THE STATION

Traditional

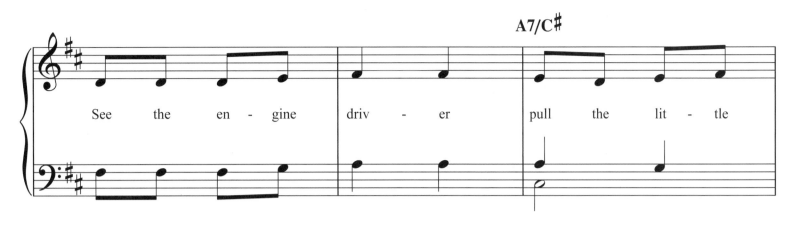

A7/C♯

See the en - gine driv - er pull the lit - tle

D

han - dle. Choo! Choo! Toot! Toot!

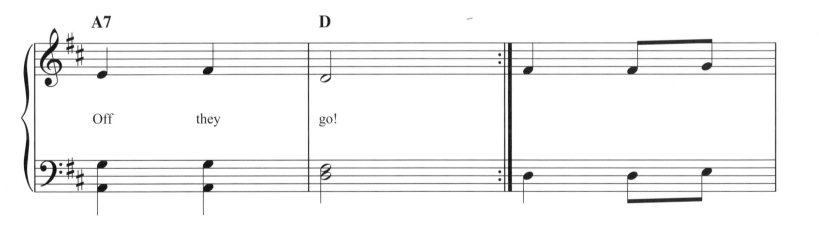

A7   **D**

Off they go!

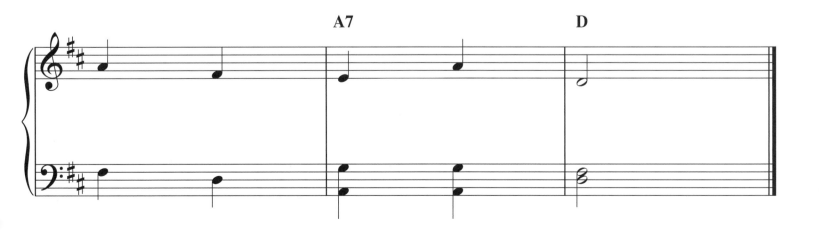

A7   **D**

EV'RYBODY WANTS TO BE A CAT

from Walt Disney's THE ARISTOCATS

Words by FLOYD HUDDLESTON
Music by AL RINKER

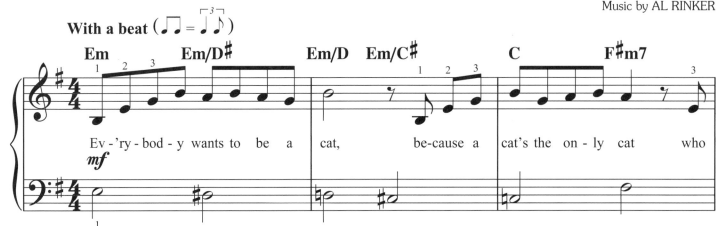

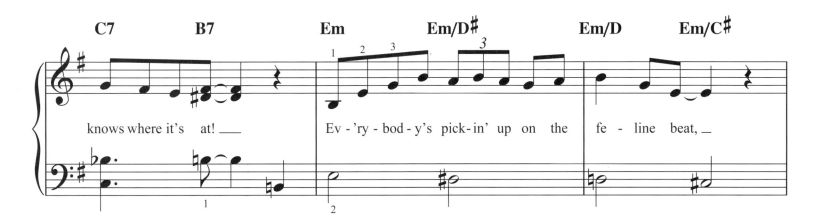

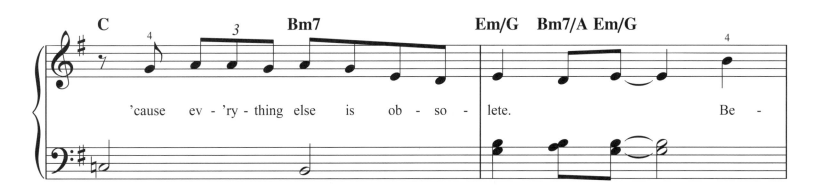

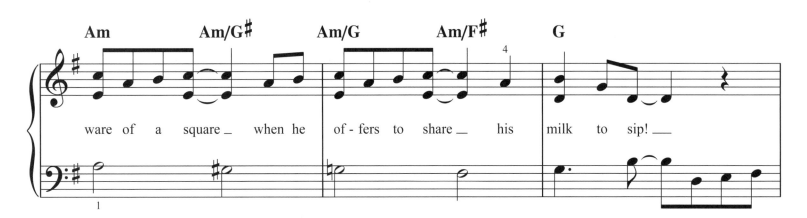

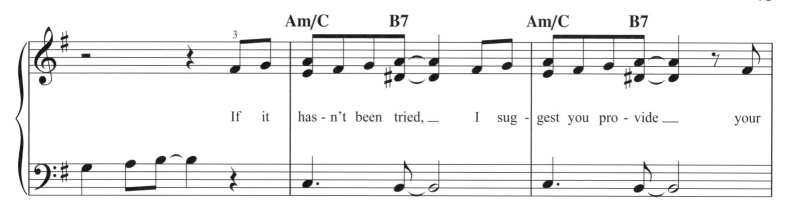

If it has - n't been tried, __ I sug - gest you pro - vide __ your

own cat - nip. __ I've heard some corn - y birds who tried to

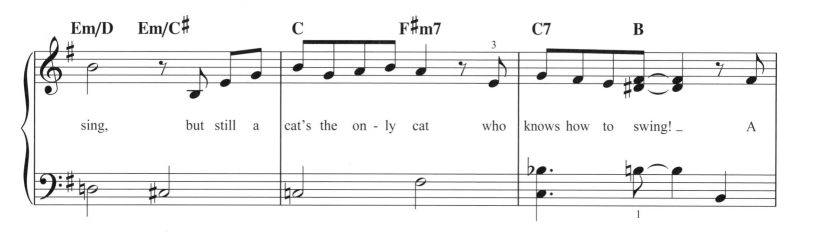

sing, but still a cat's the on - ly cat who knows how to swing! __ A

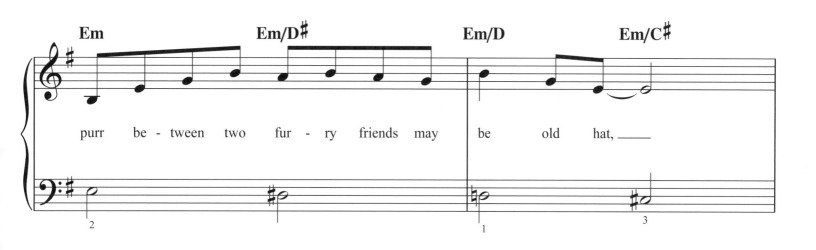

purr be - tween two fur - ry friends may be old hat, ____

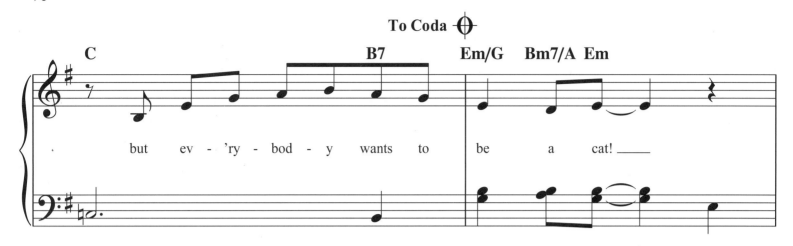

but ev - 'ry - bod - y wants to be a cat! ____

Come on, scat cat, turn me on. I'll

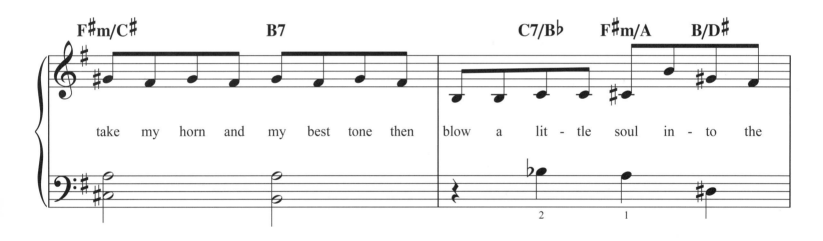

take my horn and my best tone then blow a lit - tle soul in - to the

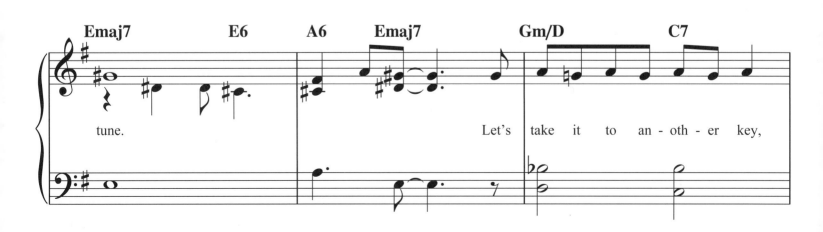

tune. Let's take it to an - oth - er key,

mod - u - late, then wait for me, I'll take a few ad libs and pret - ty soon the

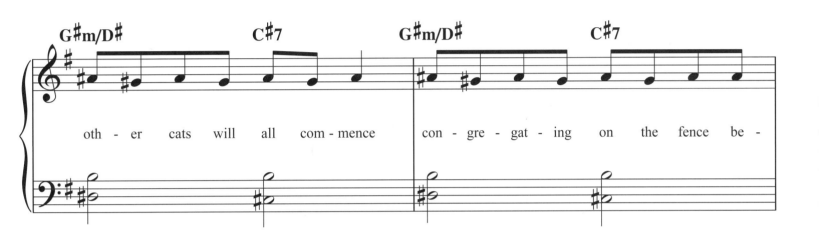

oth - er cats will all com - mence con - gre - gat - ing on the fence be -

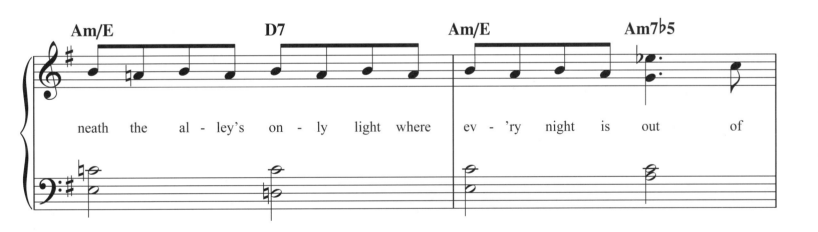

neath the al - ley's on - ly light where ev - 'ry night is out of

D.C. al Coda

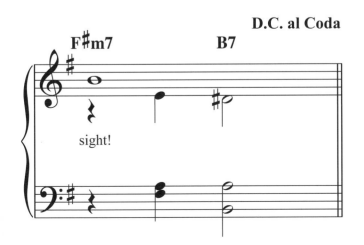

sight!

CODA

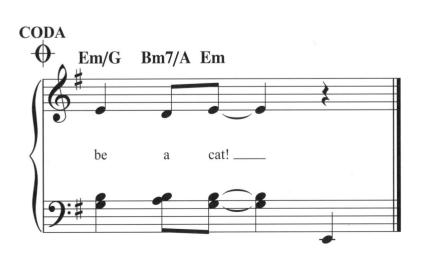

be a cat! ____

FOOD, GLORIOUS FOOD

Words and Music by
LIONEL BART

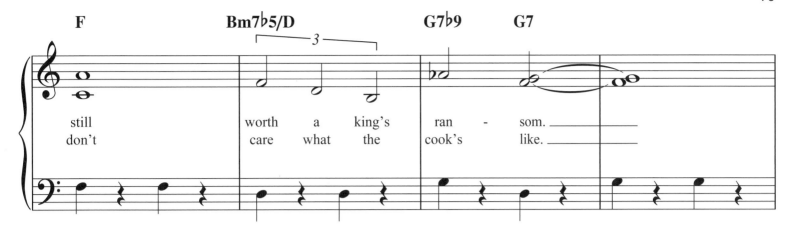

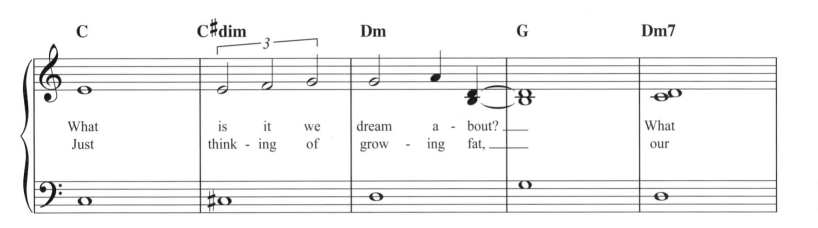

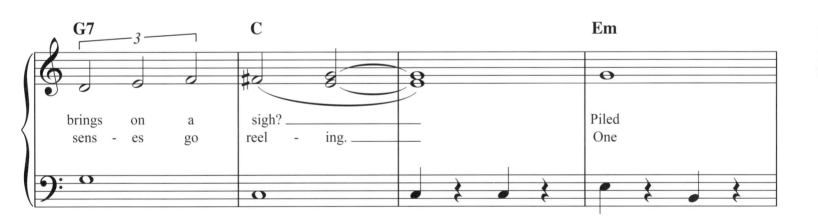

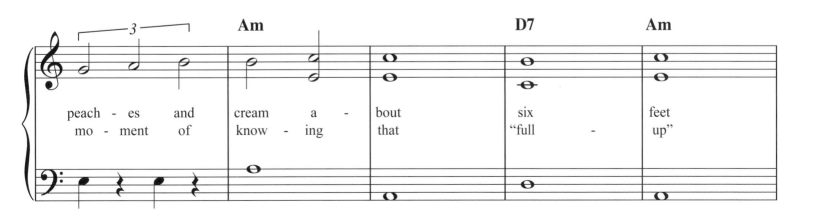

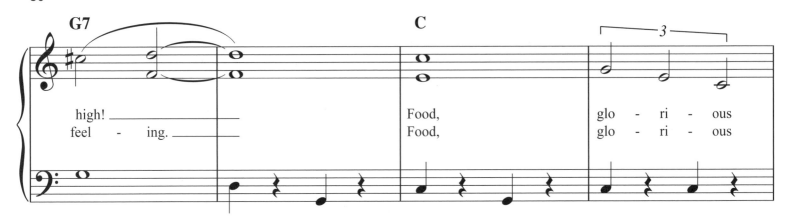

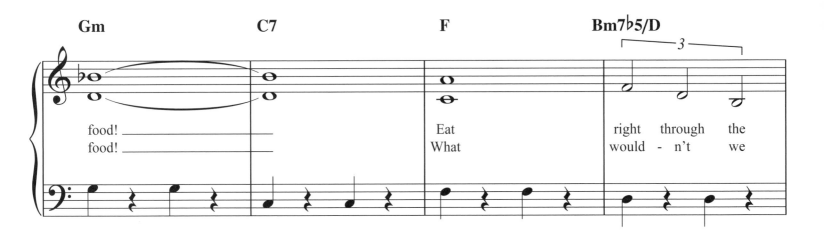

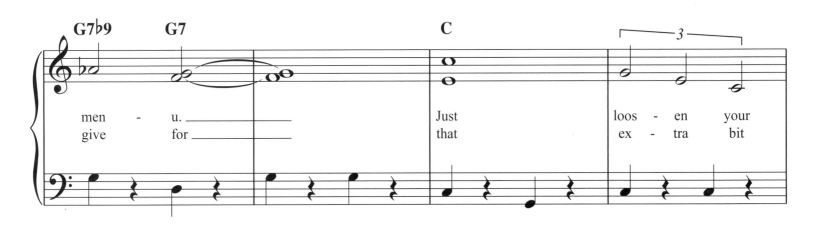

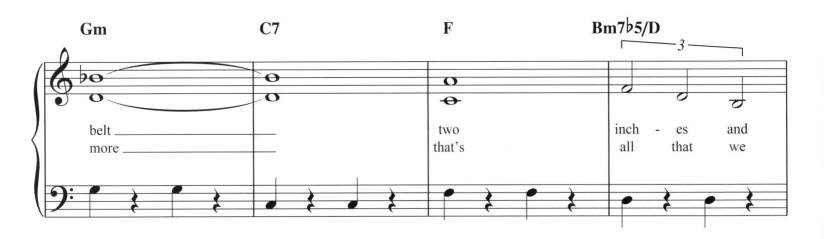

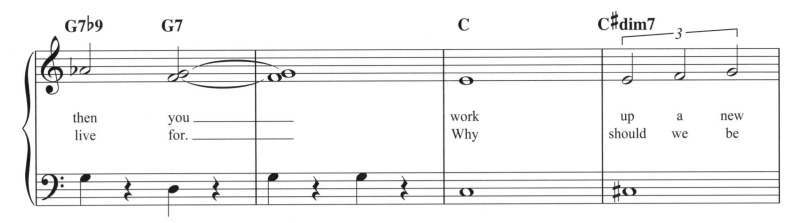

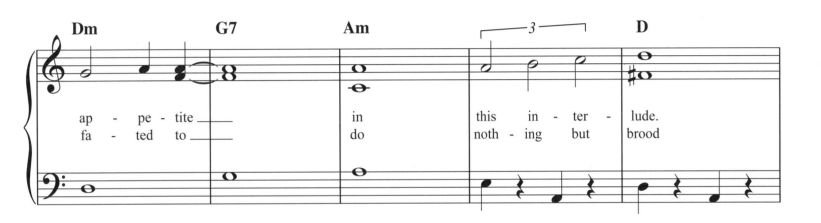

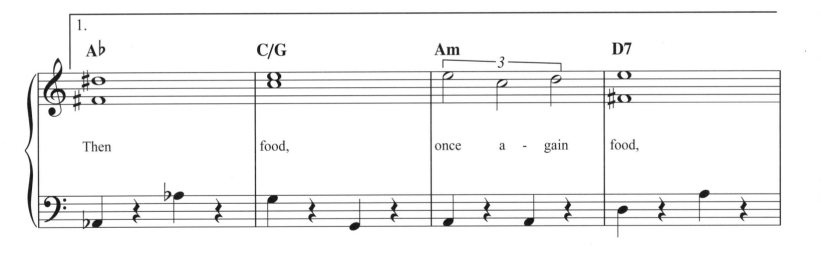

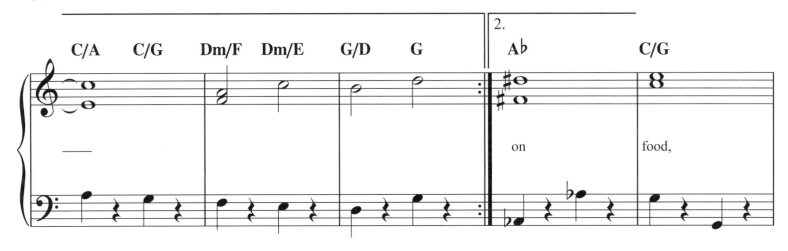

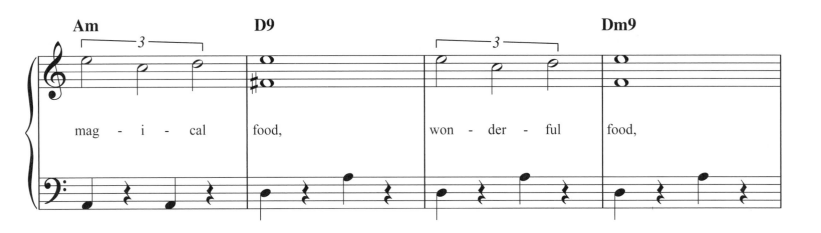

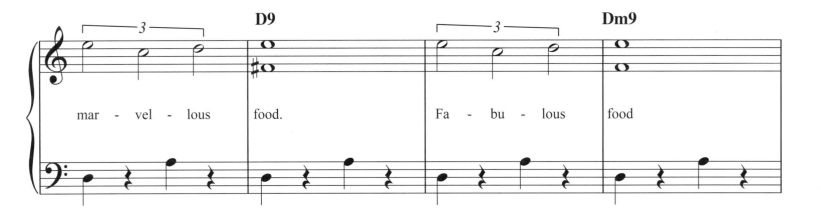

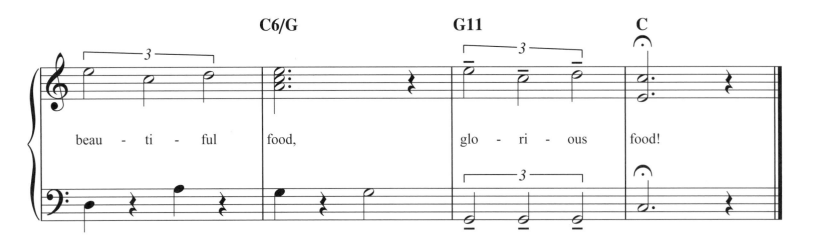

FRÈRE JACQUES
(Are You Sleeping?)

Traditional

Happily

Frè - re Jac - ques,
Are you sleep - ing,

Frè - re Jac - ques,
are you sleep - ing,

dor - mez vouz,
Broth - er John,

dor - mez vous?
Broth - er John?

Son - nez les ma - ti - nes,
Morn - ing bells are ring - ing,

son - nez les ma - ti - nes.
morn - ing bells are ring - ing.

Ding, ding, dong,

ding, ding, dong.

FRIEND LIKE ME
from Walt Disney's ALADDIN

Music by ALAN MENKEN
Lyrics by HOWARD ASHMAN

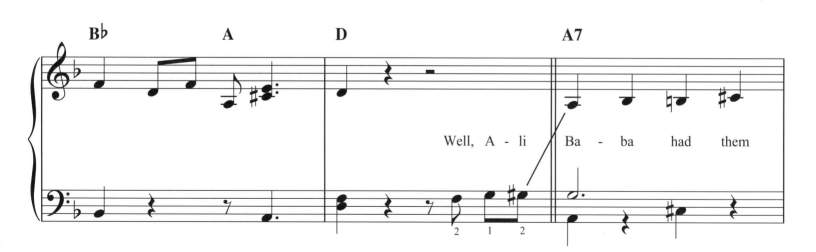

Well, A - li Ba - ba had them

for - ty thieves. Sche - her - a - za - de had a thou - sand tales. But, mas - ter,

you in luck 'cause up your sleeves __ you got a brand of mag - ic nev - er

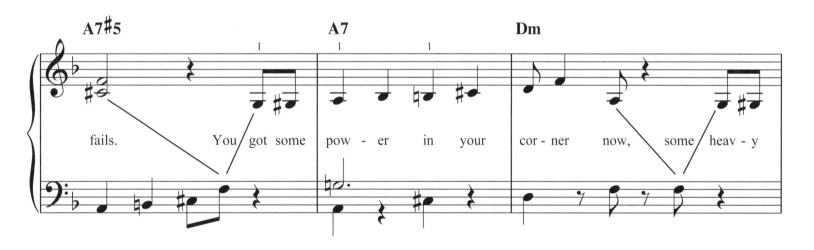

fails. You got some pow - er in your cor - ner now, some heav - y

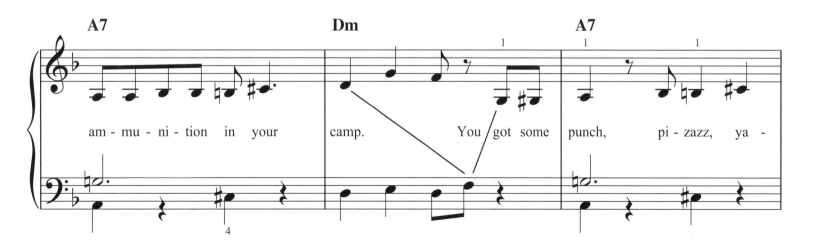

am - mu - ni - tion in your camp. You got some punch, pi - zazz, ya -

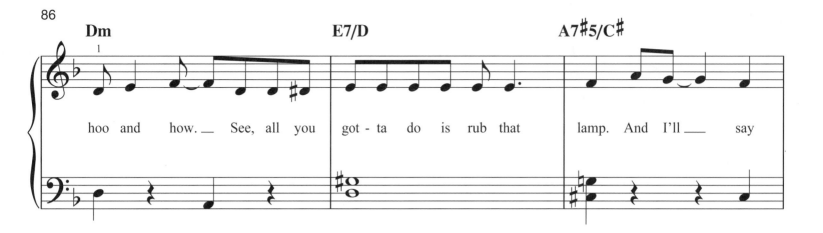

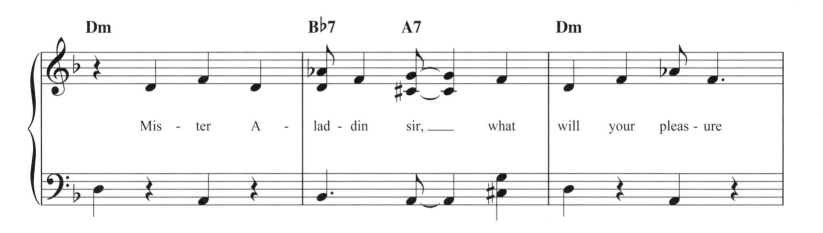

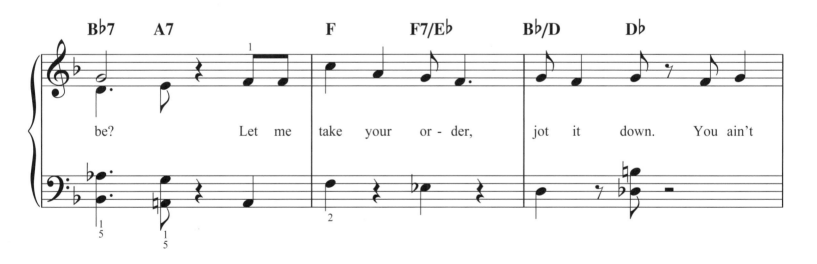

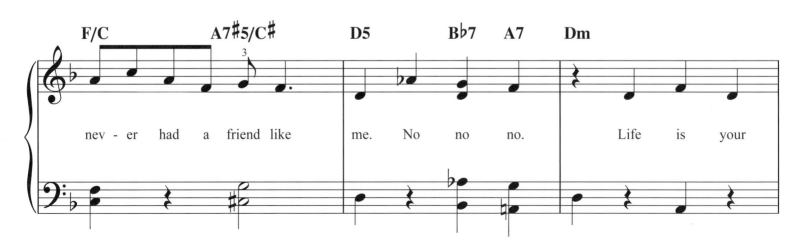

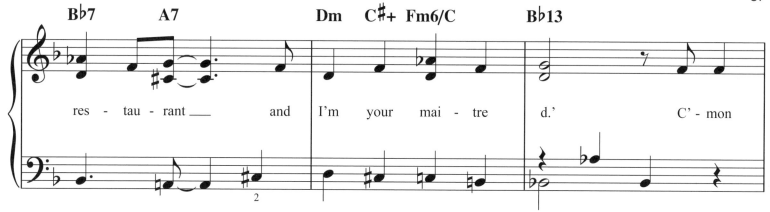

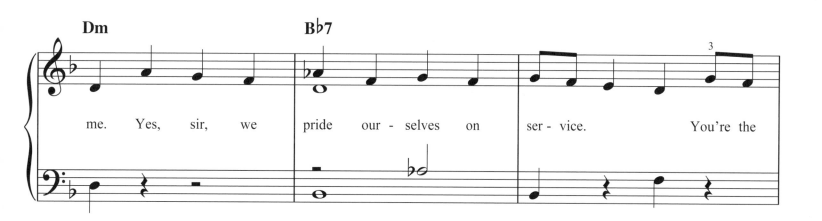

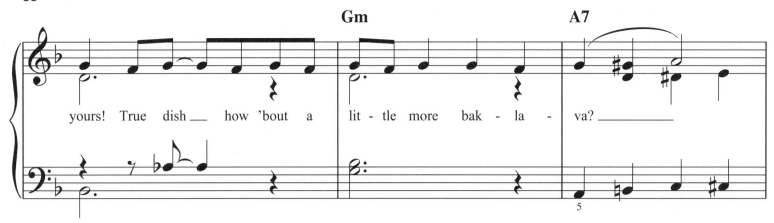

yours! True dish___ how 'bout a lit - tle more bak - la - va?___

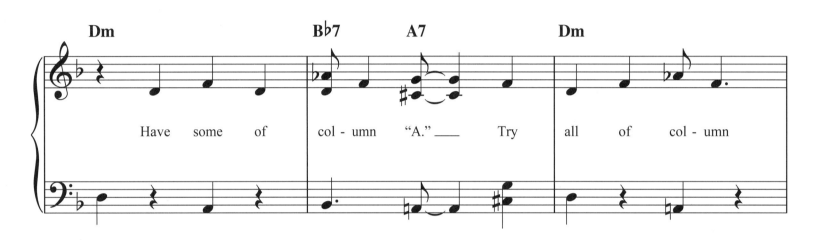

Have some of col - umn "A."___ Try all of col - umn

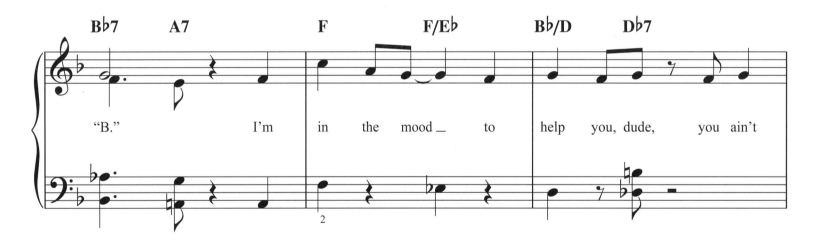

"B." I'm in the mood___ to help you, dude, you ain't

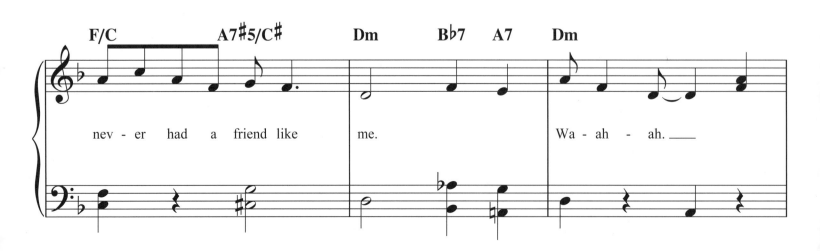

nev - er had a friend like me. Wa - ah - ah.___

Oh my. Wa - ah - ah. No no.

Wa - ah - ah. Na na na.

Can your friends do this? Can your friends do

that? Can your friends pull this

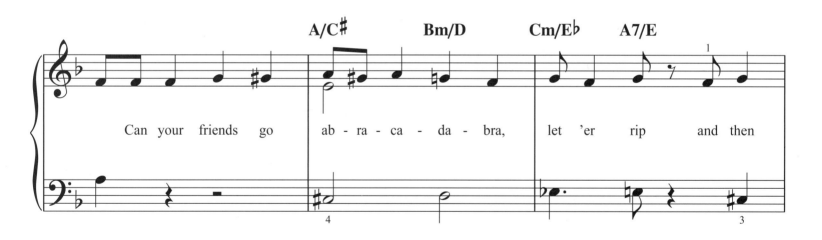

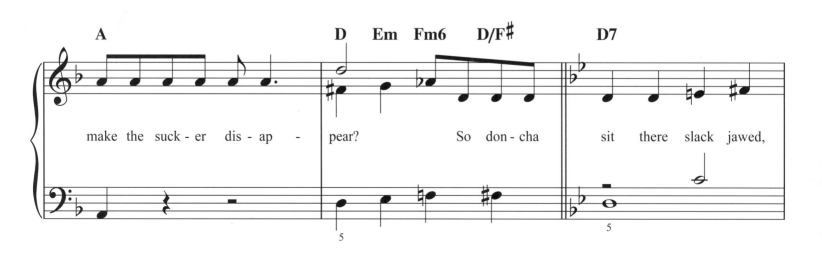

bug - gy eyed. I'm here to an - swer all your mid - day prayers. You got me

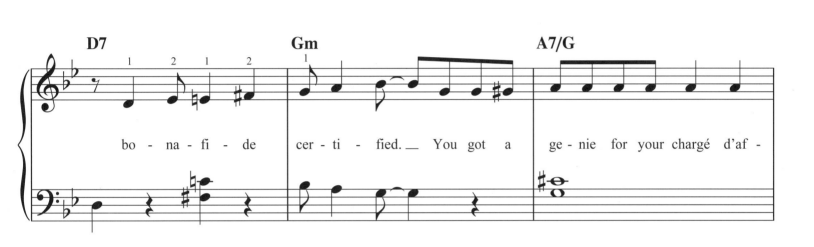

bo - na - fi - de cer - ti - fied. __ You got a ge - nie for your chargé d'af -

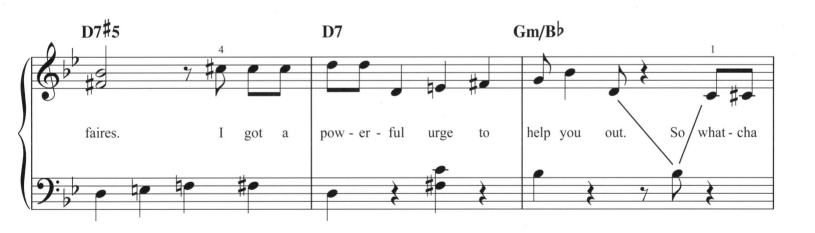

faires. I got a pow - er - ful urge to help you out. So what - cha

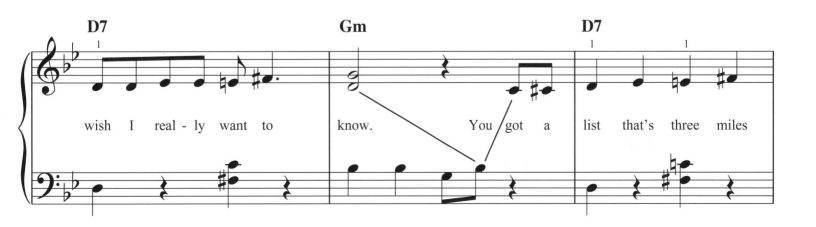

wish I real - ly want to know. You got a list that's three miles

long no doubt. Well, all you got - ta do is rub like so. And oh._____

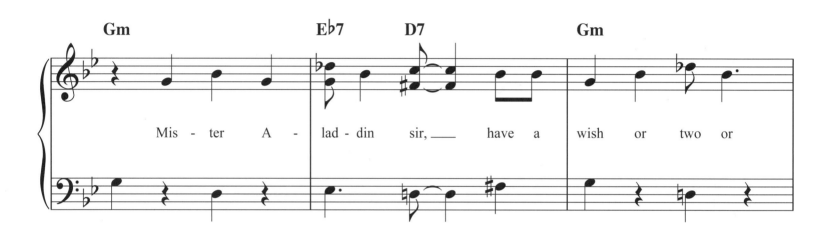

Mis - ter A - lad - din sir,____ have a wish or two or

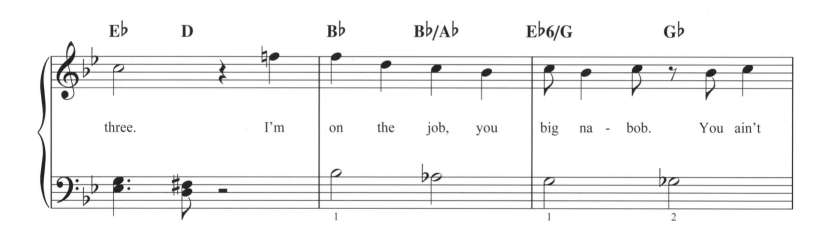

three. I'm on the job, you big na - bob. You ain't

nev - er had a friend, nev - er had a friend, you ain't nev - er had a friend, nev - er

had a friend. You ain't nev - er _____ had a _____

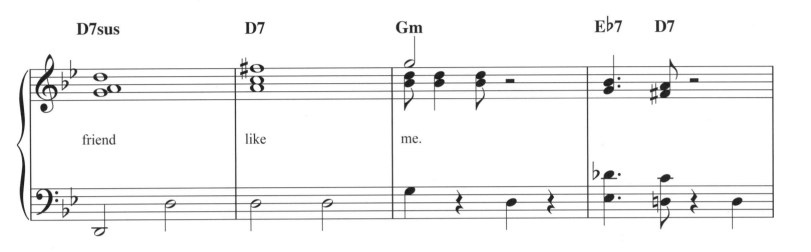

friend like me.

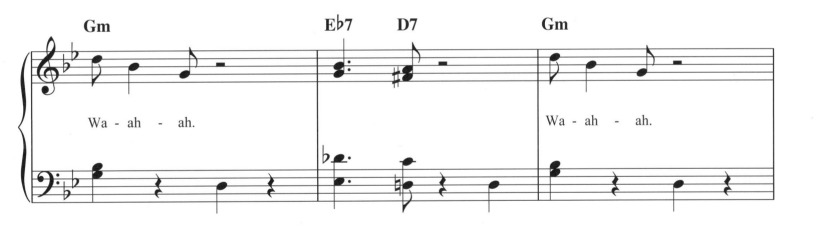

Wa - ah - ah. Wa - ah - ah.

You ain't nev - er had a friend like me. Ha!

GETTING TO KNOW YOU
from THE KING AND I

Lyrics by OSCAR HAMMERSTEIN II
Music by RICHARD RODGERS

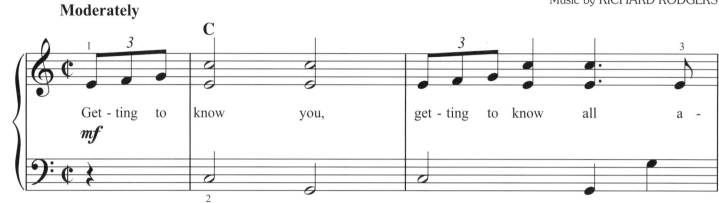

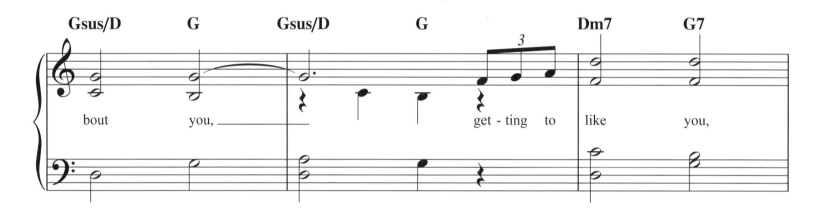

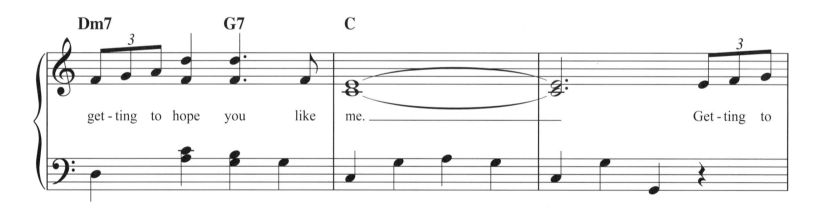

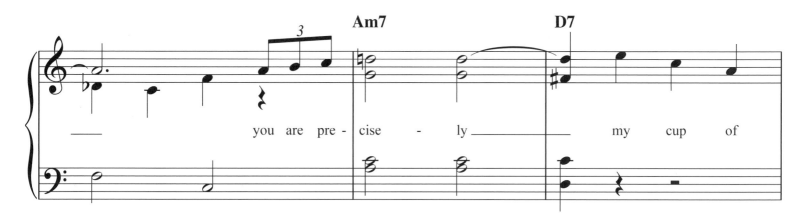

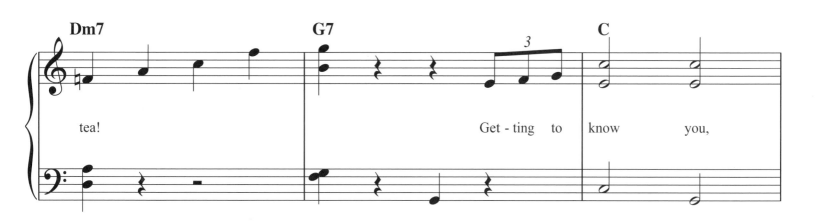

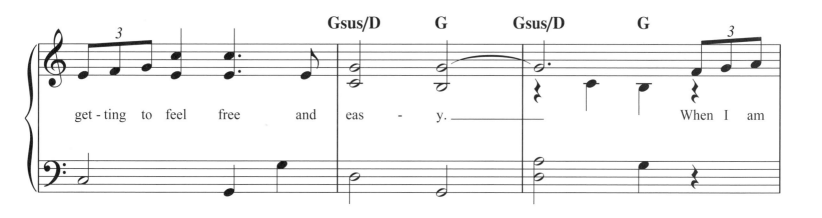

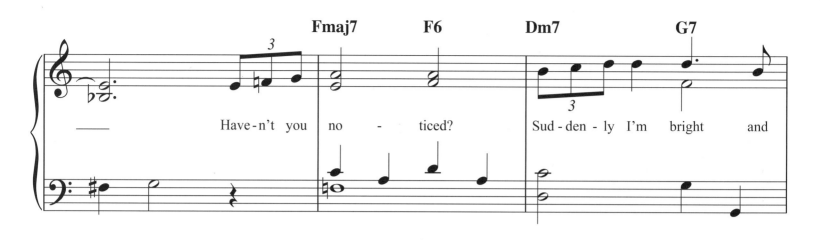

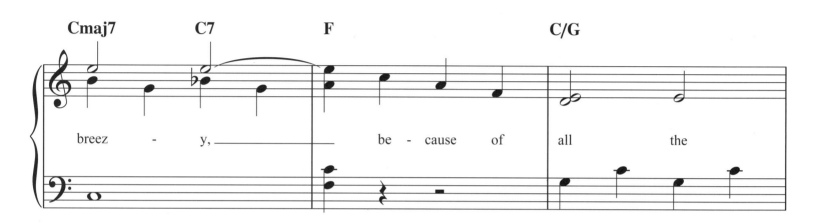

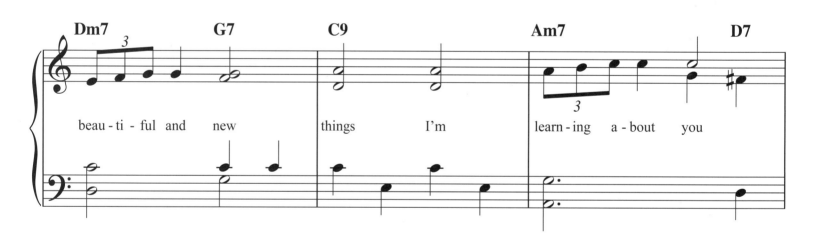

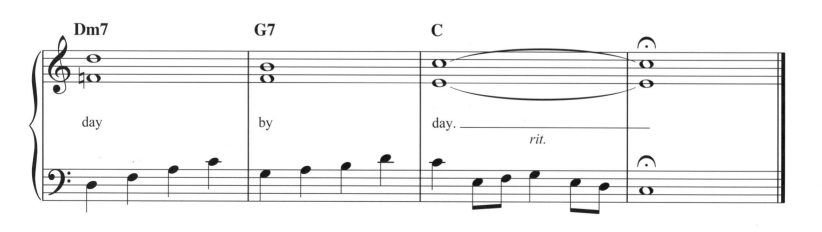

GOOD NIGHT

Words and Music by JOHN LENNON
and PAUL McCARTNEY

Slowly and dreamily

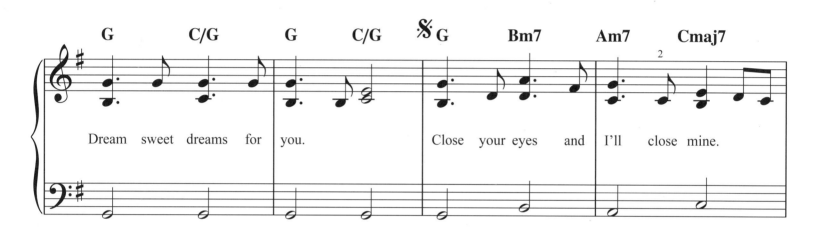

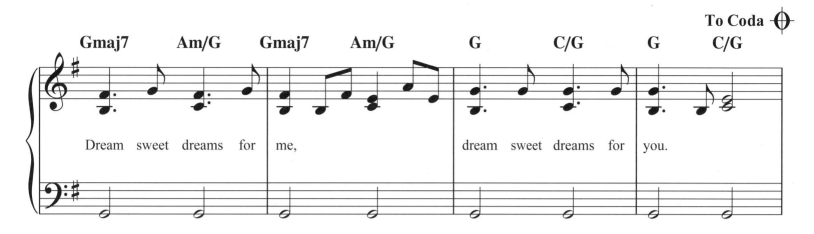
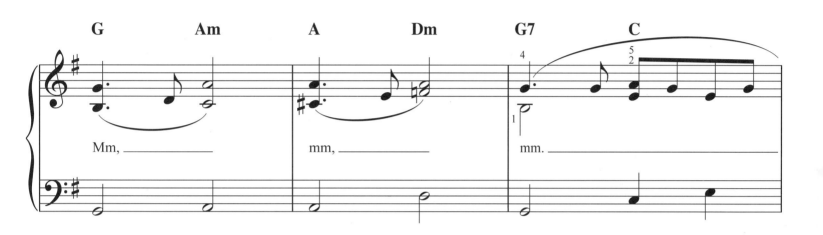
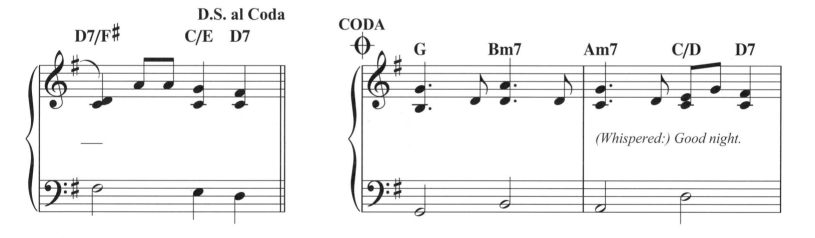
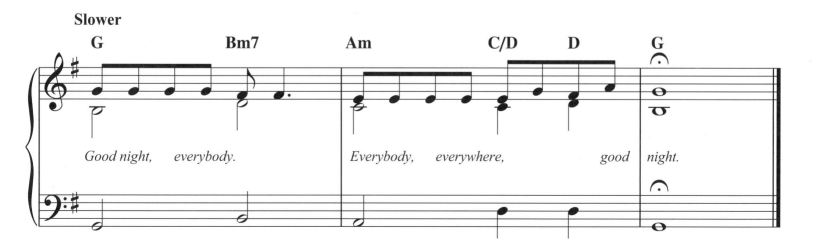

GIVE A LITTLE WHISTLE

from Walt Disney's PINOCCHIO

Words by NED WASHINGTON
Music by LEIGH HARLINE

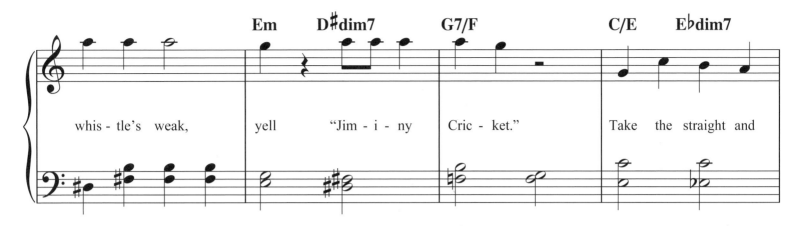

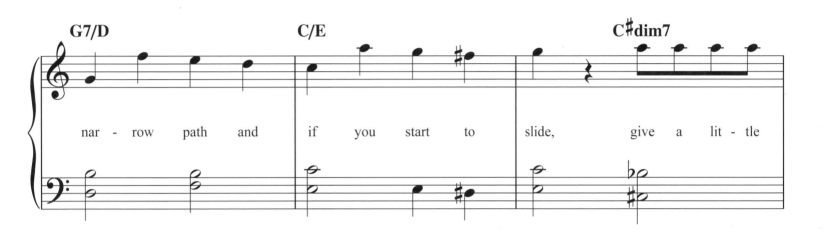

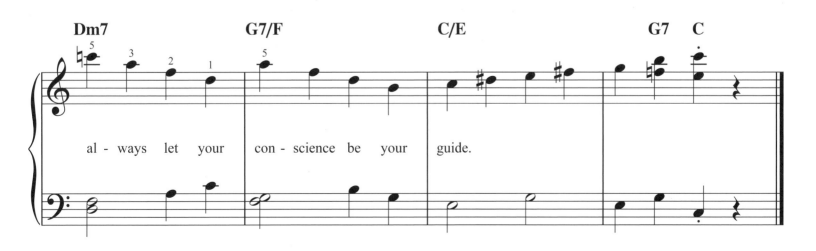

GOLDEN SLUMBERS

Words and Music by JOHN LENNON
and PAUL McCARTNEY

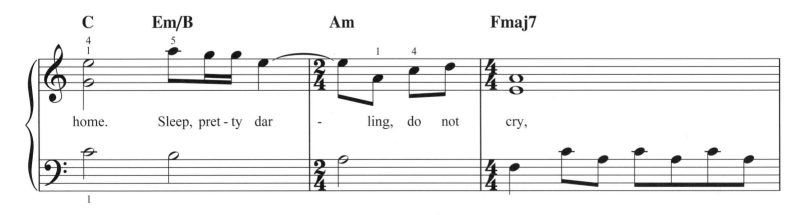

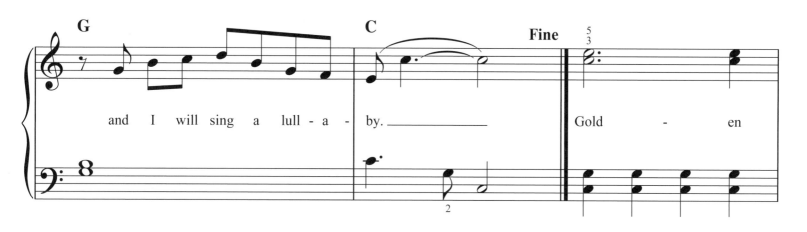

and I will sing a lull - a - by. _____ Gold - en

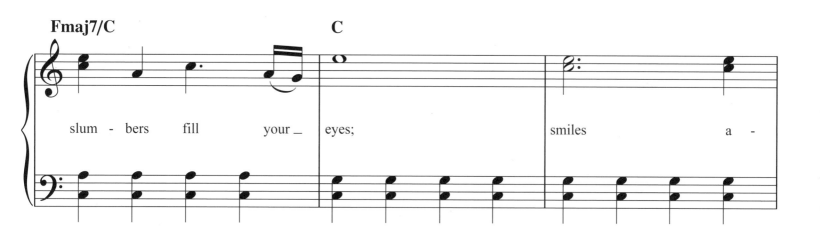

slum - bers fill your _ eyes; smiles a -

wake you when you _ rise. Sleep, pret - ty dar - ling, do not

cry, and I will sing a lull - a - by. _____

HAKUNA MATATA
from Walt Disney Pictures' THE LION KING

Music by ELTON JOHN
Lyrics by TIM RICE

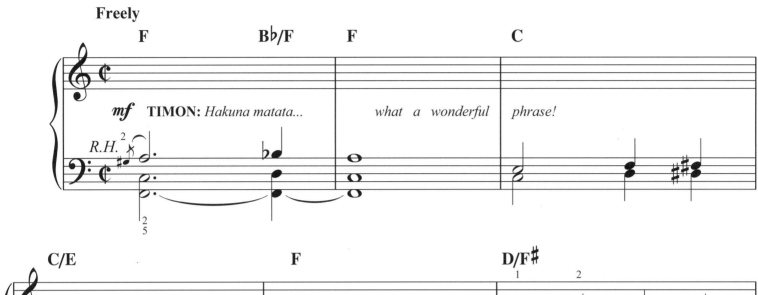

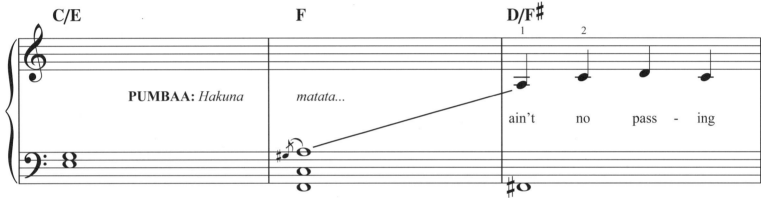

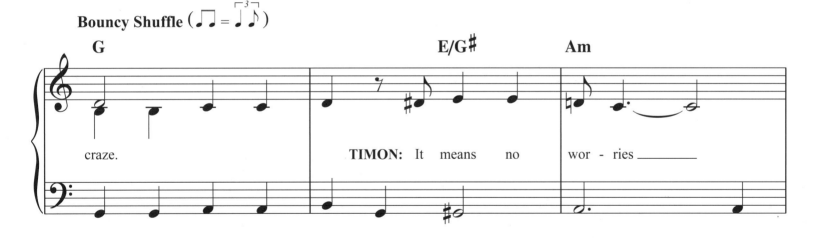

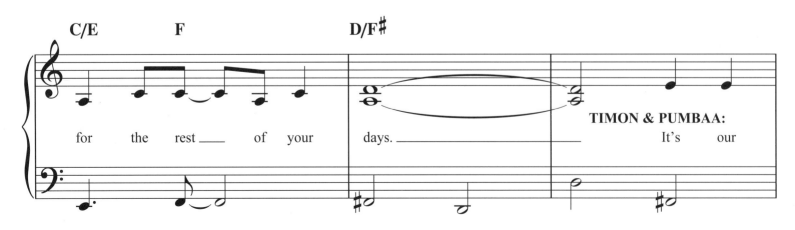

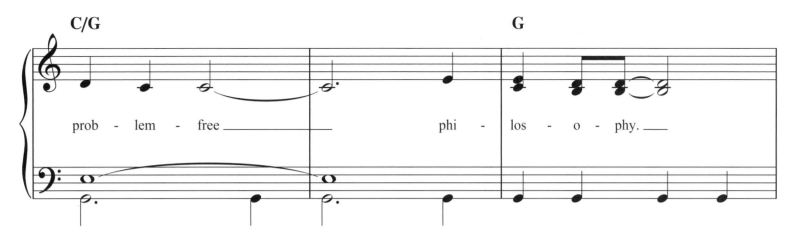

prob - lem - free _____ phi - los - o - phy. ____

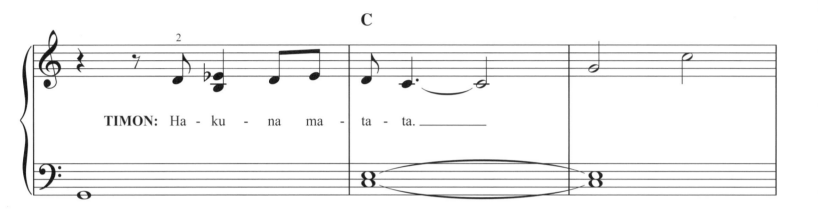

TIMON: Ha - ku - na ma - ta - ta. ____

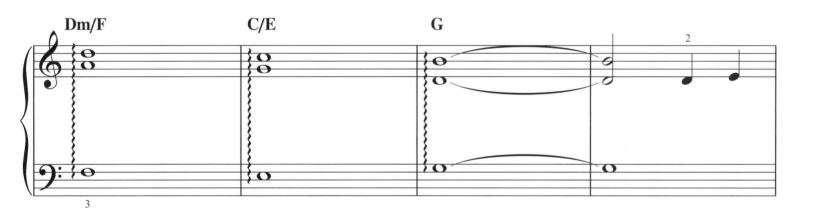

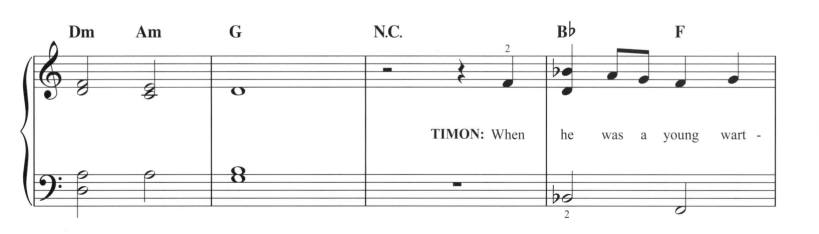

TIMON: When he was a young wart -

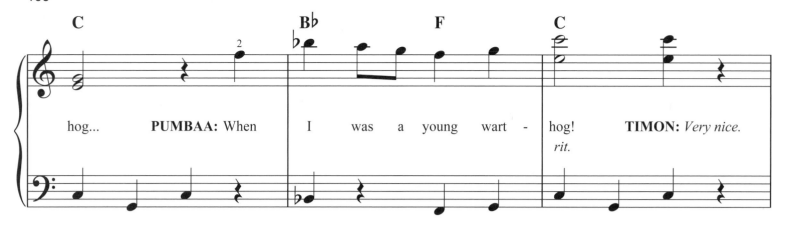

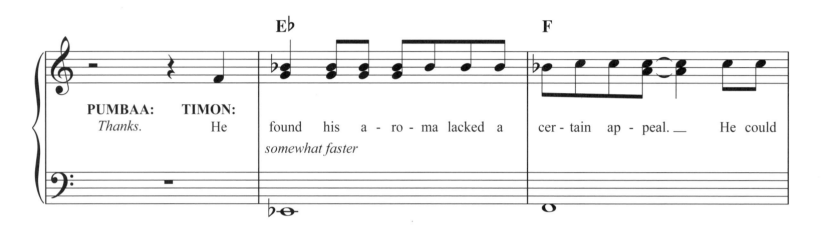

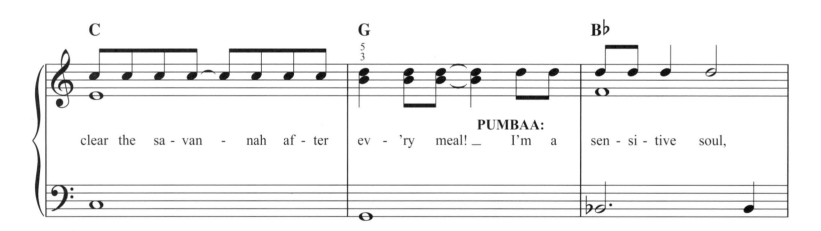

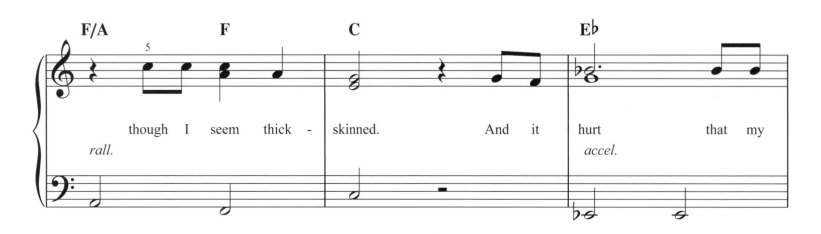

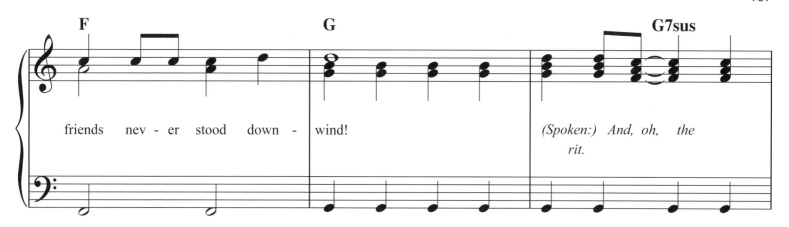

friends nev-er stood down-wind!

(Spoken:) And, oh, the rit.

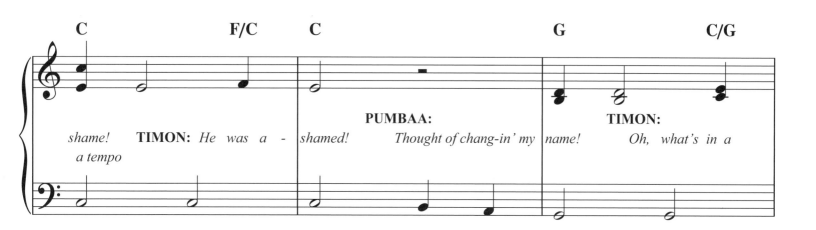

shame! **TIMON:** *He was a-shamed!* a tempo

PUMBAA: *Thought of chang-in' my name!*

TIMON: *Oh, what's in a*

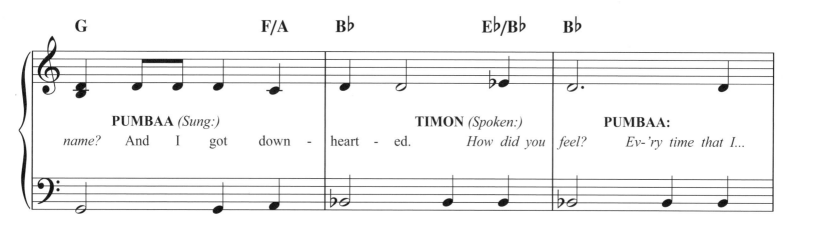

PUMBAA *(Sung:)* name? *And I got down-heart-ed.*

TIMON *(Spoken:) How did you feel?*

PUMBAA: *Ev-'ry time that I...*

TIMON: *Hey, Pumbaa, not in front of the kids.*

PUMBAA: *Oh, sorry.*

TIMON & PUMBAA: Ha - ku - na ma -

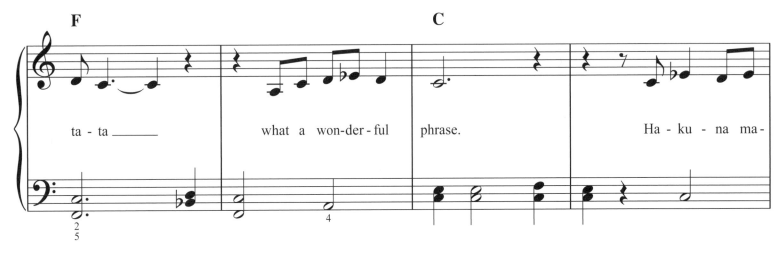

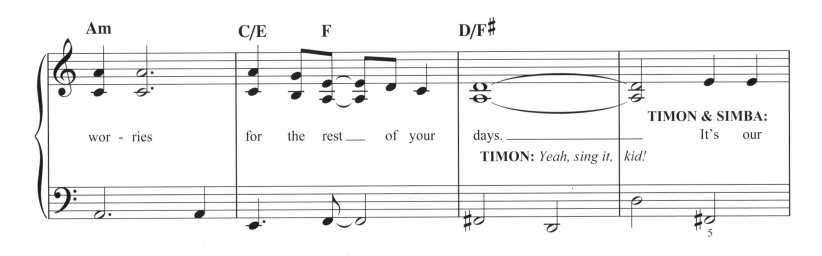

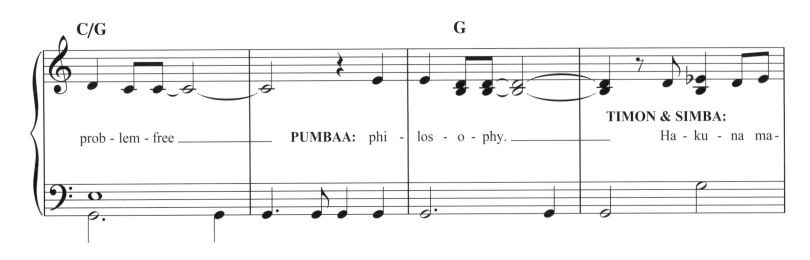

ta - ta.

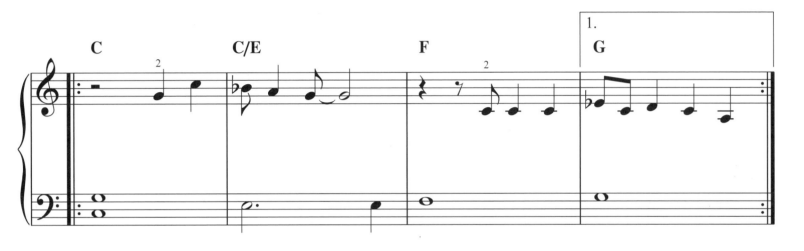

2.

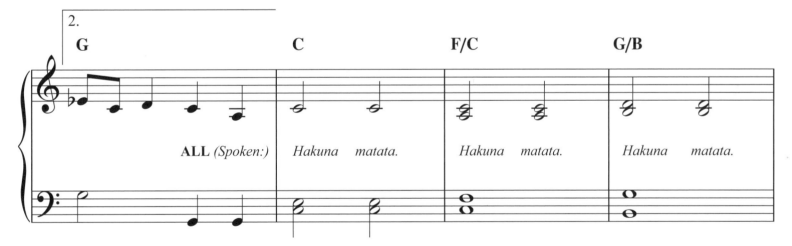

ALL *(Spoken:)*   *Hakuna matata.*   *Hakuna matata.*   *Hakuna matata.*

Hakuna matata.   *Hakuna matata.*   *Hakuna matata.*   *Hakuna matata.*

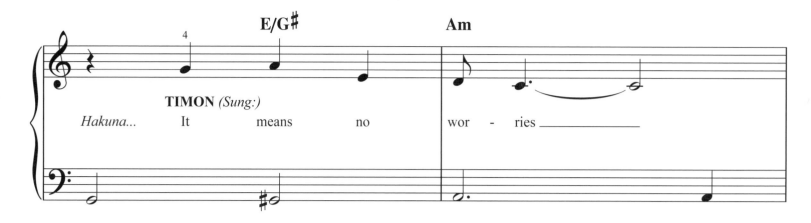

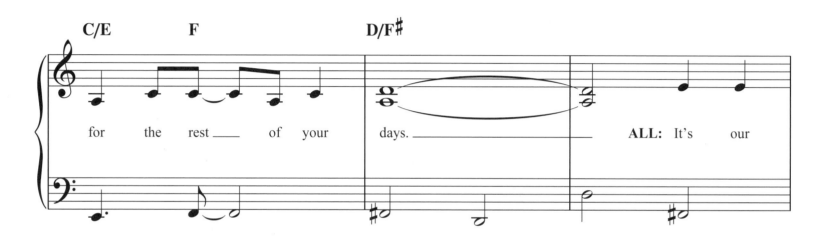

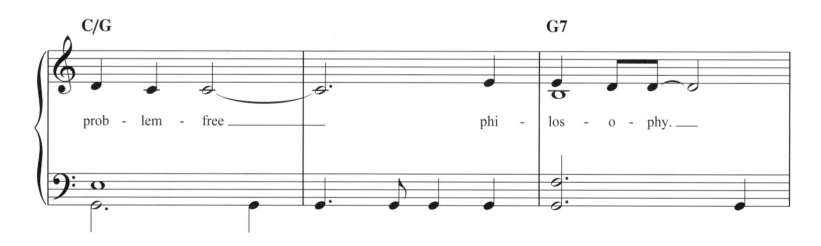

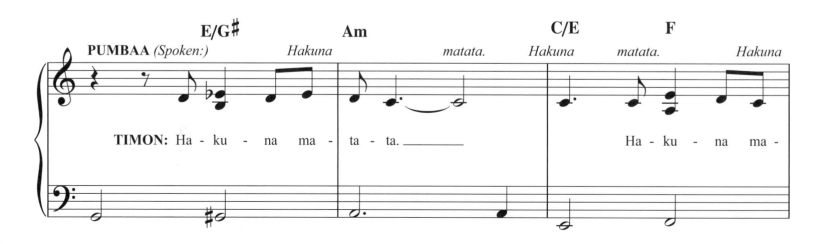

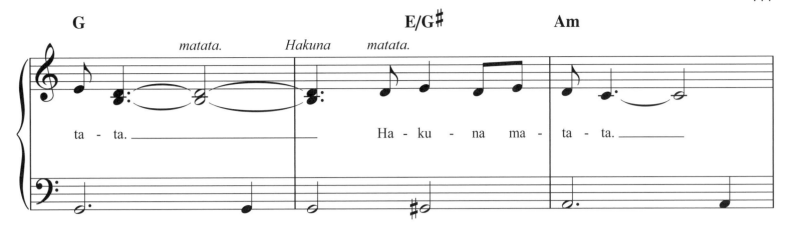

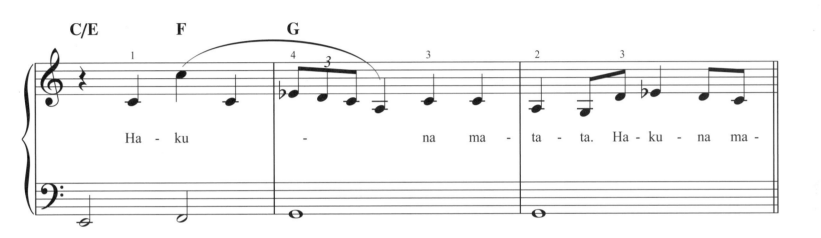

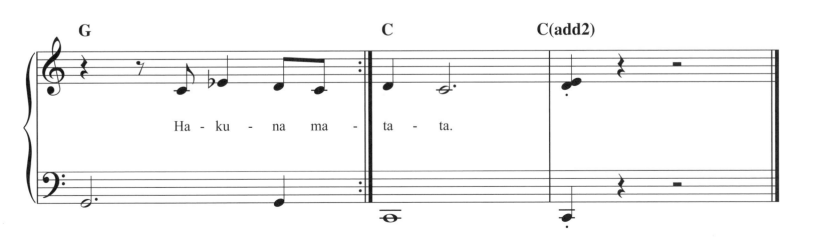

HAPPY BIRTHDAY TO YOU

Words and Music by MILDRED J. HILL
and PATTY S. HILL

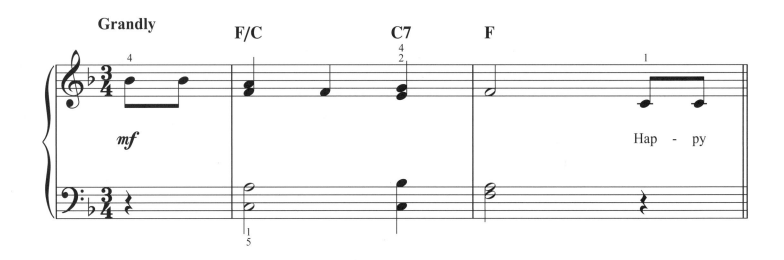

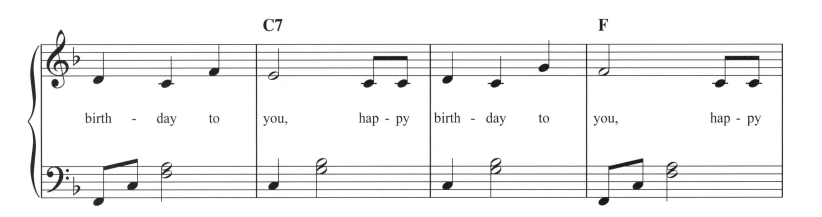

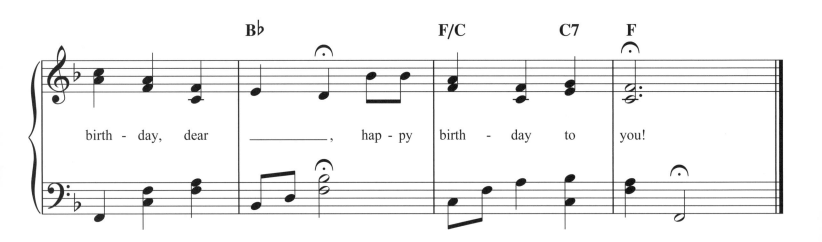

HEIGH-HO
The Dwarfs' Marching Song
from Walt Disney's SNOW WHITE AND THE SEVEN DWARFS

Words by LARRY MOREY
Music by FRANK CHURCHILL

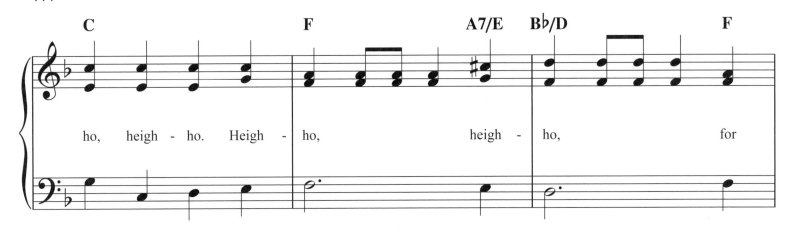

ho, heigh - ho. Heigh - ho, heigh - ho, for

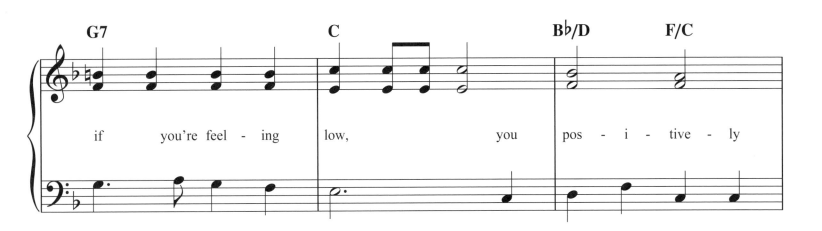

if you're feel - ing low, you pos - i - tive - ly

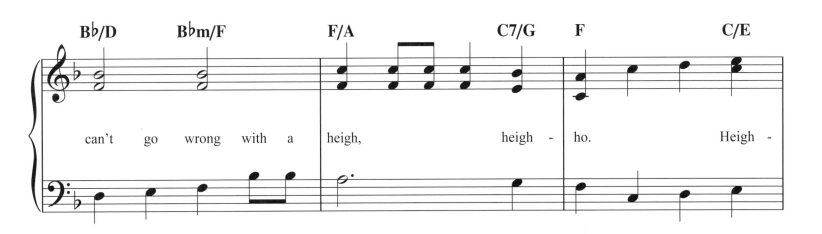

can't go wrong with a heigh, heigh - ho. Heigh -

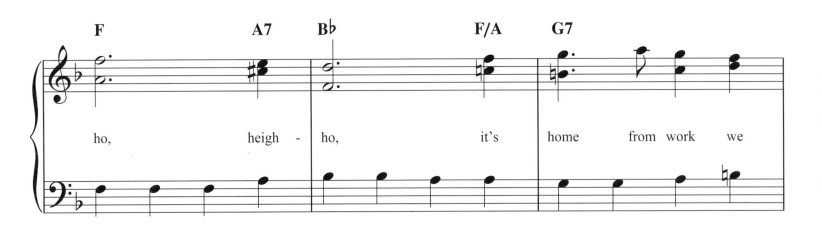

ho, heigh - ho, it's home from work we

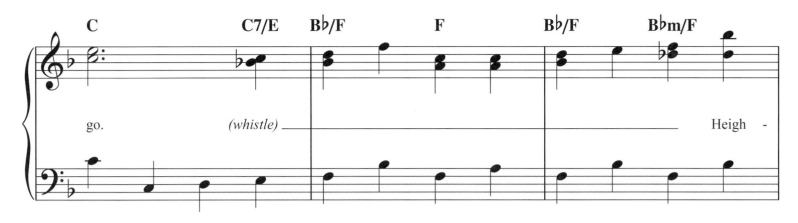

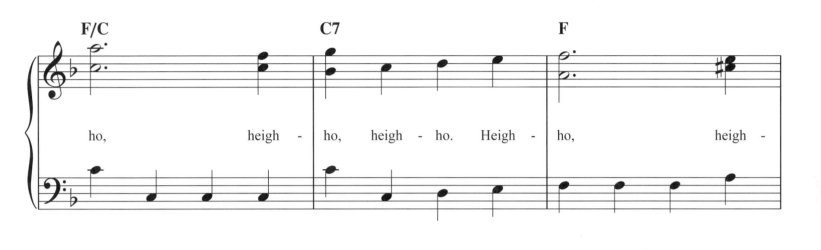

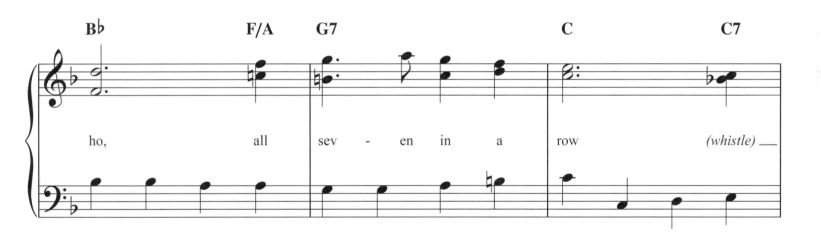

HAPPY TRAILS

from the Television Series THE ROY ROGERS SHOW

Words and Music by
DALE EVANS

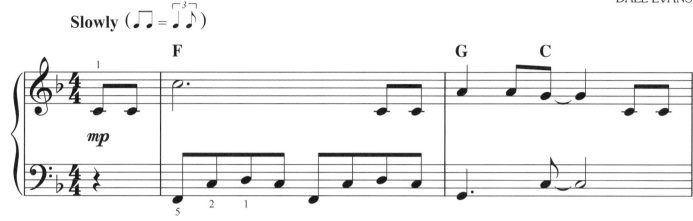

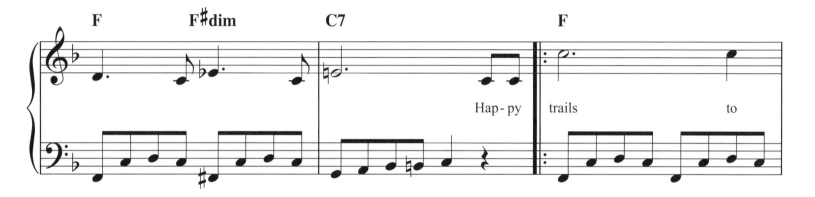

F

then.　　Who　cares　a - bout　the　clouds　when　we're　to -

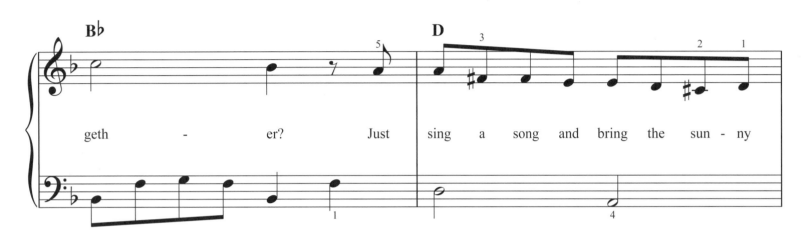

B♭　　　　　　　　　**D**

geth　-　　er?　　Just　sing　a　song　and　bring　the　sun - ny

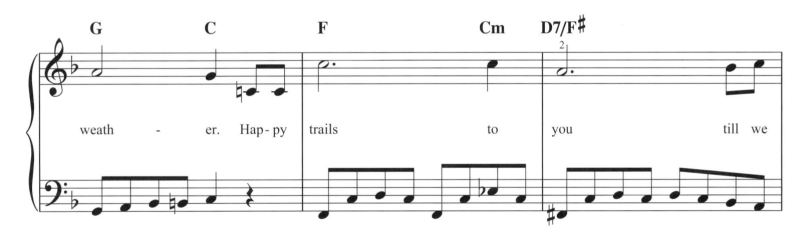

G　　　**C**　　　**F**　　　**Cm**　　**D7/F♯**

weath　-　er.　Hap - py　trails　　　　to　　you　　　　till　we

Gm　　　　**C/G**　　　　**F**　　　　　　　**F**　　**B♭/D**　　**F6**

1.

2.

meet　　a　-　　gain.　　　　Hap - py　　gain.

rit.

HEART AND SOUL

from the Paramount Short Subject A SONG IS BORN

Words by FRANK LOESSER
Music by HOAGY CARMICHAEL

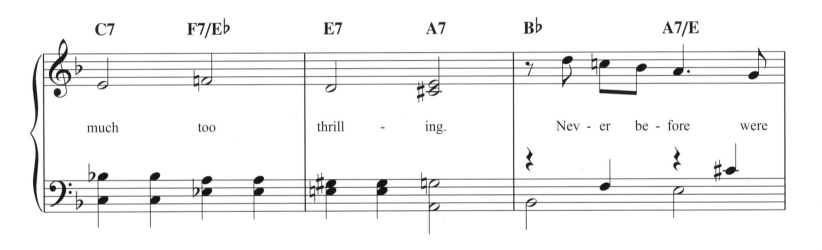

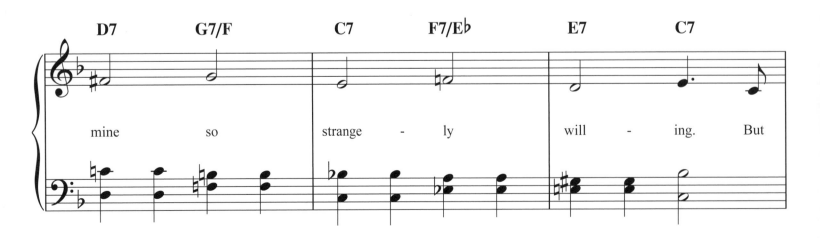

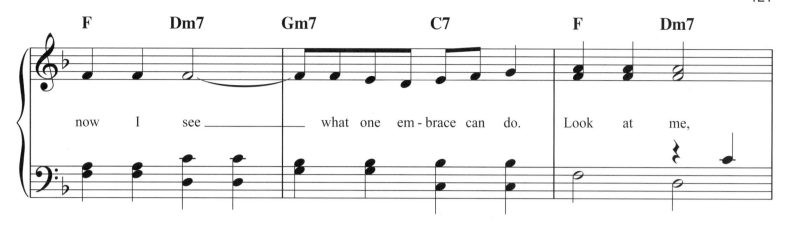

now I see _____ what one em-brace can do. Look at me,

it's got me lov-ing you mad — ly, that lit-tle kiss you

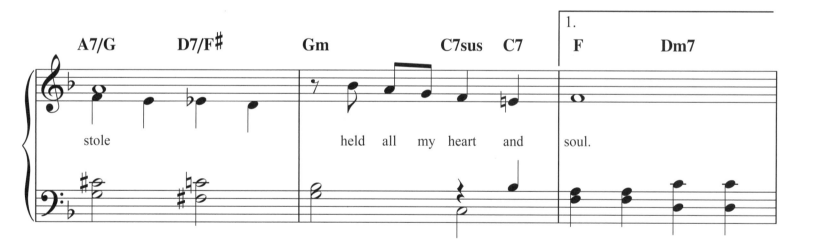

stole held all my heart and soul.

1.

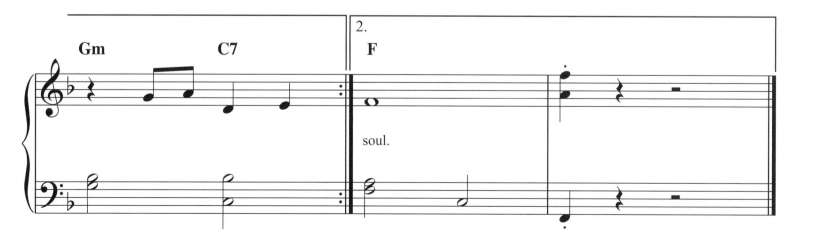

2.

soul.

soul.

THE HOKEY POKEY

Words and Music by CHARLES P. MACAK,
TAFFT BAKER and LARRY LaPRISE

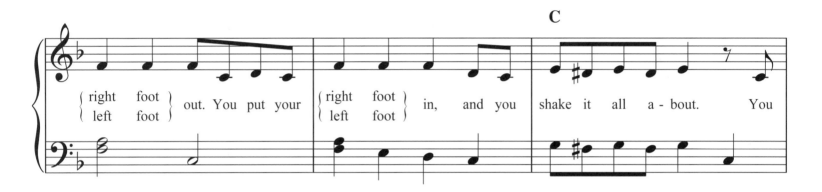

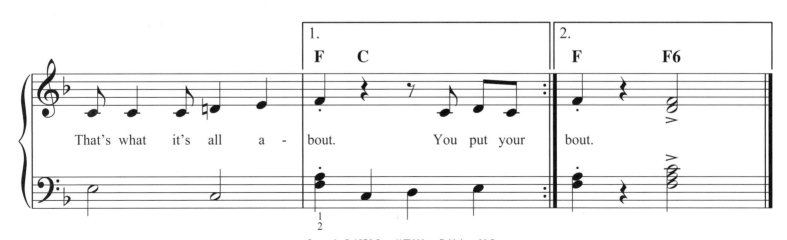

HOW MUCH IS THAT DOGGIE IN THE WINDOW

Words and Music by
BOB MERRILL

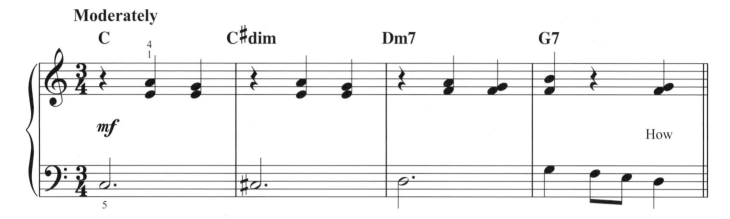

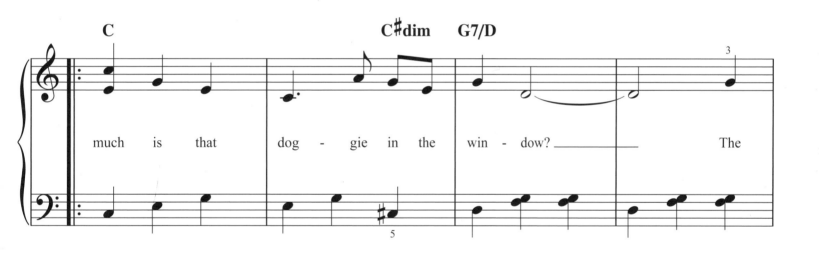

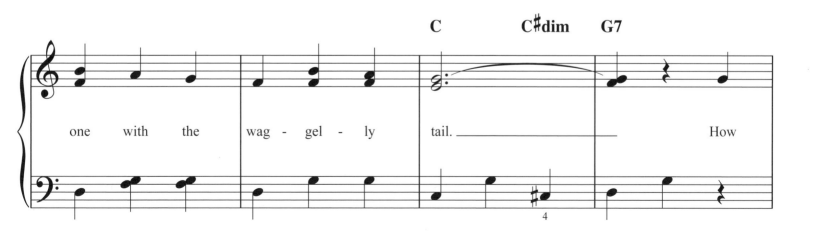

124

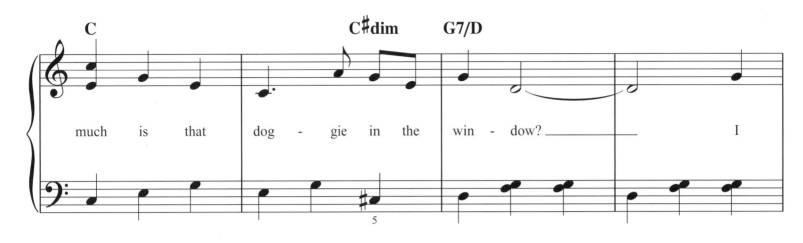

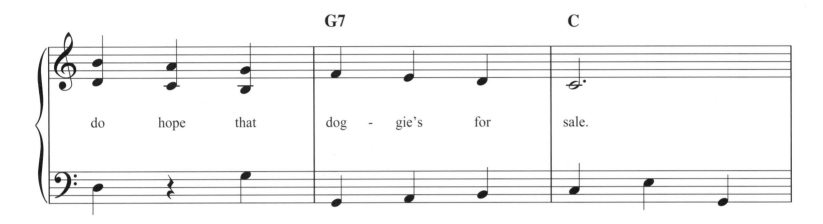

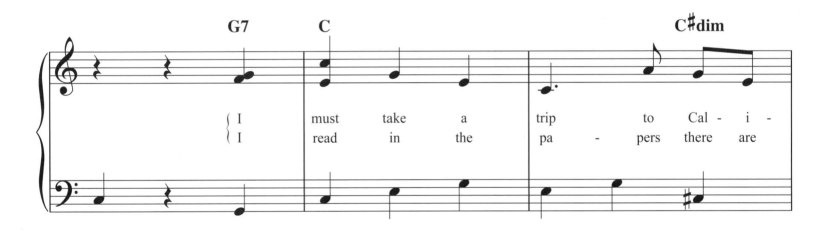

I WHISTLE A HAPPY TUNE

from THE KING AND I

Lyrics by OSCAR HAMMERSTEIN II
Music by RICHARD RODGERS

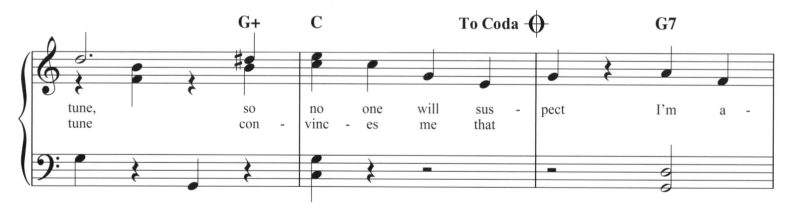

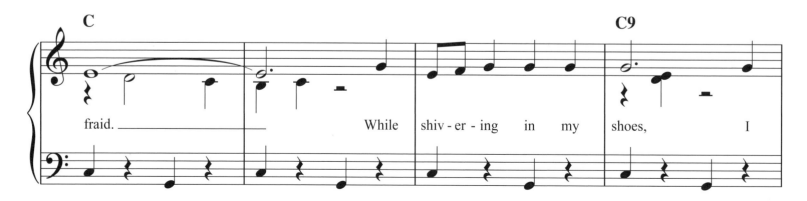

strike a care - less pose and whis - tle a hap - py

tune and no one ev - er knows I'm a - fraid._____

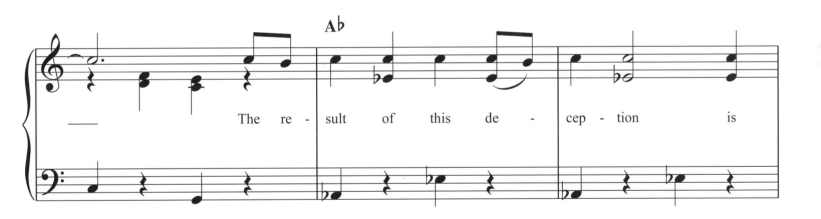

_____ The re - sult of this de - cep - tion is

ver - y strange to ____ tell, for when I fool the

Gm6 · **D9** · **G7** · **D.S. al Coda**

peo - ple I fear, I fool my - self as well! I

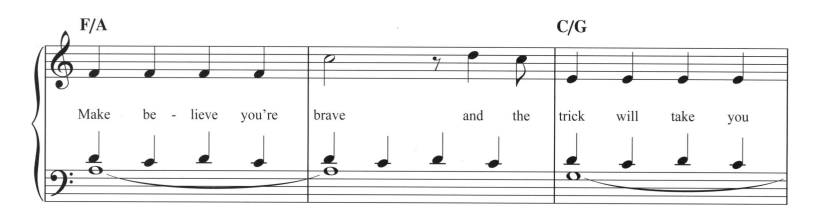

CODA · **G7** · **C**

I'm not a - fraid.

F/A · **C/G**

Make be - lieve you're brave and the trick will take you

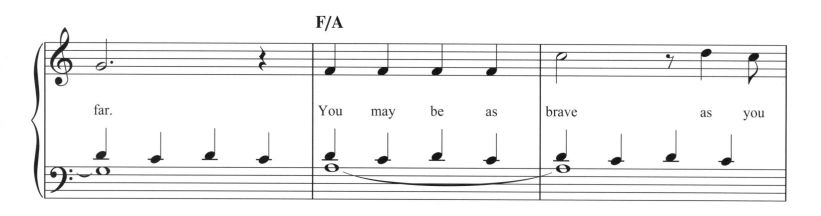

F/A

far. You may be as brave as you

129

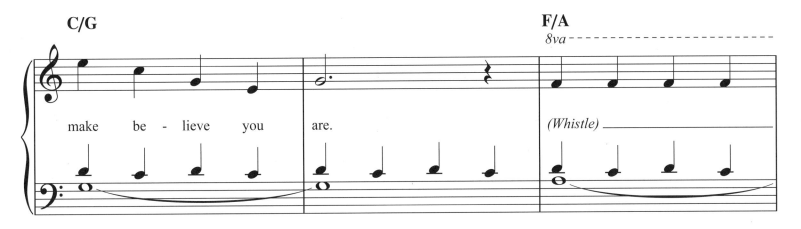

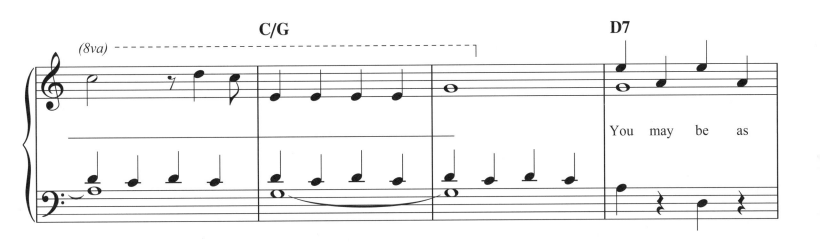

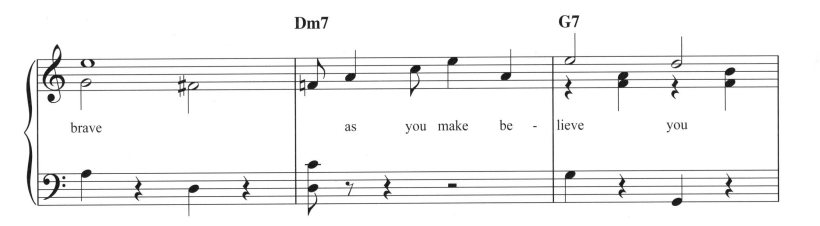

I'M LATE
from Walt Disney's ALICE IN WONDERLAND

Words by BOB HILLIARD
Music by SAMMY FAIN

With nervous energy, in 2

I'm late, I'm late for a

ver-y im-por-tant date. No time to say hel-

lo, good-bye, I'm late, I'm late, I'm late, I'm late, and

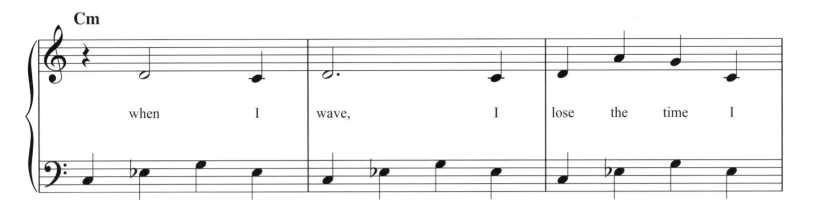

Cm

when I wave, I lose the time I

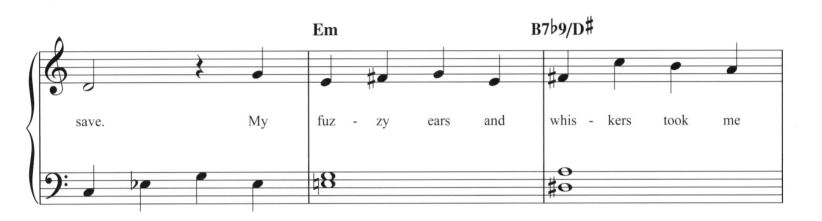

save. My fuz - zy ears and whis - kers took me

Em   **B7♭9/D♯**

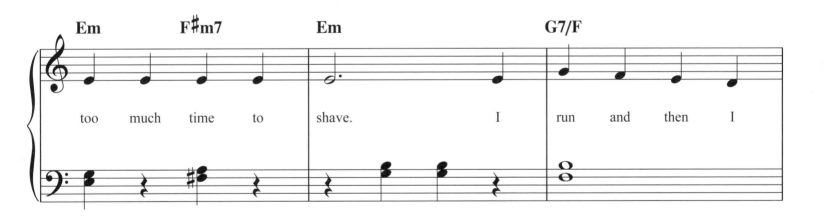

Em   **F♯m7**   **Em**   **G7/F**

too much time to shave. I run and then I

C6/G   **G7/F**   **C6/G**

hop, hop, hop, I wish that I could fly. There's

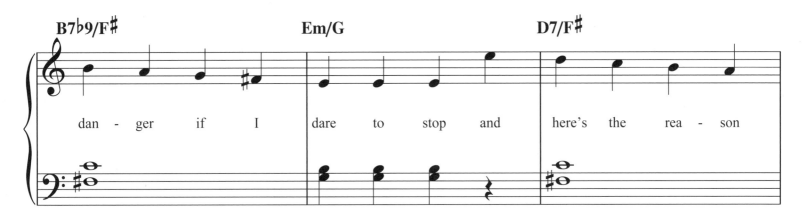

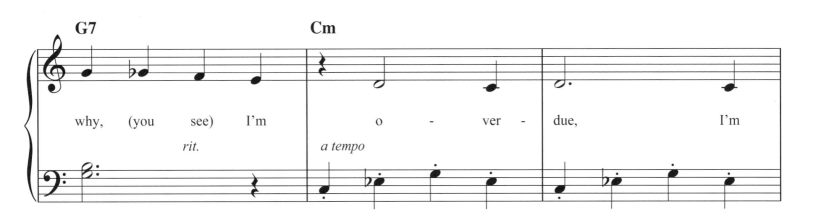

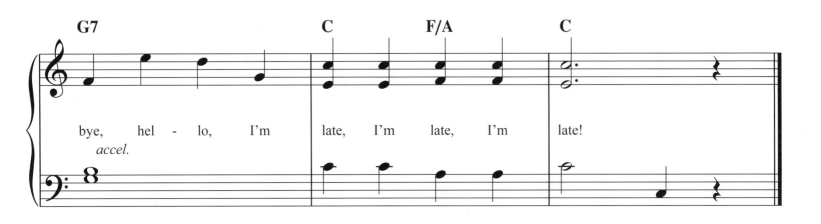

IF I ONLY HAD A BRAIN

from THE WIZARD OF OZ

Lyric by E.Y. "YIP" HARBURG
Music by HAROLD ARLEN

trou - ble or in pain.
gard - ing love and art.
fate I don't de - serve.

With the
I'd be
But I

thoughts I'd be think - in' I could
friends with the spar - rows and the
could show my prow - ess, be a

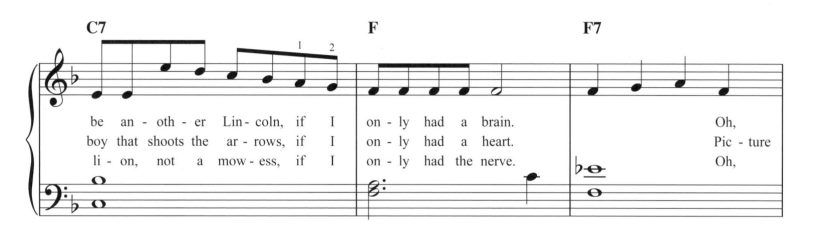

be an - oth - er Lin - coln, if I
boy that shoots the ar - rows, if I
li - on, not a mow - ess, if I

on - ly had a brain.
on - ly had a heart.
on - ly had the nerve.

Oh,
Pic - ture
Oh,

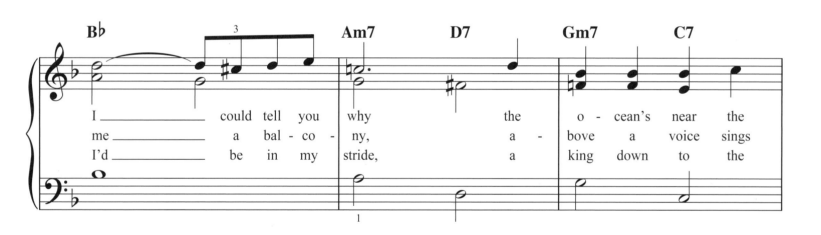

I _____ could tell you
me _____ a bal - co -
I'd _____ be in my

why
ny,
stride,

the
a -
a

o - cean's near the
bove a voice sings
king down to the

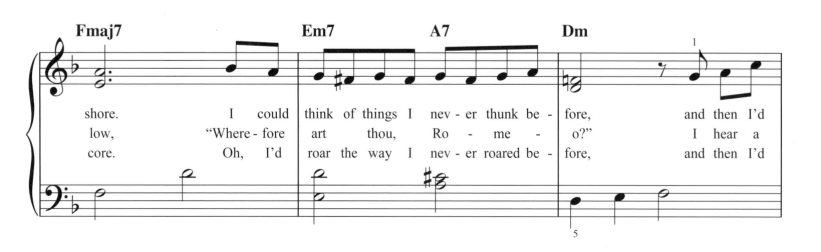

shore.
low,
core.

I could
"Where - fore
Oh, I'd

think of things I nev - er thunk be -
art thou, Ro - me -
roar the way I nev - er roared be -

fore,
o?"
fore,

and then I'd
I hear a
and then I'd

G C7 F

sit and think some more. I would not be just a nuff-in' my
beat. How sweet! Just to reg-is-ter e-mo-tion,
rrrwoof, and roar some more. I would show the di-no-sau-rus who's

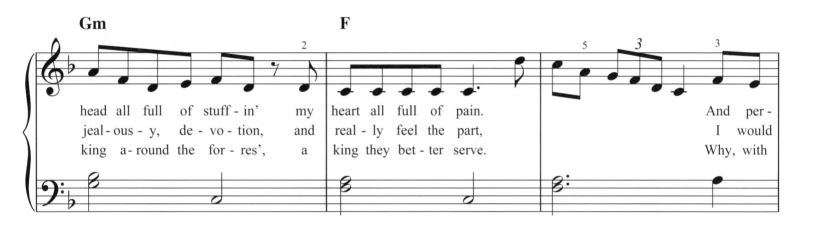

Gm F

head all full of stuff-in' my heart all full of pain. And per-
jeal-ous-y, de-vo-tion, and real-ly feel the part, I would
king a-round the for-res', a king they bet-ter serve. Why, with

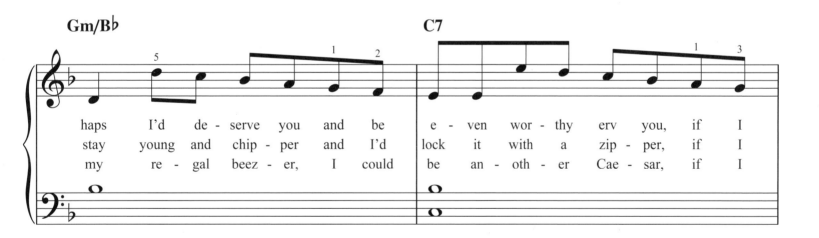

Gm/Bb C7

haps I'd de-serve you and be e-ven wor-thy erv you, if I
stay young and chip-per and I'd lock it with a zip-per, if I
my re-gal beez-er, I could be an-oth-er Cae-sar, if I

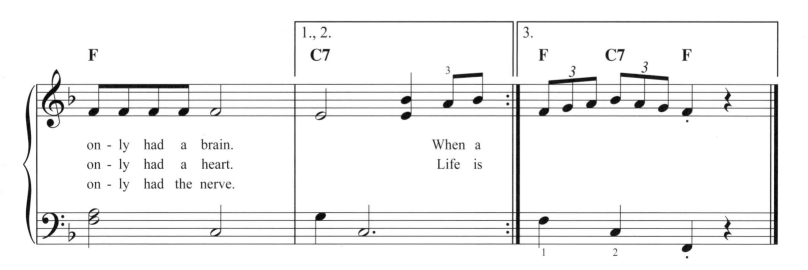

F 1., 2. C7 3. F C7 F

on-ly had a brain. When a Life is
on-ly had a heart.
on-ly had the nerve.

I'M POPEYE THE SAILOR MAN

Theme from the Paramount Cartoon POPEYE THE SAILOR

Words and Music by
SAMMY LERNER

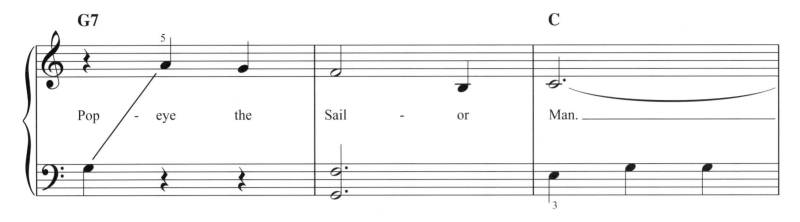

Pop - eye the Sail - or Man. _____

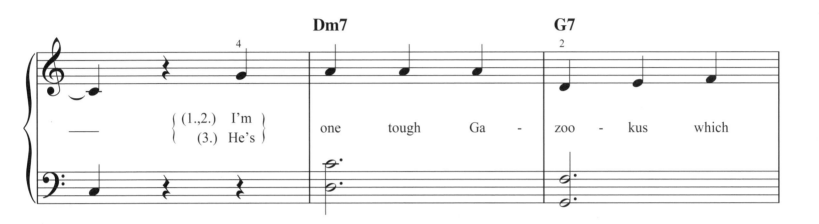

_____ { (1.,2.) I'm } { (3.) He's } one tough Ga - zoo - kus which

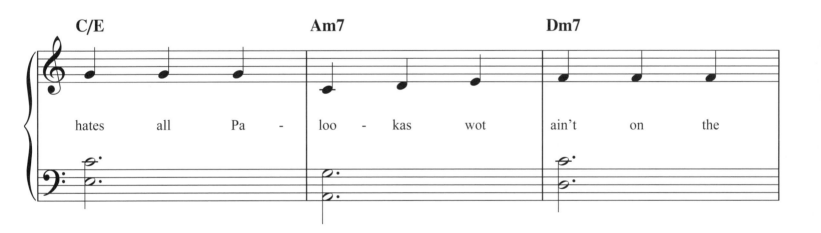

hates all Pa - loo - kas wot ain't on the

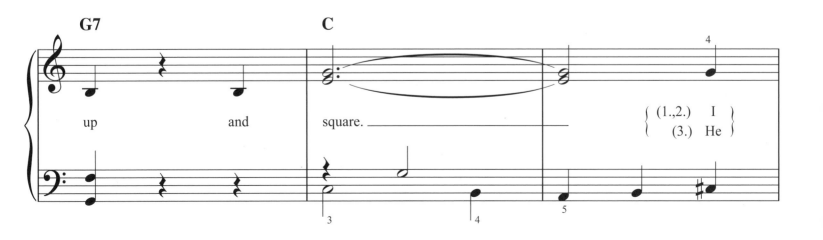

up and square. _____ { (1.,2.) I } { (3.) He }

138

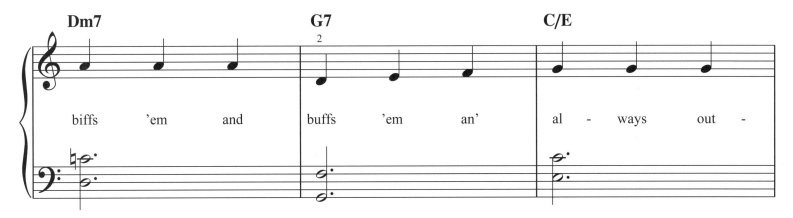

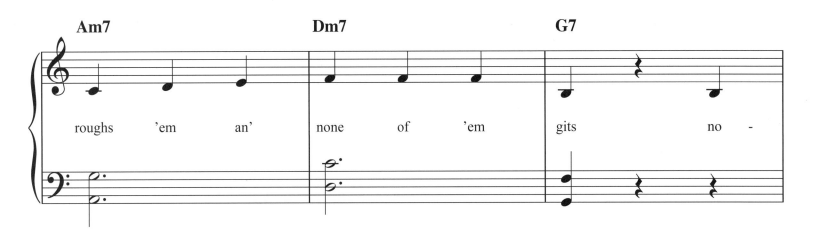

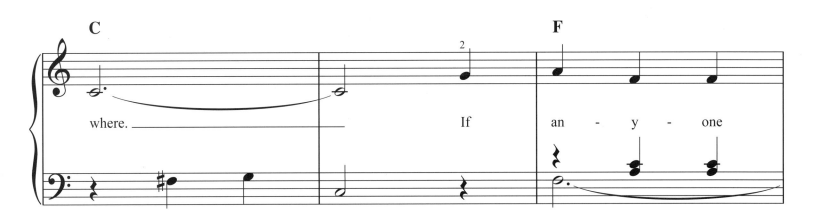

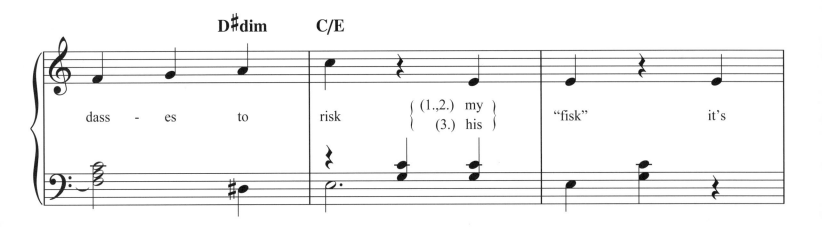

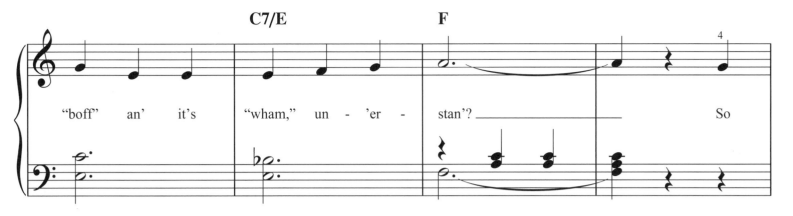

C7/E   **F**

"boff" an' it's "wham," un - 'er - stan'? _____ So

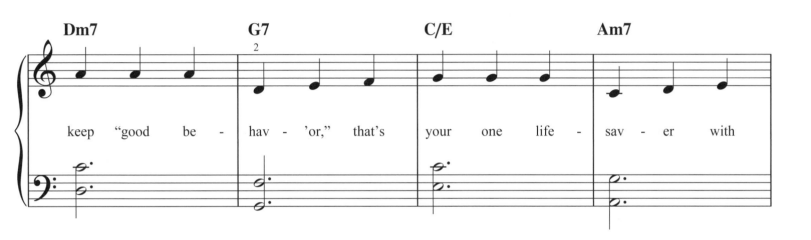

Dm7   **G7**   **C/E**   **Am7**

keep "good be - hav - 'or," that's your one life - sav - er with

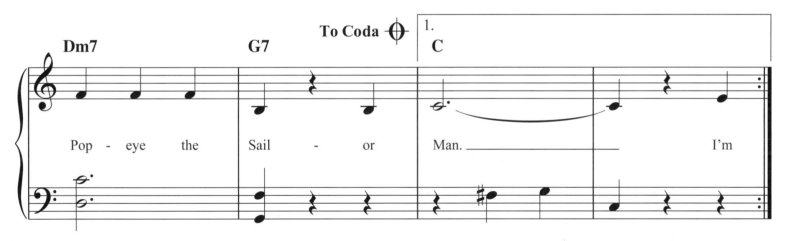

Dm7   **G7**   **To Coda** ⊕   **1.** **C**

Pop - eye the Sail - or Man. _____ I'm

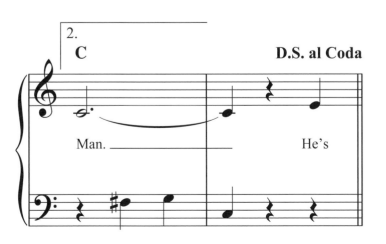

2. **C**   **D.S. al Coda**

Man. _____ He's

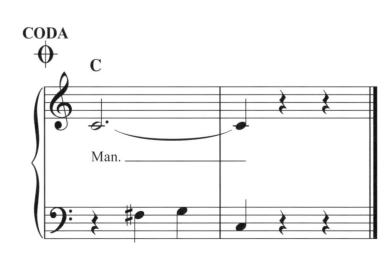

CODA ⊕   **C**

Man. _____

I'VE BEEN WORKING ON THE RAILROAD

American Folksong

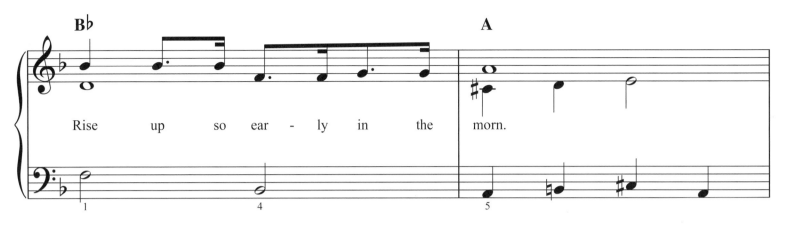

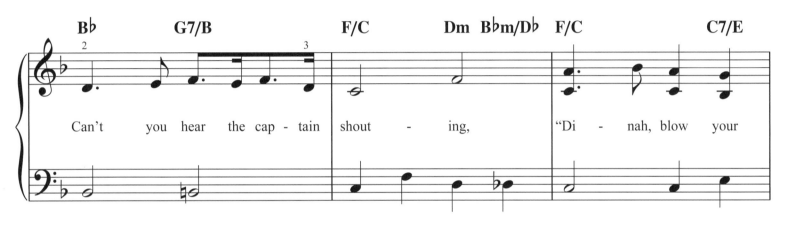

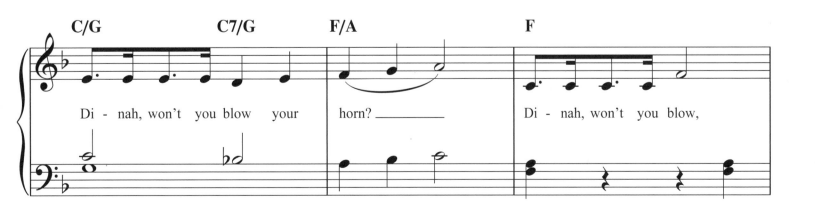

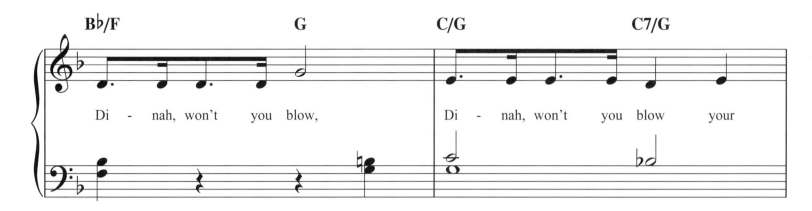

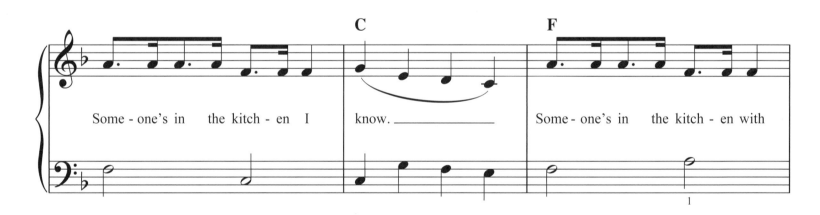

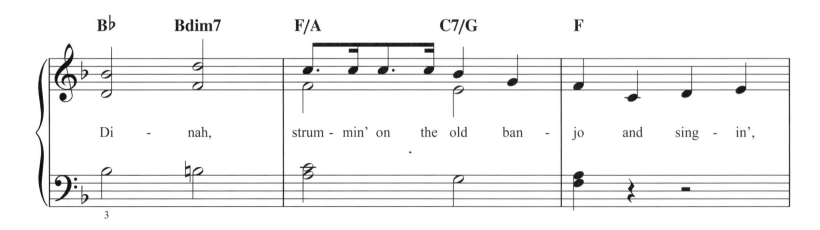

"Fee,   fi,   fid - dle - ee - i   -   o,   fee,   fi,   fid - dle - ee - i -

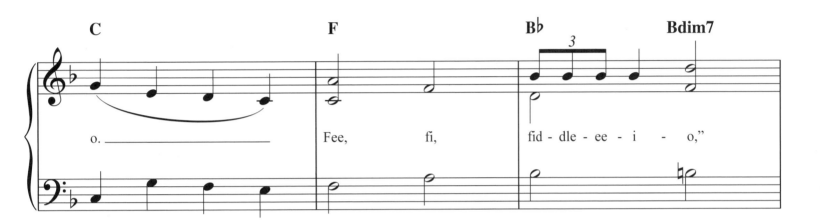

o. _____   Fee,   fi,   fid - dle - ee - i - o,"

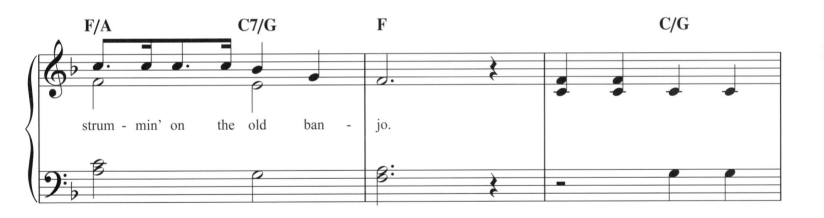

strum - min' on   the old ban - jo.

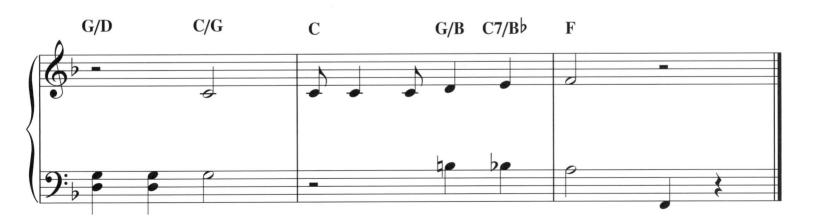

I'VE GOT NO STRINGS
from Walt Disney's PINOCCHIO

Words by NED WASHINGTON
Music by LEIGH HARLINE

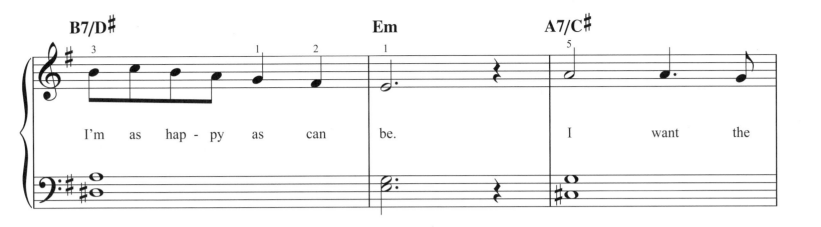

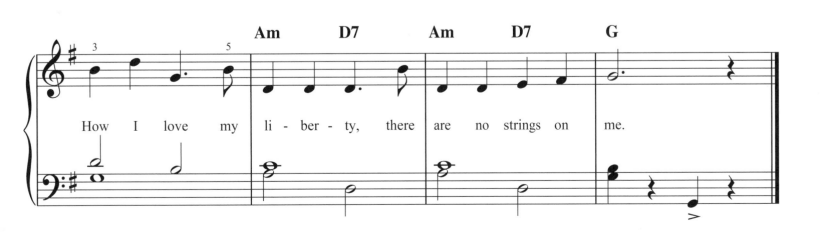

IMAGINE

Words and Music by
JOHN LENNON

Slowly

I - mag - ine there's   no   heav -
I - mag - ine there's   no   coun -
I - mag - ine   no   pos - ses -

en.   It's   eas - y   if   you   try.
tries.   It   is - n't   hard   to   do.
sions.   I   won - der   if   you   can.

No   hell   be - low   us,
Noth - ing   to   kill   or   die   for
No   need for   greed   or   hun -   ger,

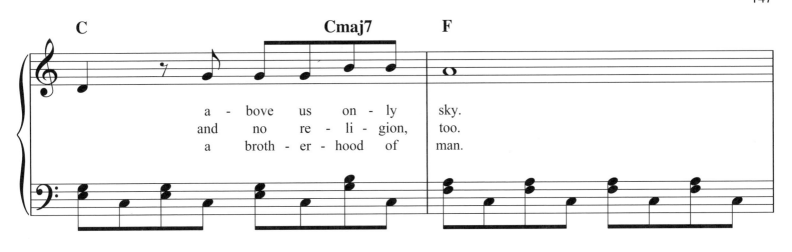

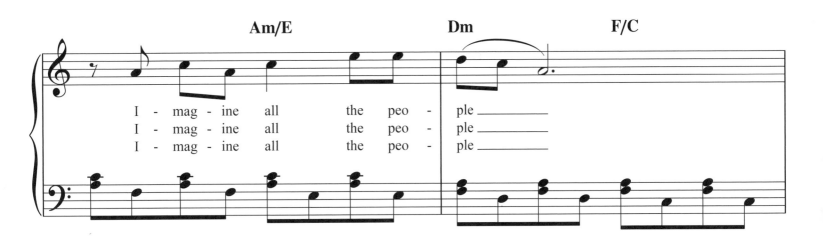

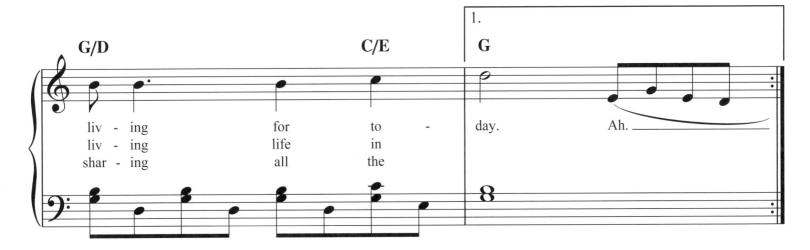

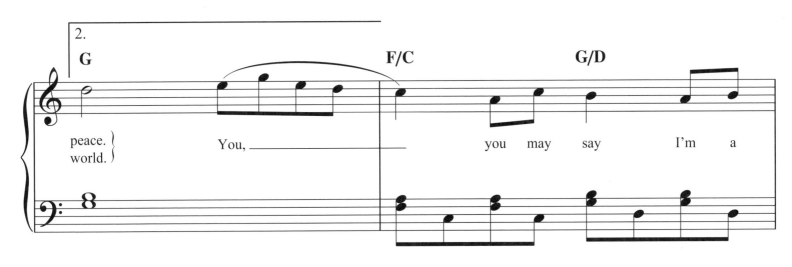

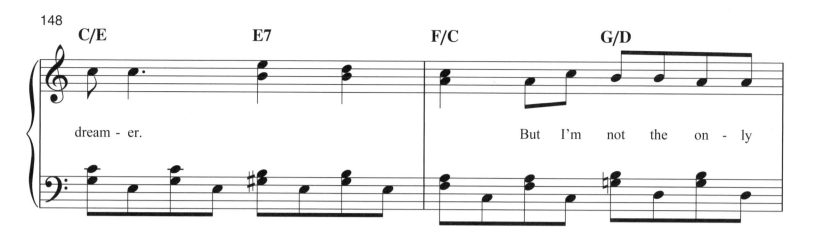

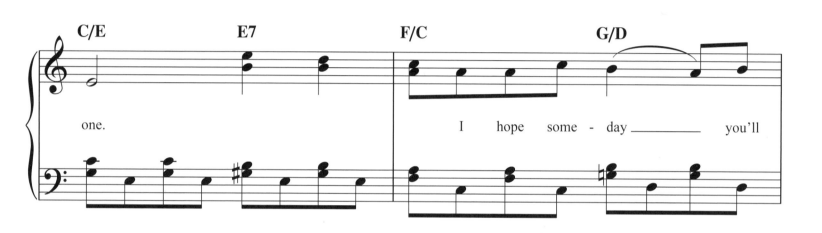

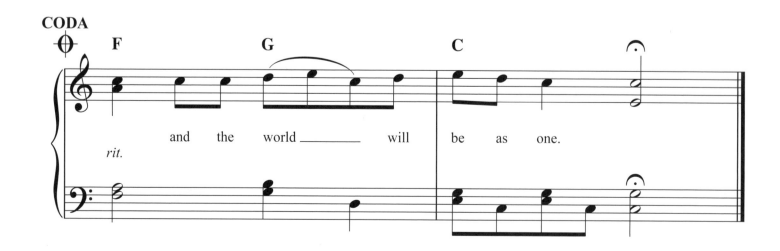

JOHN JACOB JINGLEHEIMER SCHMIDT

Traditional

IT'S A SMALL WORLD

from Disneyland Resort® and Magic Kingdom® Park

Words and Music by RICHARD M. SHERMAN
and ROBERT B. SHERMAN

Brisk March tempo

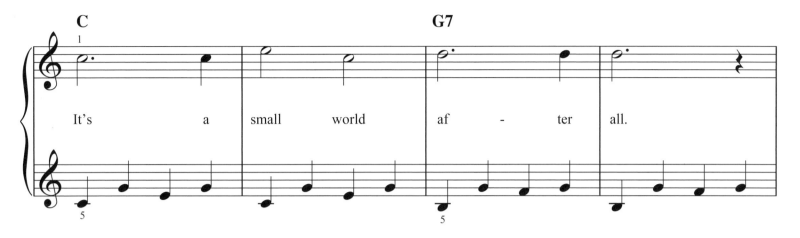

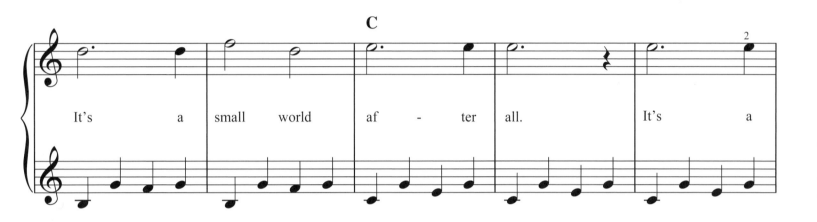

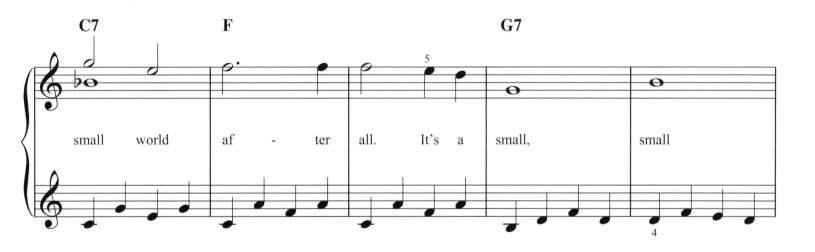

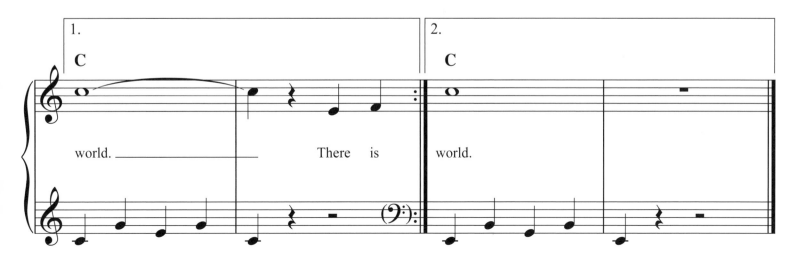

KUMBAYA

Congo Folksong

Slowly, like a hymn

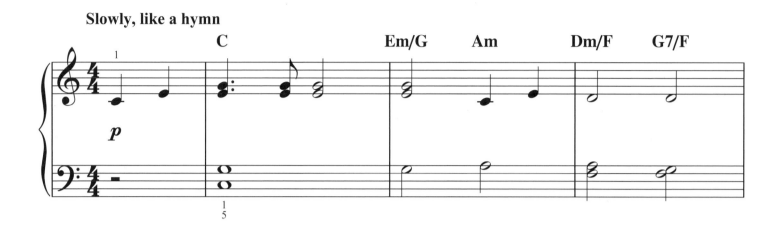

Kum - ba - ya, my Lord, _____ kum - ba -
cry - ing, Lord, _____ kum - ba -
pray - ing, Lord, _____ kum - ba -
need you, Lord, _____ kum - ba -

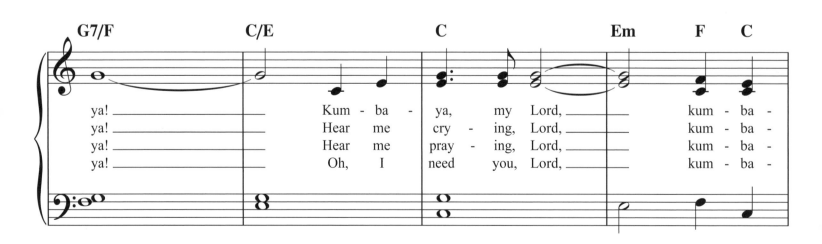

ya! _____ Kum - ba - ya, my Lord, _____ kum - ba -
ya! _____ Hear me cry - ing, Lord, _____ kum - ba -
ya! _____ Hear me pray - ing, Lord, _____ kum - ba -
ya! _____ Oh, I need you, Lord, _____ kum - ba -

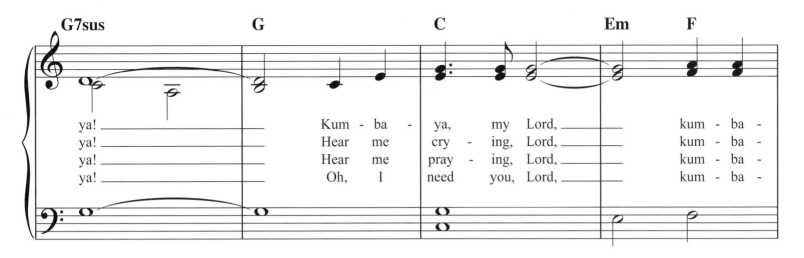

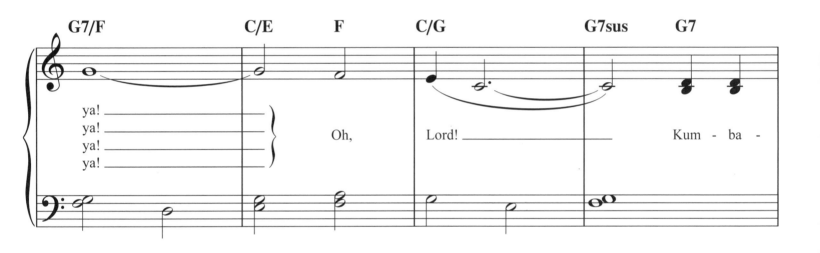

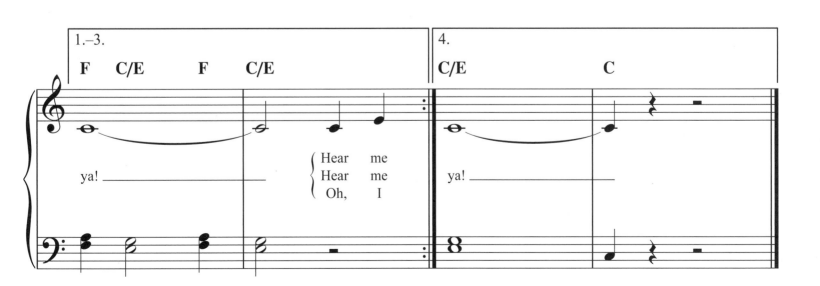

LAVENDER BLUE
(Dilly Dilly)
from Walt Disney's SO DEAR TO MY HEART

Words by LARRY MOREY
Music by ELIOT DANIEL

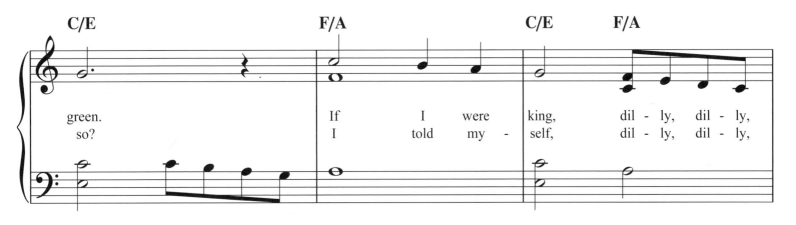

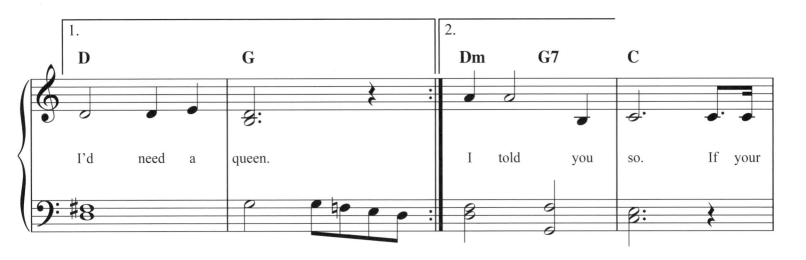

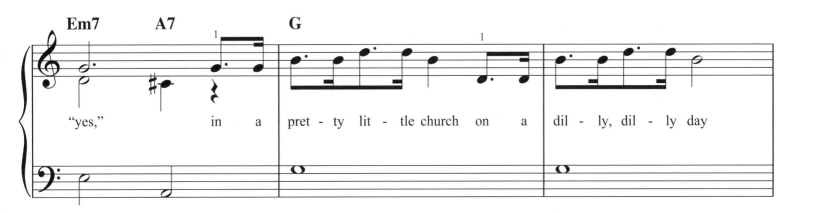

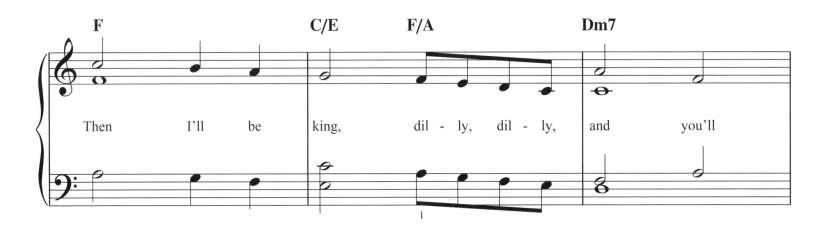

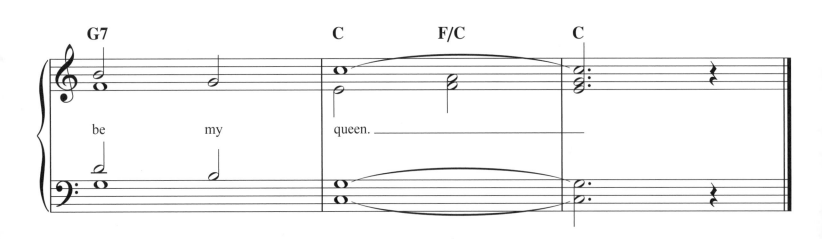

LET IT GO
from Disney's Animated Feature FROZEN

Music and Lyrics by KRISTEN ANDERSON-LOPEZ
and ROBERT LOPEZ

Half-time feel, mysterious

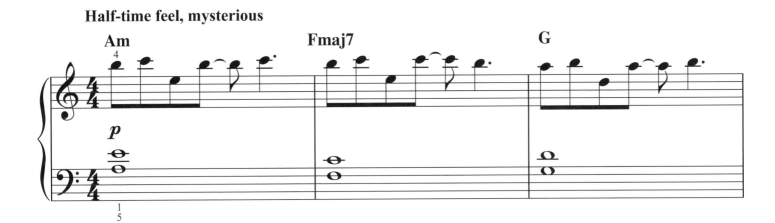

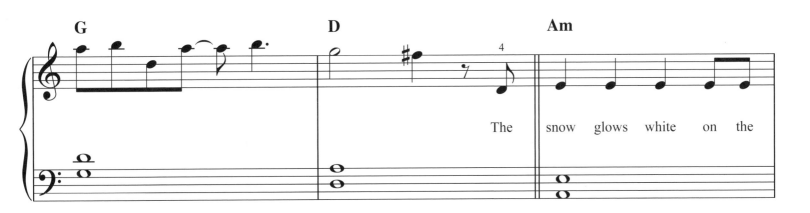

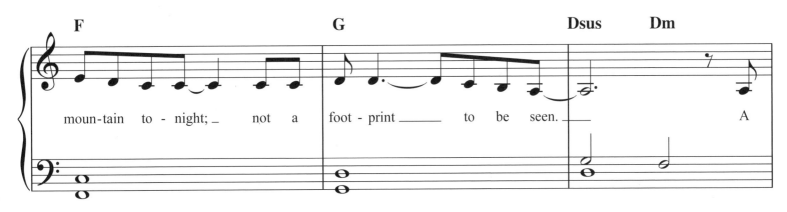

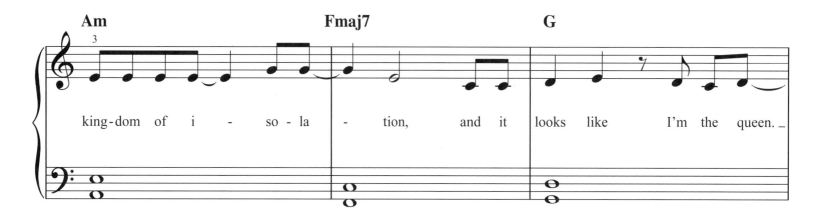

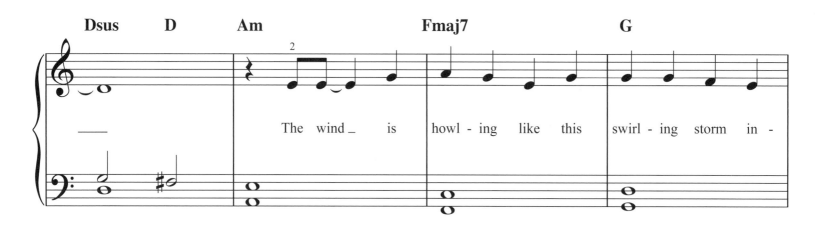

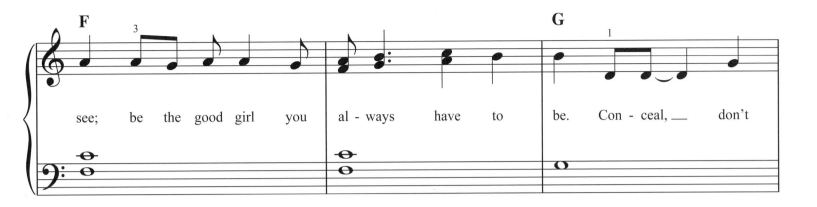

see; be the good girl you al - ways have to be. Con - ceal, __ don't

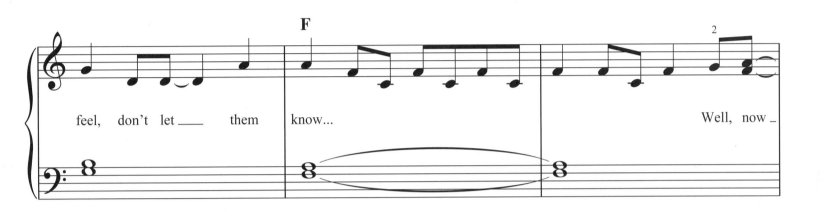

feel, don't let __ them know... Well, now __

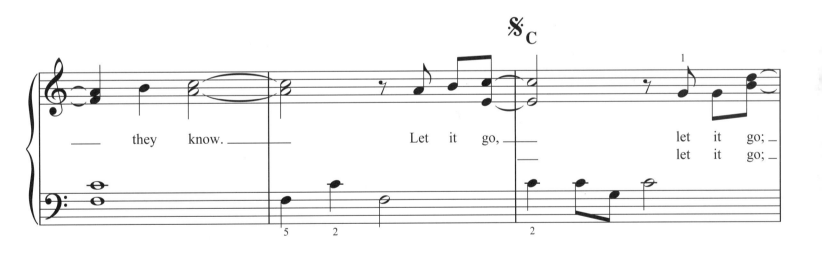

__ they know. __ Let it go, __ let it go; __
let it go; __

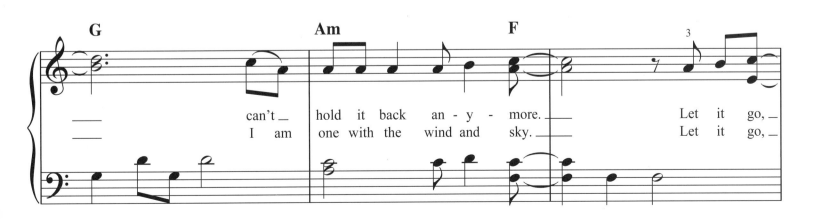

can't __ hold it back an - y - more. __ Let it go, __
I am one with the wind and sky. Let it go, __

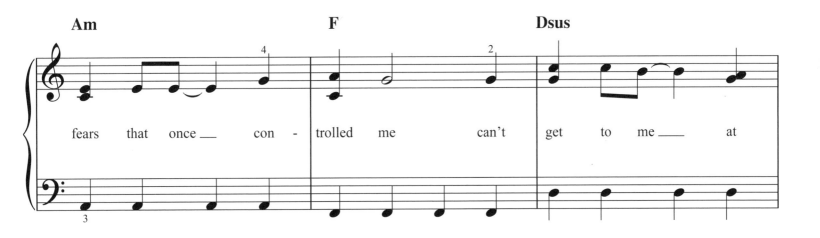

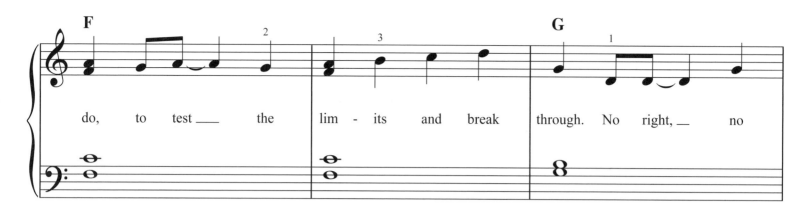

do, to test ___ the lim - its and break through. No right, ___ no

wrong, no rules for me, ___ I'm free!

D.S. al Coda

Let it go, ___

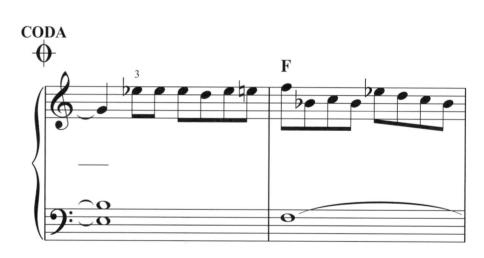

CODA

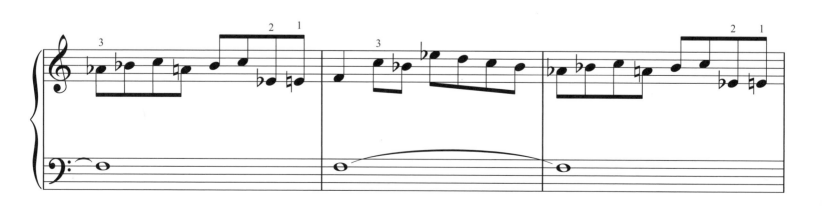

My pow – er · flur – ries through the · air in – to the

ground. · My soul __ is · spi – ral – ing in

fro – zen frac – tals · all a – round. __ · And one __ thought

cry – stal – liz – es · like an i – cy · blast:

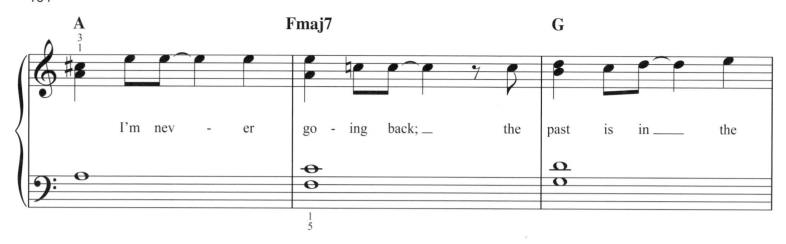

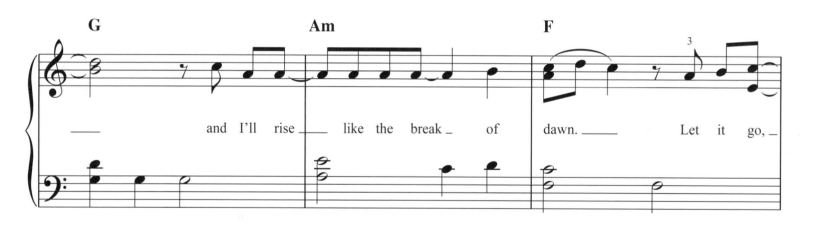

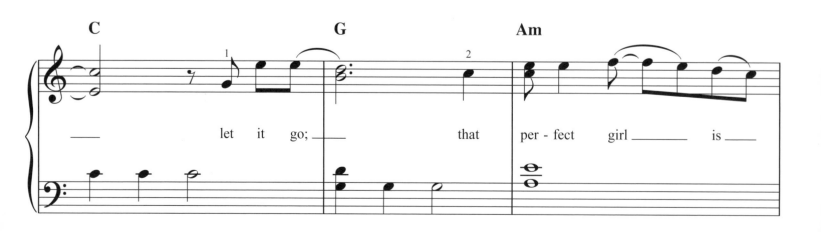

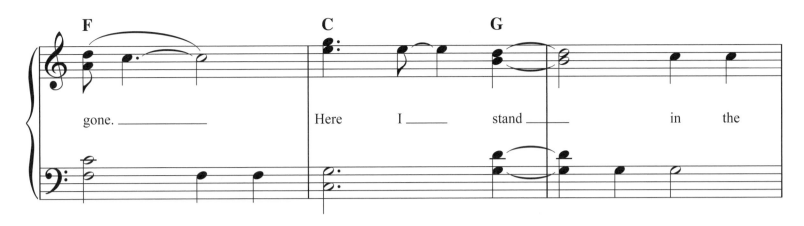

gone. _____ Here I _____ stand _____ in the

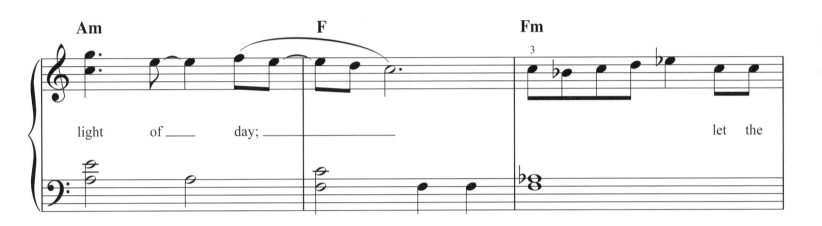

light of ___ day; _____ let the

storm rage ___ on. _____ The

cold nev - er both - ered me an - y - way. _____

LET ME ENTERTAIN YOU

from GYPSY

Lyrics by STEPHEN SONDHEIM
Music by JULE STYNE

LITTLE PEOPLE
from LES MISÉRABLES

Music by CLAUDE-MICHEL SCHÖNBERG
Lyrics by ALAIN BOUBLIL,
JEAN-MARC NATEL and HERBERT KRETZMER

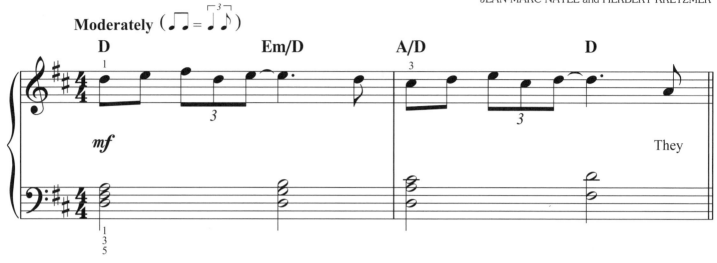

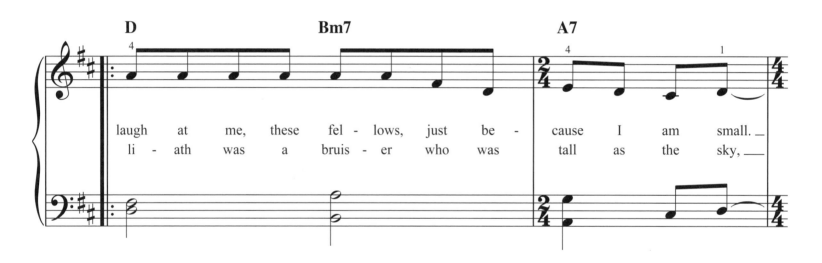

laugh at me, these fel-lows, just be- cause I am small.
li- ath was a bruis- er who was tall as the sky,

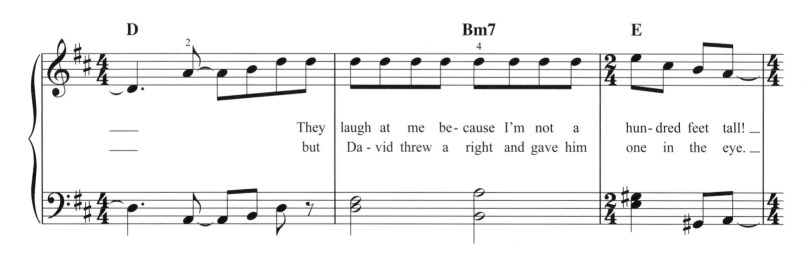

They laugh at me be-cause I'm not a hun-dred feet tall!
but Da- vid threw a right and gave him one in the eye.

fly can fly a-round Ver-sailles 'cos flies don't care! __ A spar-row in a hat can

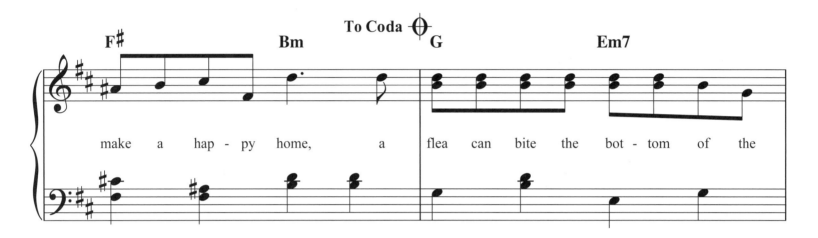

make a hap-py home, a flea can bite the bot-tom of the

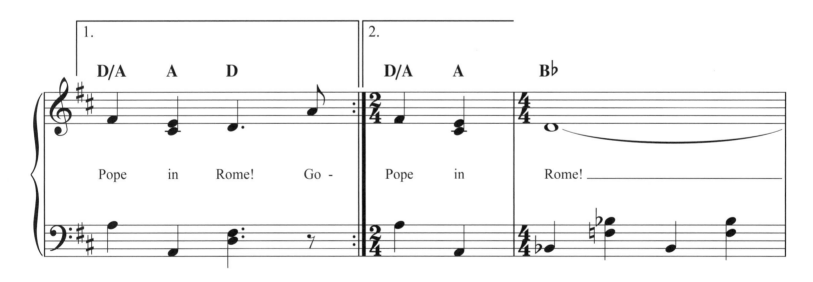

Pope in Rome! Go- Pope in Rome! ____

__ So lis-ten here, Pro-fes-sor, with your

head in the cloud. _____ It's of - ten kind of use - ful to get

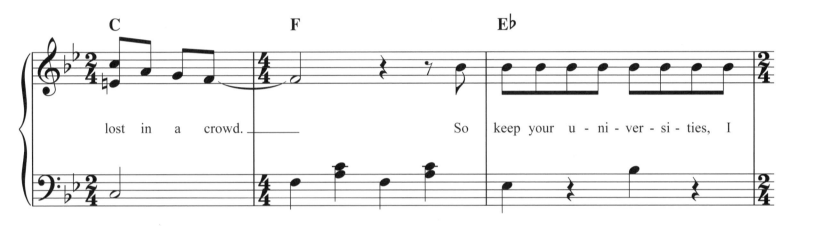

lost in a crowd. _____ So keep your u - ni - ver - si - ties, I

don't give a damn. _____ For bet - ter or for worse, it is the

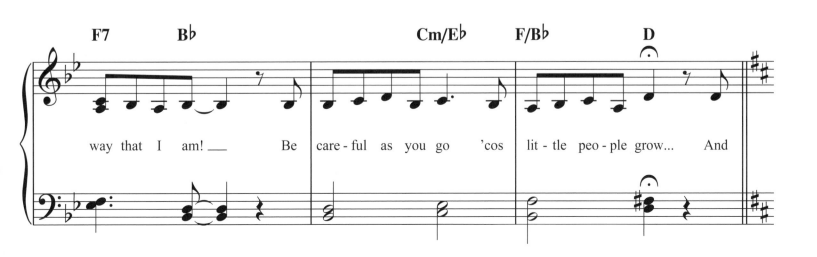

way that I am! __ Be care - ful as you go 'cos lit - tle peo - ple grow... And

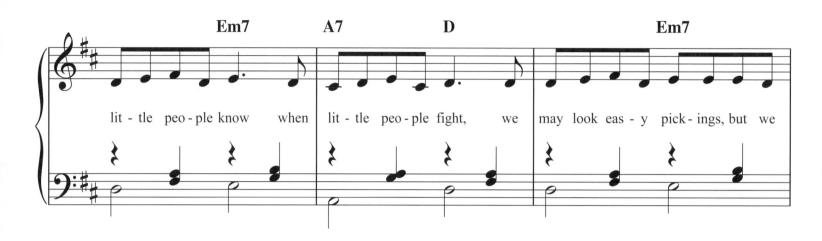

lit - tle peo - ple know when lit - tle peo - ple fight, we may look eas - y pick - ings, but we

got some bite! So nev - er kick a dog be - cause it's just a pup. You

bet - ter run for cov - er when the pup grows up! And we'll fight like twen - ty ar - mies and we

D.S. al Coda

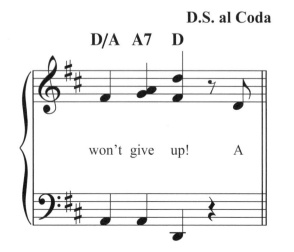

won't give up! A

CODA

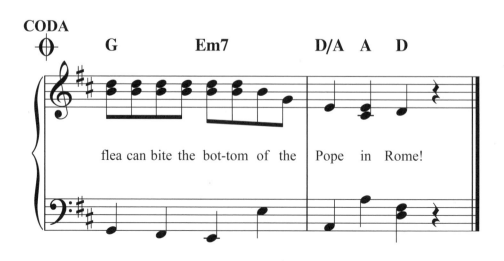

flea can bite the bot-tom of the Pope in Rome!

LITTLE APRIL SHOWER

from Walt Disney's BAMBI

Words by LARRY MOREY
Music by FRANK CHURCHILL

Moderately, with a light, staccato touch

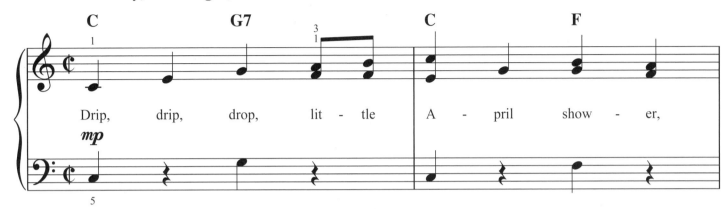

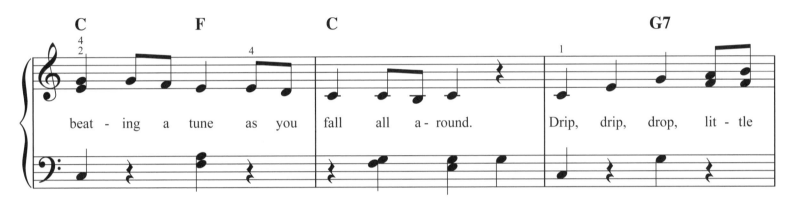

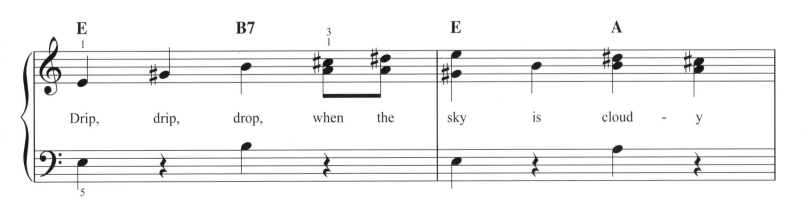

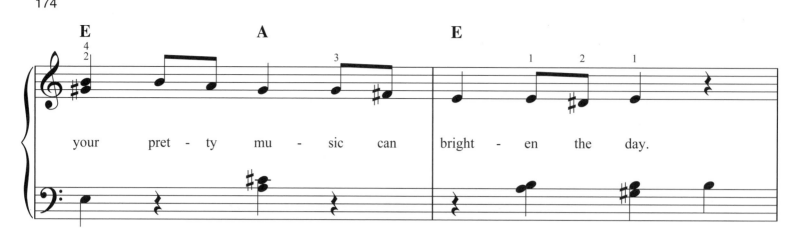

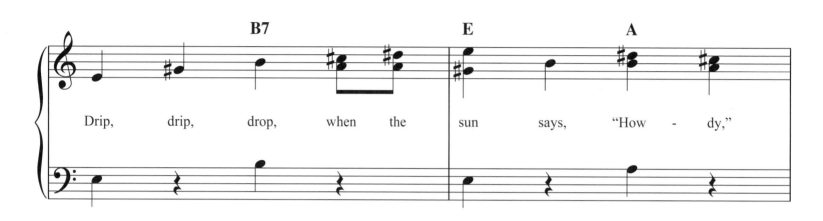

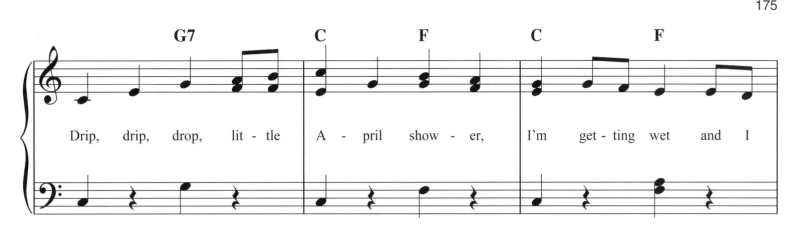

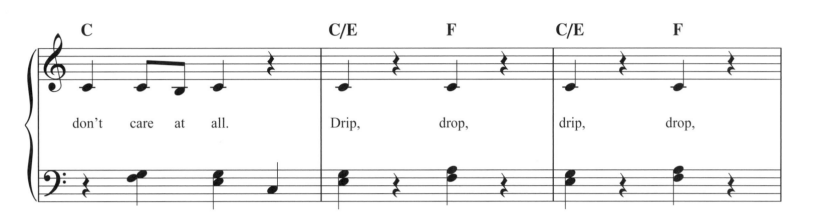

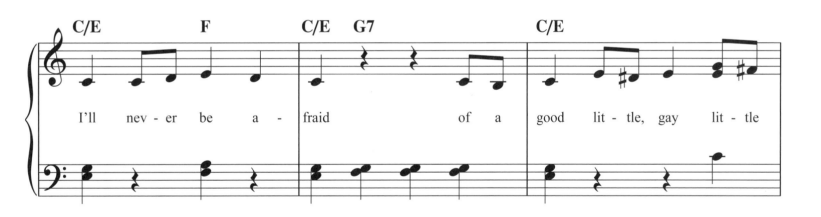

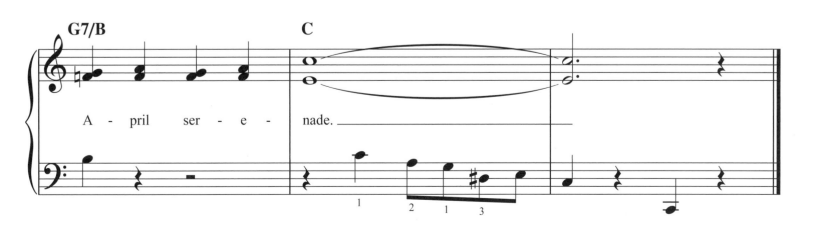

MICHAEL ROW THE BOAT ASHORE

Traditional Folksong

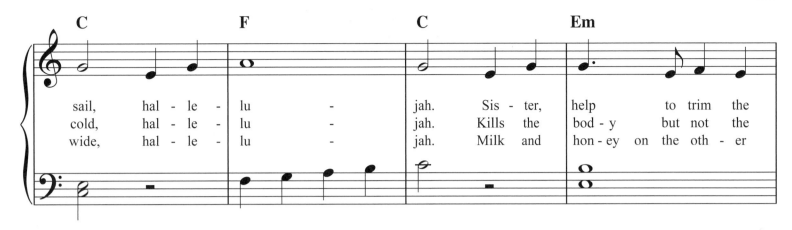

sail, hal - le - lu - jah. Sis - ter, help to trim the
cold, hal - le - lu - jah. Kills the bod - y but not the
wide, hal - le - lu - jah. Milk and hon - ey on the oth - er

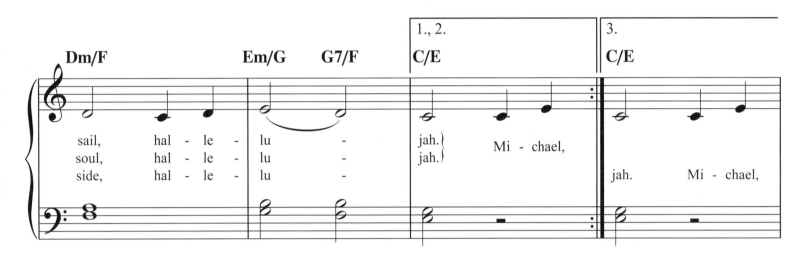

sail, hal - le - lu - jah.⌉
soul, hal - le - lu - jah.⌉ Mi - chael,
side, hal - le - lu - jah. Mi - chael,

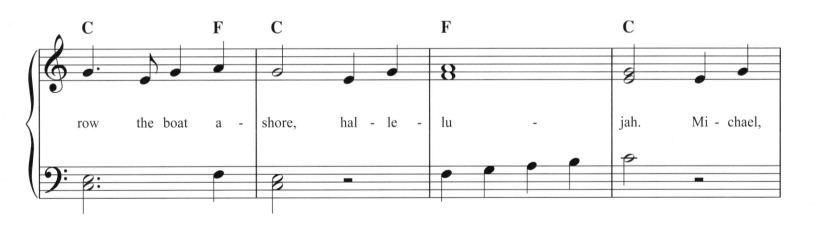

row the boat a - shore, hal - le - lu - jah. Mi - chael,

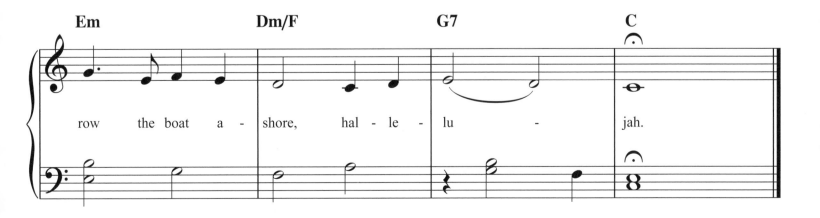

row the boat a - shore, hal - le - lu - jah.

MICKEY MOUSE MARCH

from Walt Disney's THE MICKEY MOUSE CLUB

Words and Music by
JIMMIE DODD

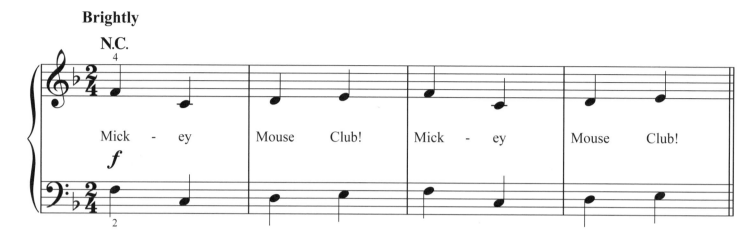

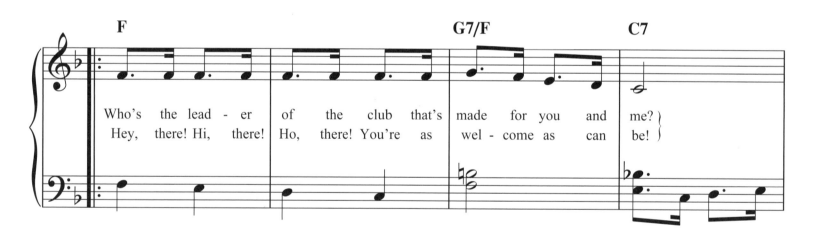

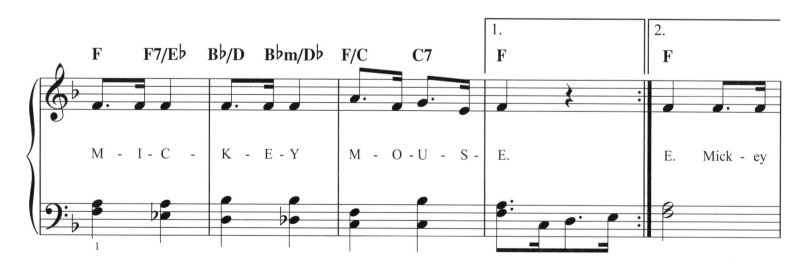

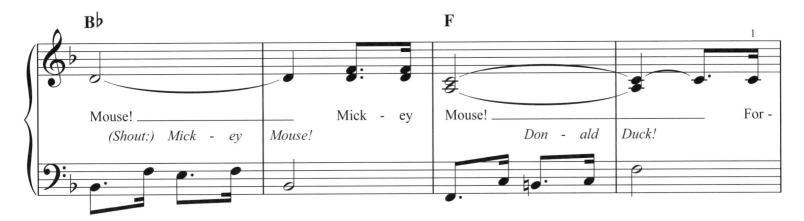

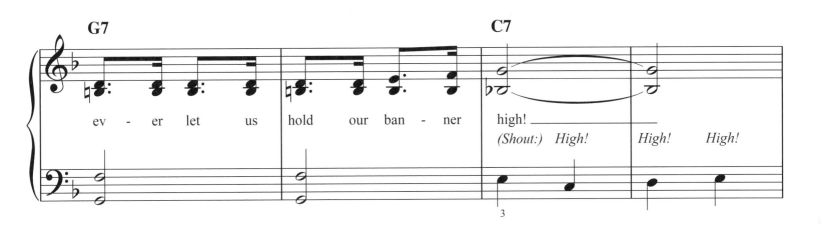

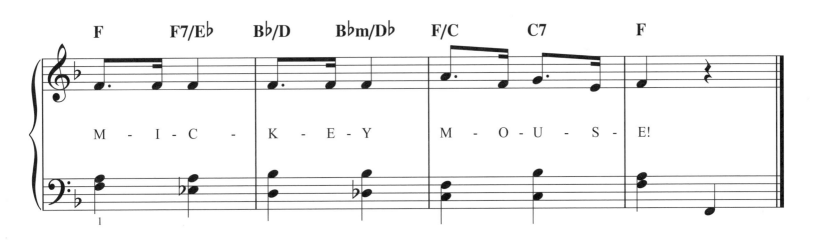

MY BONNIE LIES OVER THE OCEAN

Traditional

Flowing and spirited

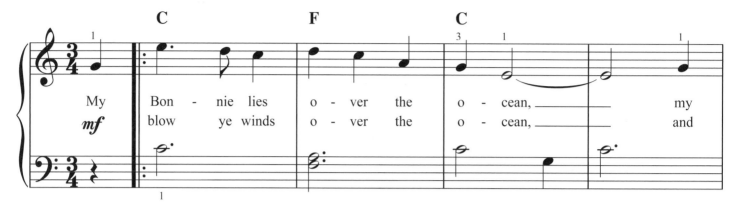

My
Bon - nie lies   o - ver the   o - cean, _____   my
blow   ye winds   o - ver the   o - cean, _____   and

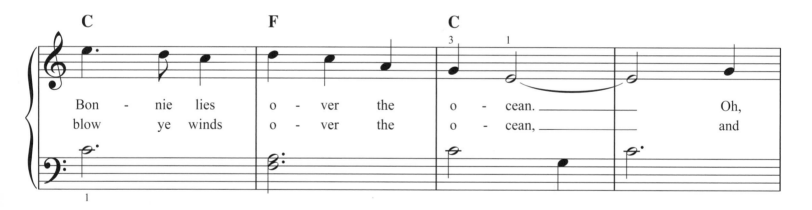

Bon - nie lies   o - ver the   sea. _____   My
blow   ye winds   o - ver the   sea. _____   Oh,

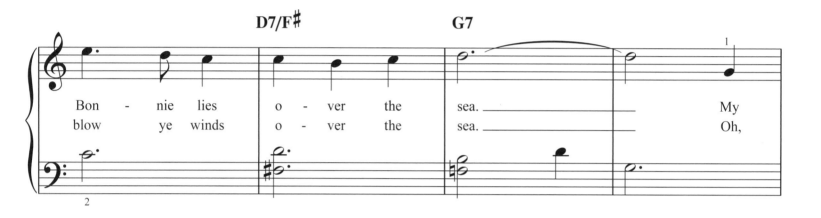

Bon - nie lies   o - ver the   o - cean. _____   Oh,
blow   ye winds   o - ver the   o - cean, _____   and

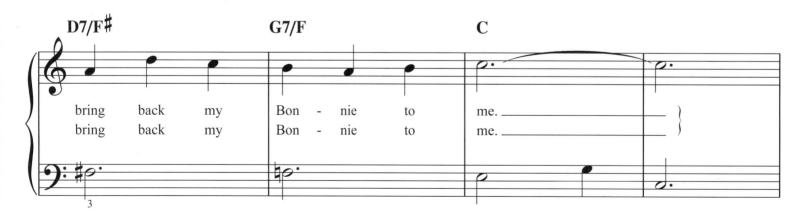

bring   back   my   Bon - nie   to   me. _____
bring   back   my   Bon - nie   to   me. _____

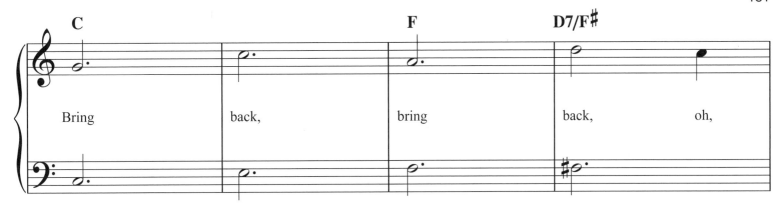

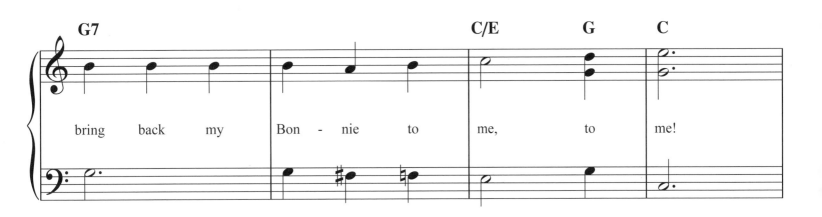

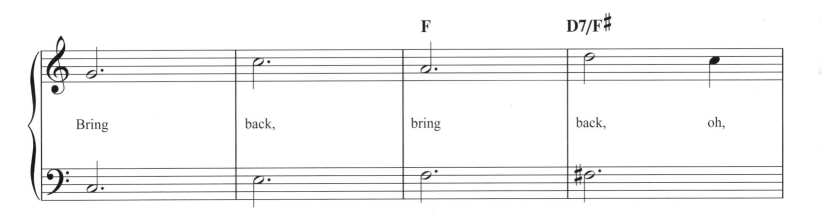

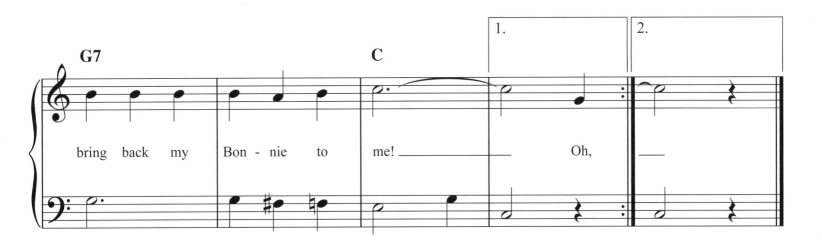

MY FAVORITE THINGS
from THE SOUND OF MUSIC

Lyrics by OSCAR HAMMERSTEIN II
Music by RICHARD RODGERS

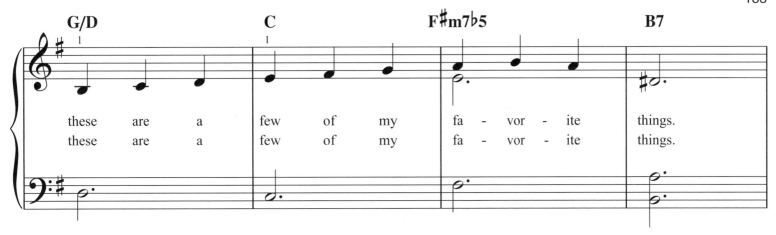

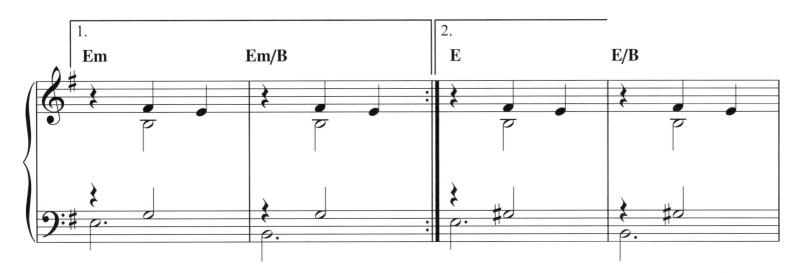

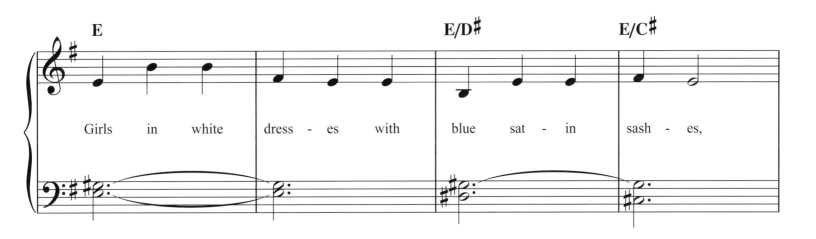

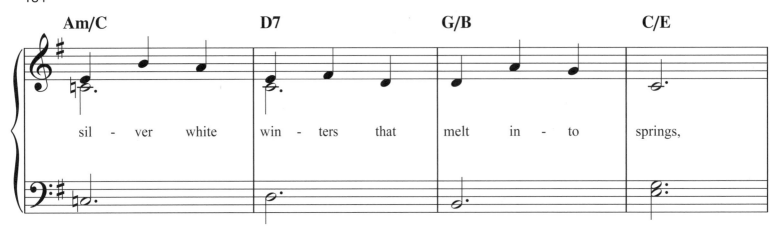

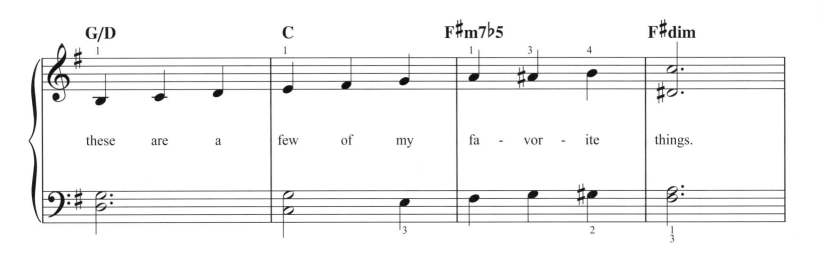

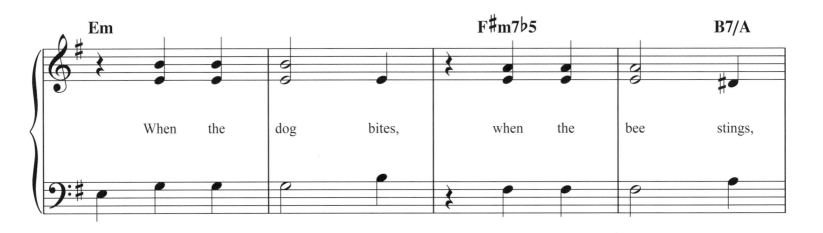

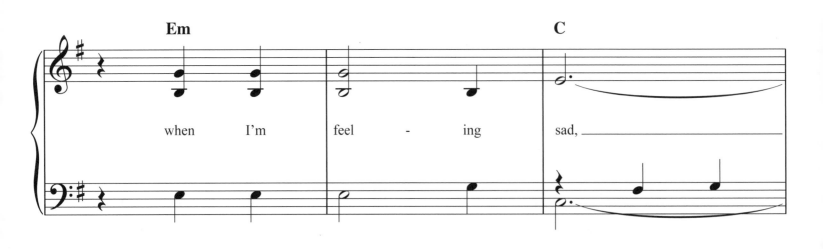

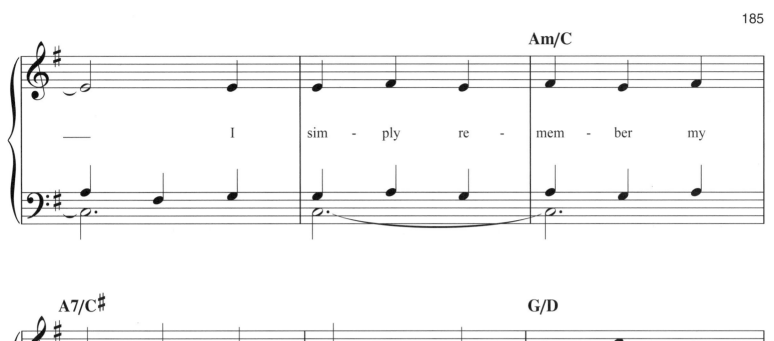

Am/C

I sim - ply re - mem - ber my

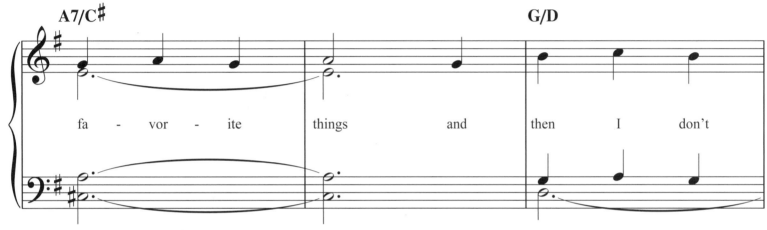

A7/C♯   G/D

fa - vor - ite   things   and   then   I   don't

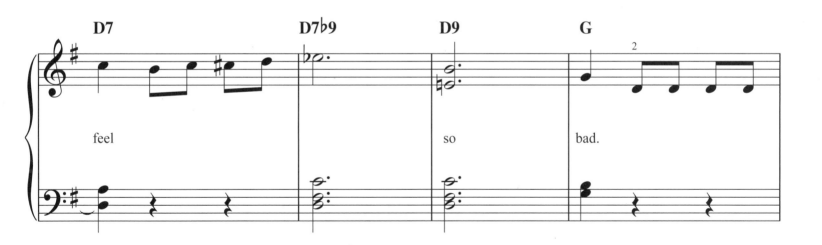

D7   D7♭9   D9   G

feel   so   bad.

B♭/D   D7   G

OH WHERE, OH WHERE HAS MY LITTLE DOG GONE

Words by SEP. WINNER
Traditional Melody

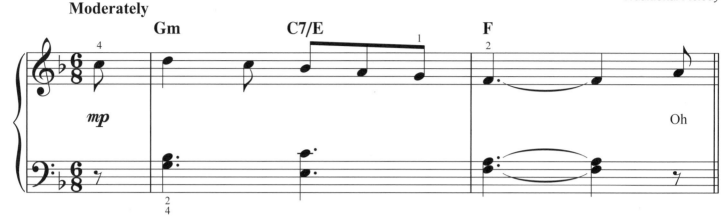

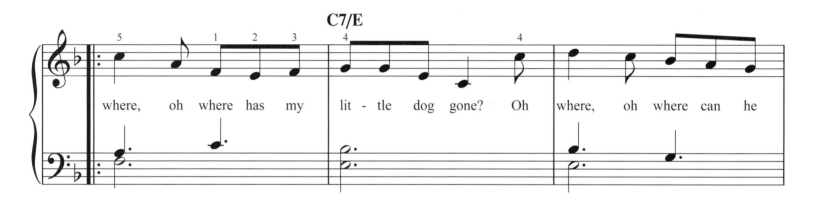

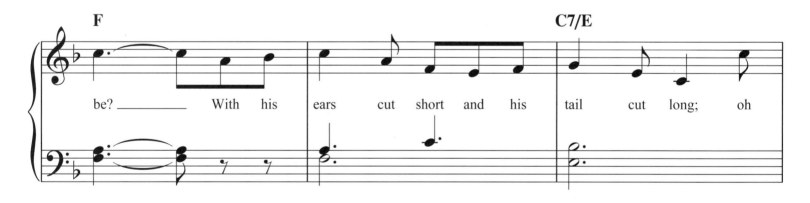

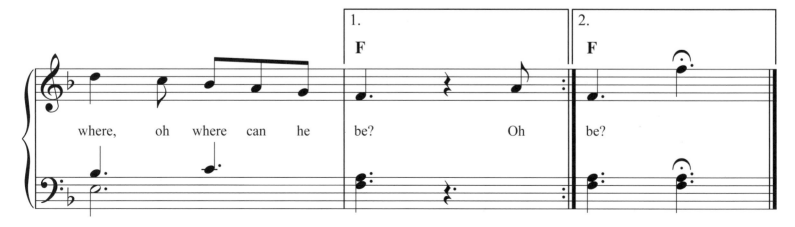

NEVER SMILE AT A CROCODILE

from Walt Disney's PETER PAN

Words by JACK LAWRENCE
Music by FRANK CHURCHILL

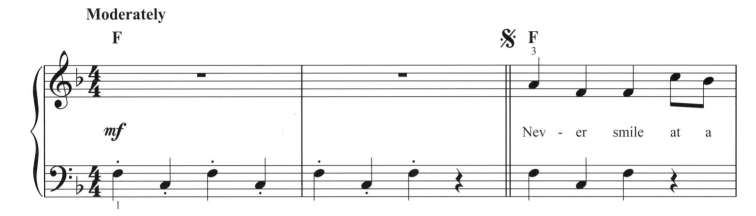

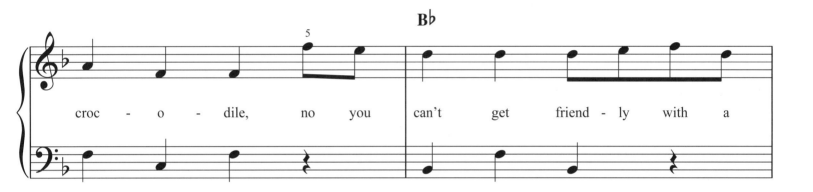

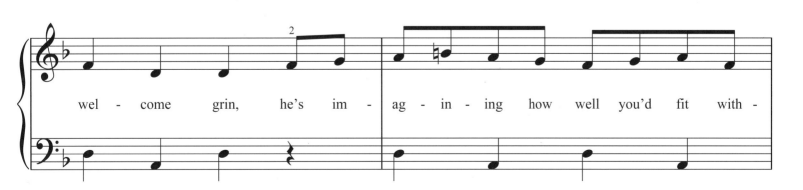

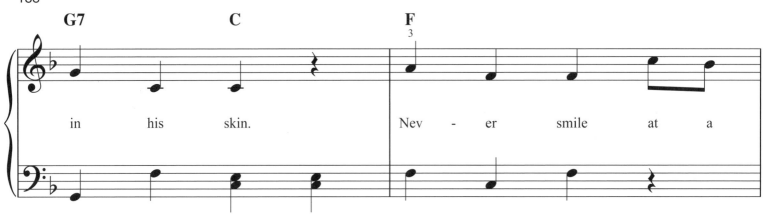

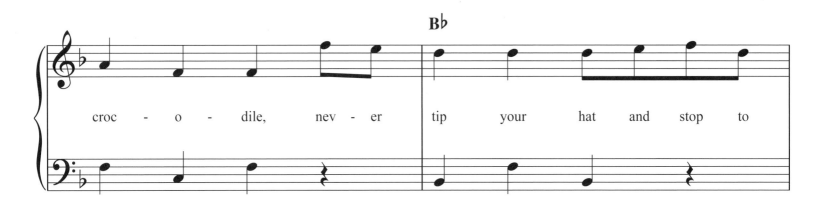

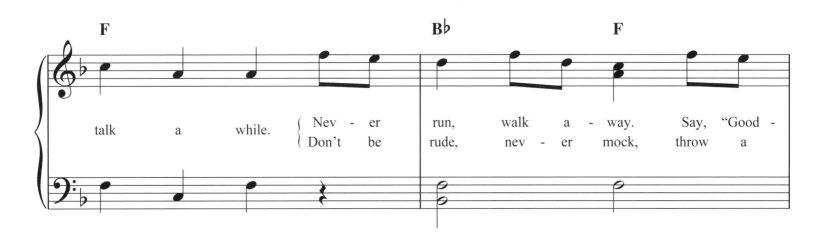

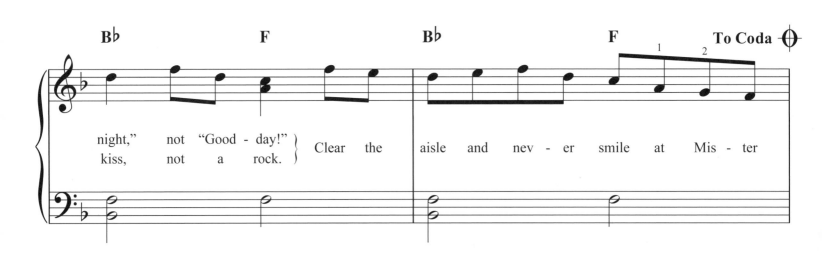

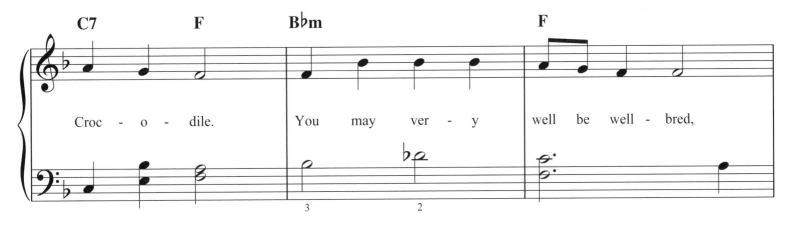

Croc - o - dile. You may ver - y well be well - bred,

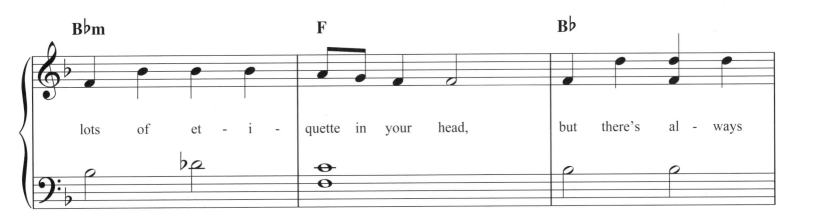

lots of et - i - quette in your head, but there's al - ways

D.S. al Coda

some spe - cial case, time, or place, to for - get et - i - quette.

CODA

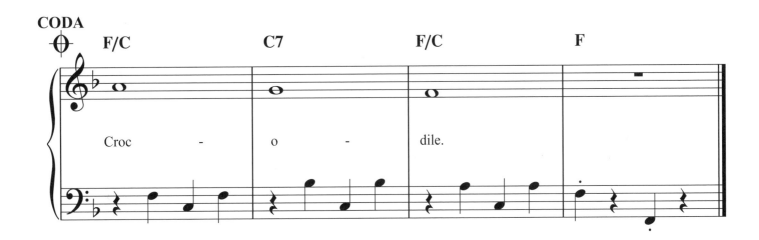

Croc - o - dile.

OCTOPUS'S GARDEN

Words and Music by
RICHARD STARKEY

Moderately bright

I'd like to be ____ under the sea ____
We would be warm ____ be-low the storm _

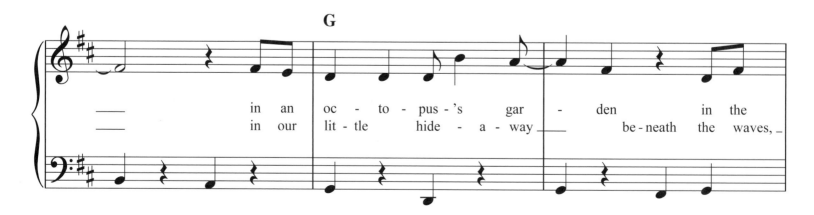

____ in an oc-to-pus's gar - den in the
____ in our lit-tle hide-a-way ____ be-neath the waves,

an oc - to - pus - 's   gar - den   with   me.
be - cause   we   know   we   can't   be   found.

I'd   like   to   be   un - der   the   sea

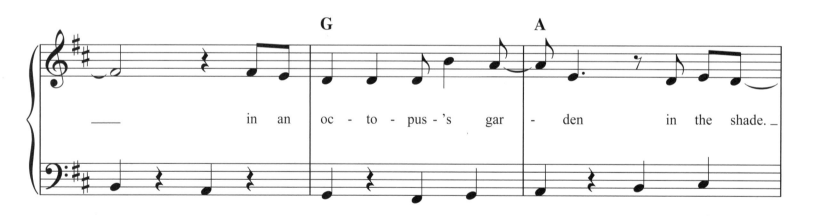

in   an   oc - to - pus - 's   gar - den   in   the   shade.

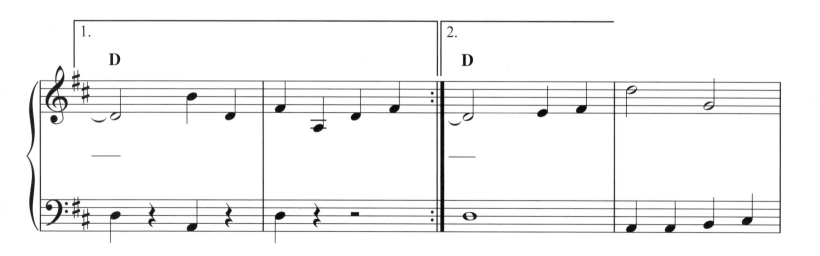

We would shout ___ and swim a - bout ___

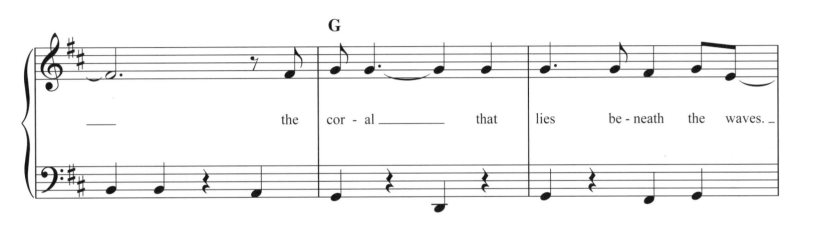

___ the cor - al ___ that lies be - neath the waves. ___

___ Oh, what joy ___ for

ev - 'ry girl and boy ___ know - ing ___ they're

hap - py   and they're   safe.   We would

be   so   hap - py   you   and   me;

no   one   there   to   tell   us   what   to   do.

I'd   like   to   be

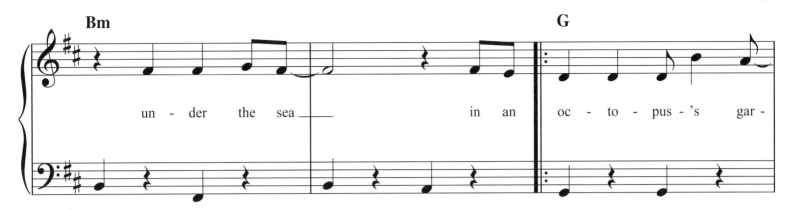

un - der the sea ___ in an oc - to - pus - 's gar -

1.

- den with you. ___ In an

2.

___ In an oc - to - pus - 's gar -

- den with you.

OLD MACDONALD HAD A FARM

Traditional

ON TOP OF SPAGHETTI

Words and Music by
TOM GLAZER

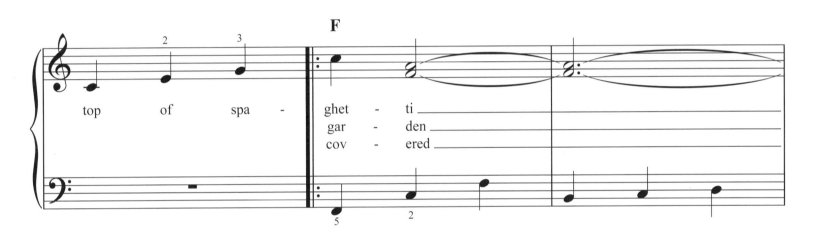

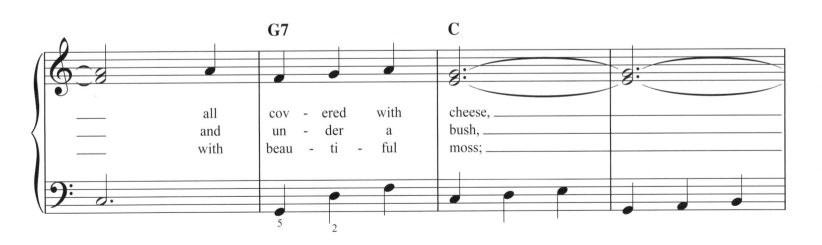

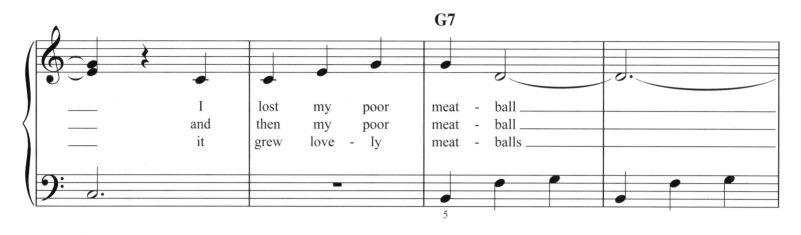

I lost my poor meat - ball ___
and then my poor meat - ball ___
it grew love - ly meat - balls ___

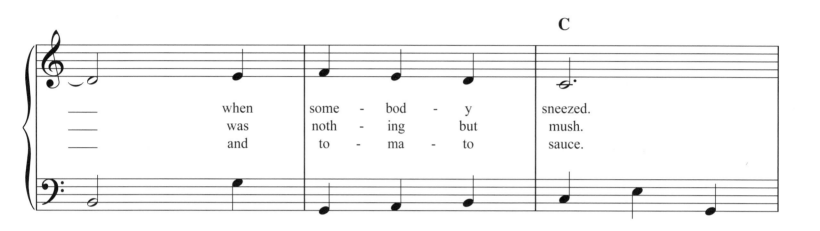

when some - bod - y sneezed.
was noth - ing but mush.
and to - ma - to sauce.

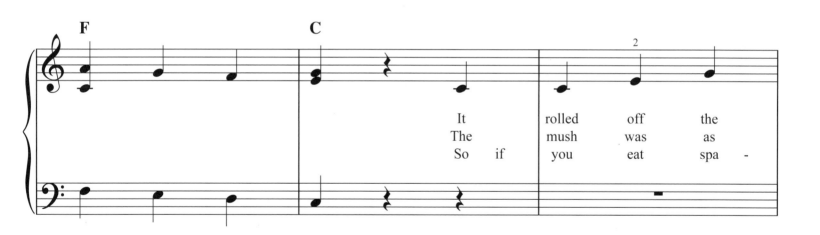

It rolled off the
The mush was as
So if you eat spa -

ta - ble ___ and on - to the
tast - y ___ as tast - y could
ghet - ti ___ all cov - ered with

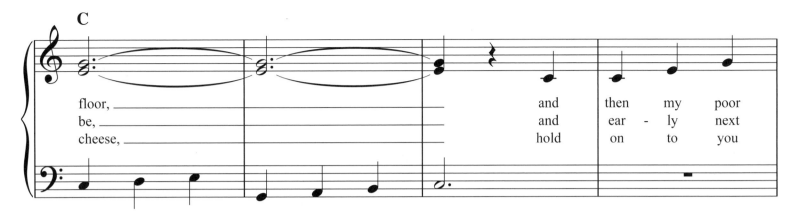

C

floor, _____ and then my poor
be, _____ and ear - ly next
cheese, _____ hold on to you

G7

meat - ball _____ rolled out of the
sum - mer, _____ it grew in - to a
meat - balls _____ and don't ev - er

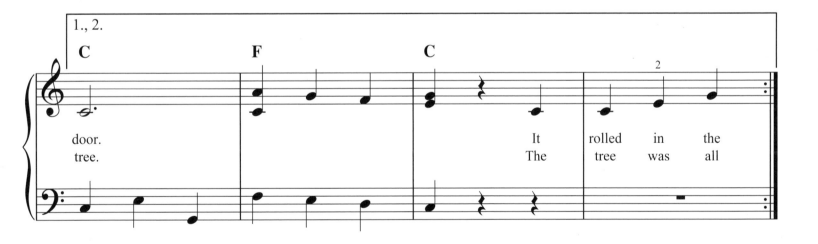

1., 2.

C   F   C   2

door.   It rolled in the
tree.   The tree was all

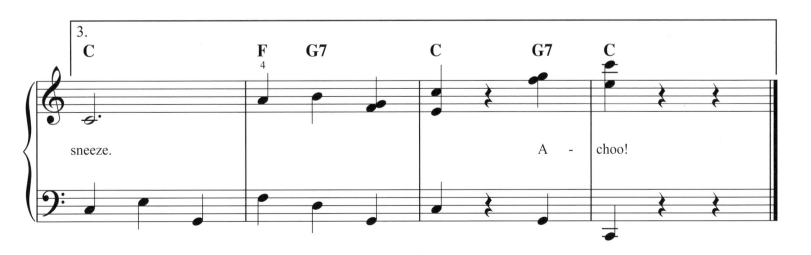

3.

C   F   G7   C   G7   C

sneeze.   A - choo!

ONCE UPON A DREAM
from Walt Disney's SLEEPING BEAUTY

Words and Music by SAMMY FAIN
and JACK LAWRENCE
Adapted from a Theme by TCHAIKOVSKY

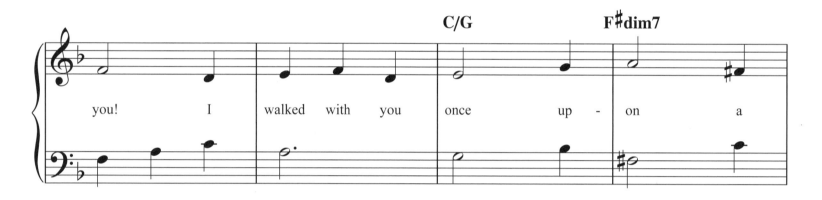

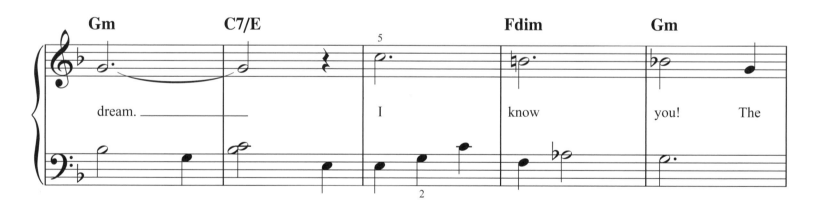

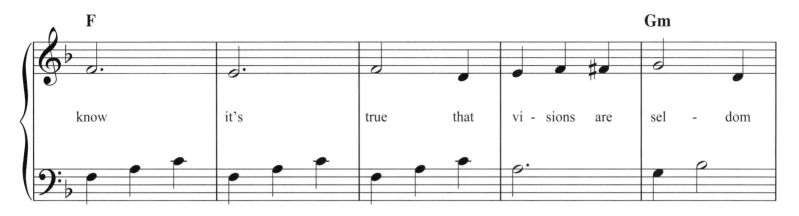

know   it's   true   that   vi - sions are   sel - dom

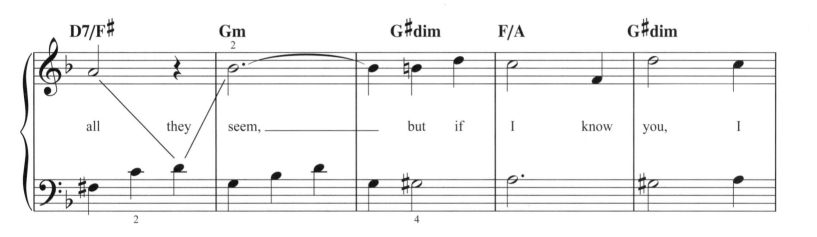

all   they   seem, _____   but if   I   know you,   I

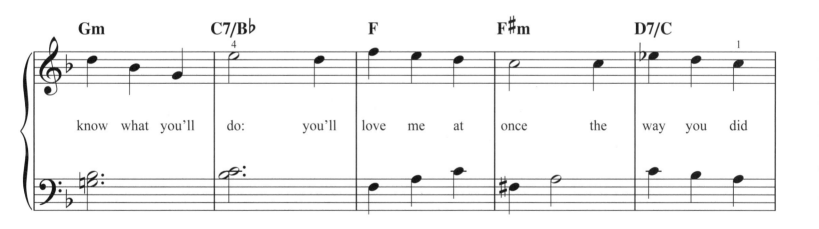

know what you'll   do: you'll   love me at   once   the   way you did

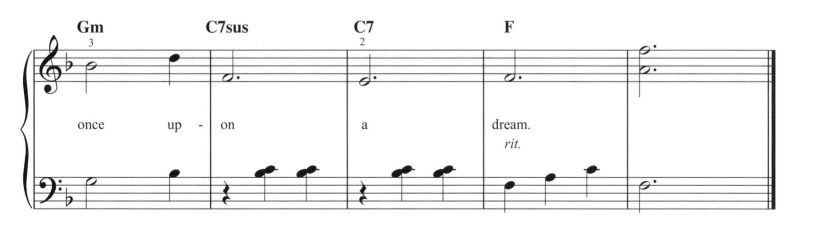

once   up - on   a   dream.
rit.

PART OF YOUR WORLD
from Walt Disney's THE LITTLE MERMAID

Music by ALAN MENKEN
Lyrics by HOWARD ASHMAN

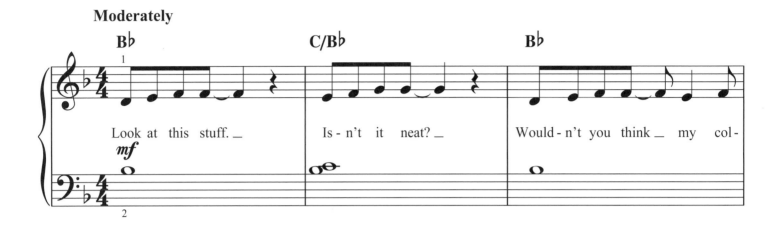

Look at this stuff. __ Is-n't it neat? __ Would-n't you think __ my col-

lec-tion's com-plete? Would-n't you think __ I'm the girl, ___ the girl who has

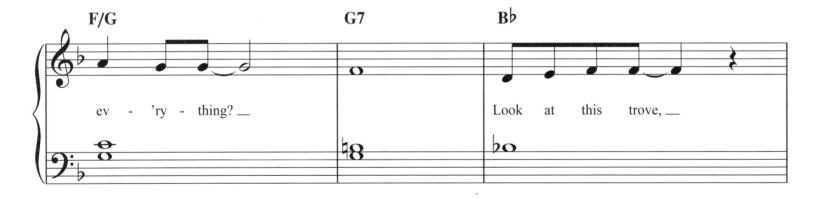

ev - 'ry - thing? __ Look at this trove, __

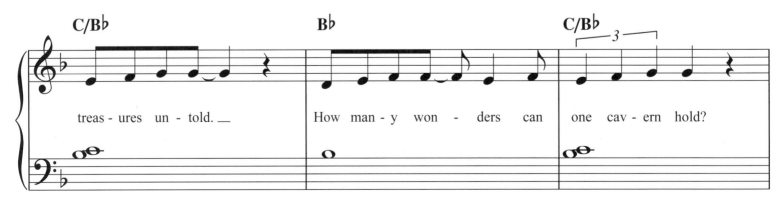

treas-ures un-told. __ How man-y won-ders can one cav-ern hold?

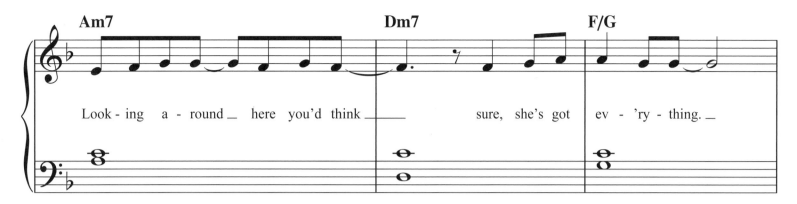

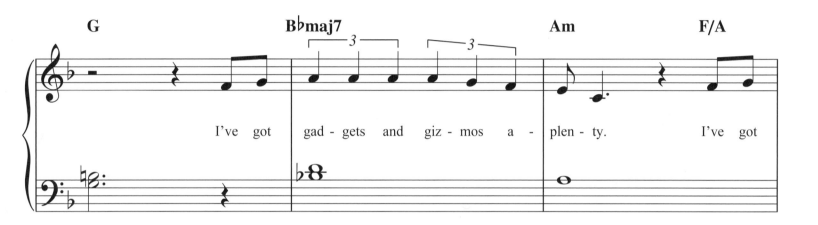

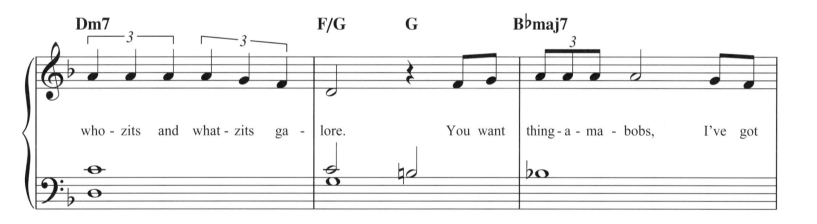

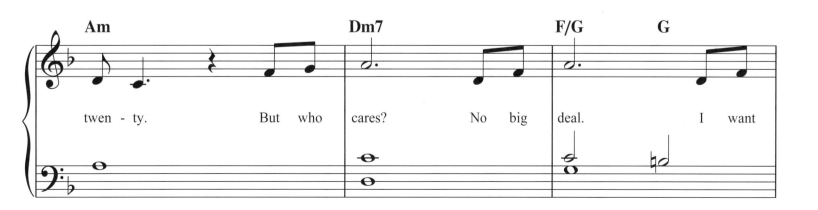

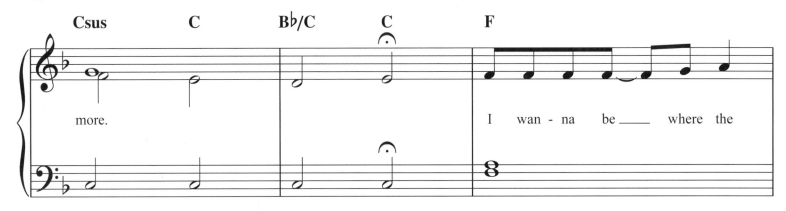

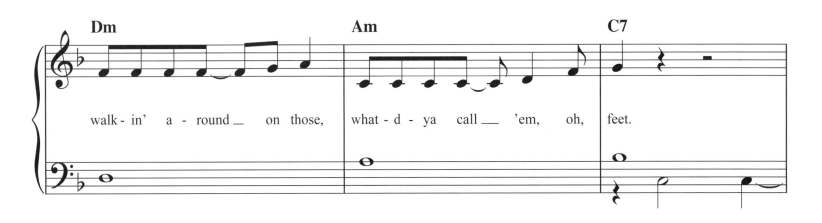

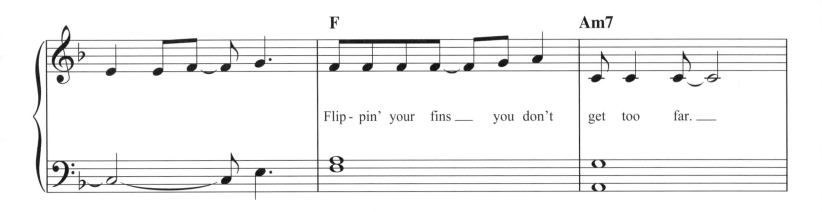

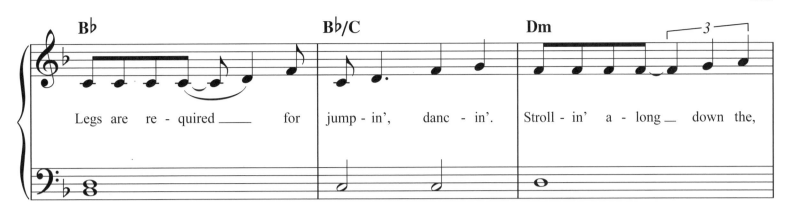

B♭

Legs are re - quired _____ for

B♭/C

jump - in', danc - in'.

Dm

Stroll - in' a - long _ down the,

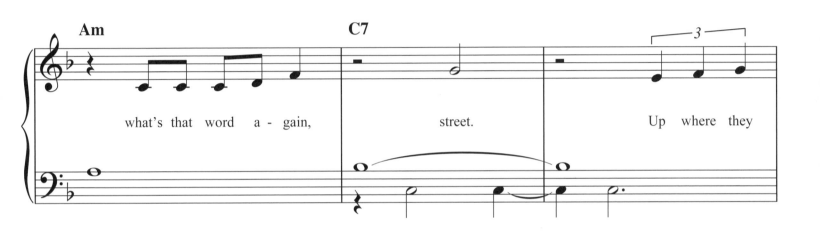

Am

what's that word a - gain,

C7

street.

Up where they

F

walk, up where they

F/E♭

run, up where they

B♭/D

stay all day _ in the sun. _

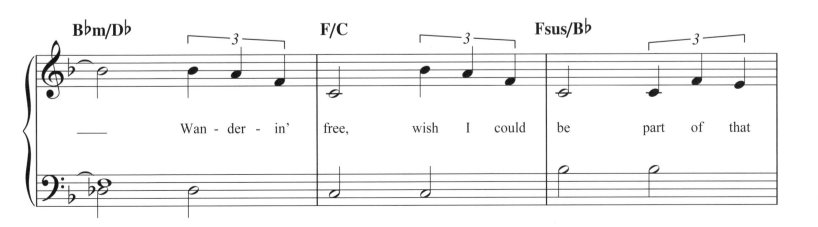

B♭m/D♭

_____ Wan - der - in'

F/C

free, wish I could

Fsus/B♭

be part of that

world. _____ What would I give if I could

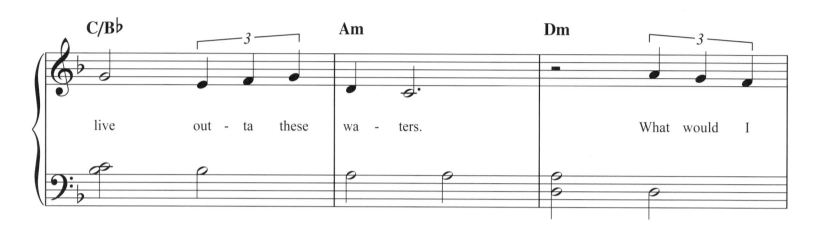

live out - ta these wa - ters. What would I

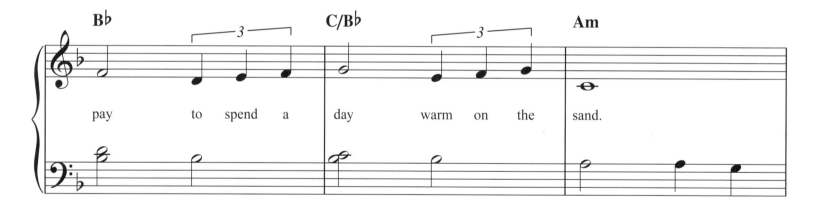

pay to spend a day warm on the sand.

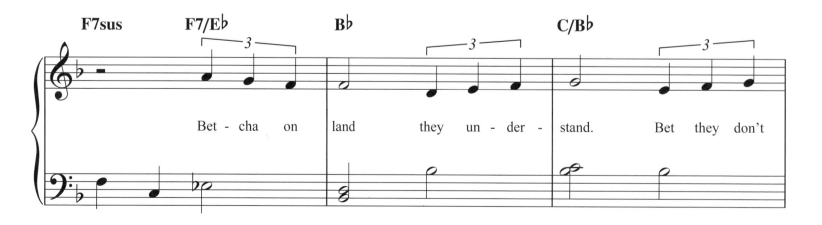

Bet - cha on land they un - der - stand. Bet they don't

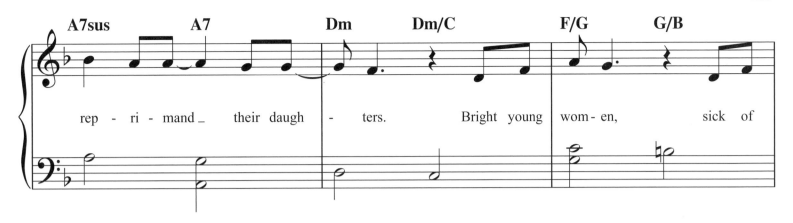

rep - ri - mand _ their daugh - ters. Bright young wom - en, sick of

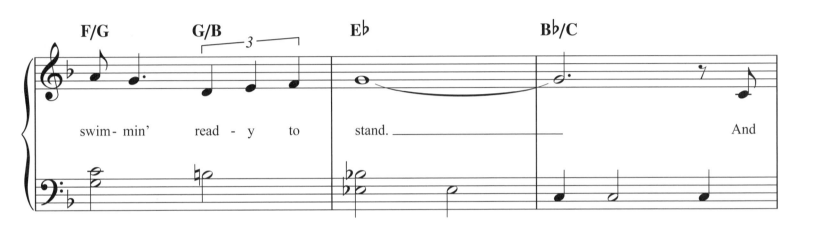

swim- min' read - y to stand. _____ And

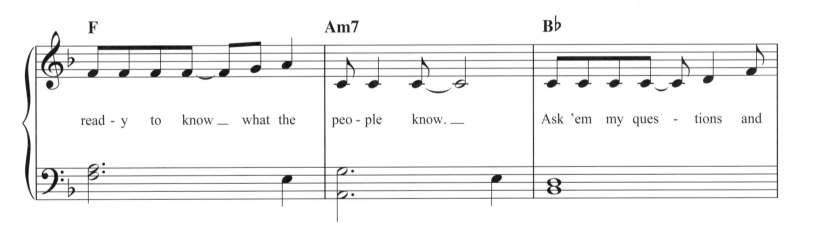

read - y to know _ what the peo - ple know. _ Ask 'em my ques - tions and

get some an - swers. What's a fire, _____ and why does it, what's the word,

Gm   C7   F

burn.   When's __ it my turn? Would - n't I

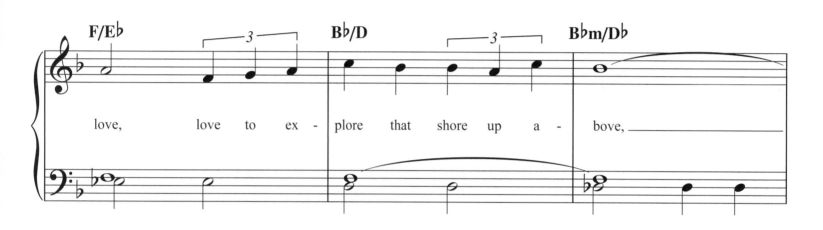

F/E♭   B♭/D   B♭m/D♭

love,   love to ex - plore that shore up a - bove, _____

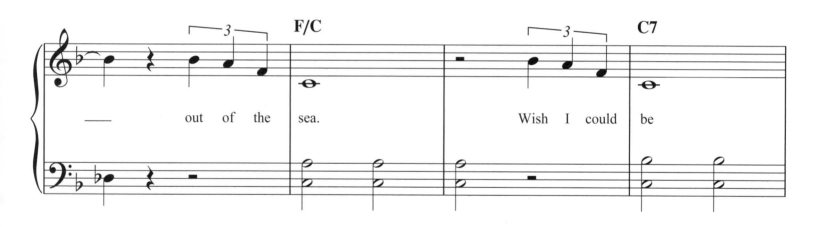

F/C   C7

_____ out of the sea.   Wish I could be

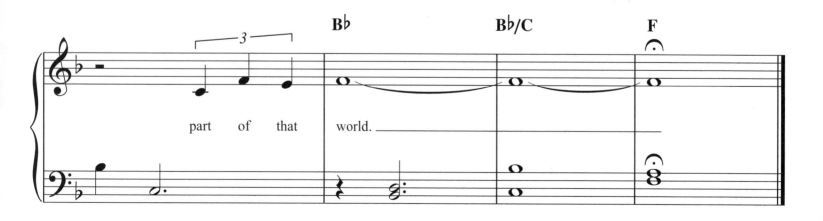

B♭   B♭/C   F

part of that world. _____

OVER THE RAINBOW
from THE WIZARD OF OZ

Music by HAROLD ARLEN
Lyric by E.Y. "YIP" HARBURG

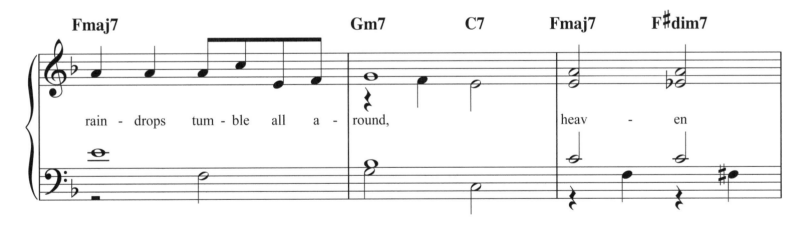

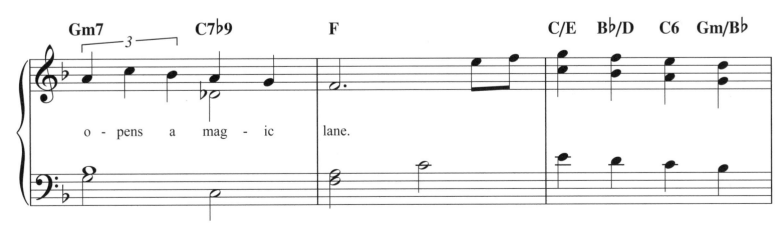

F　　　　　　　　　**B♭/F**　　　　　**Fmaj7**

When all the clouds dark-en up the sky-way, there's a rain-bow high-way to be

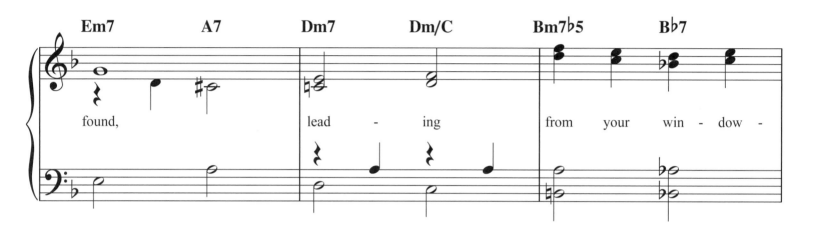

Em7　　**A7**　　**Dm7**　　**Dm/C**　　**Bm7♭5**　　**B♭7**

found,　　　　lead - ing　　　from your win - dow -

Am7　　**A♭7**　　**Gm7**　　**C7**　　**Am7**　　**A♭7**

pane _____ to a place be - hind the sun, _____

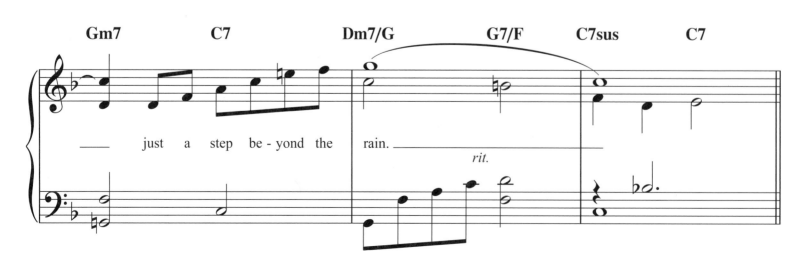

Gm7　　**C7**　　**Dm7/G**　　**G7/F**　　**C7sus**　　**C7**

___ just a step be - yond the rain. _____
rit.

211

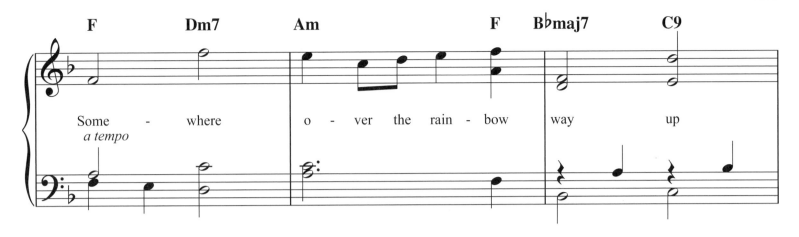

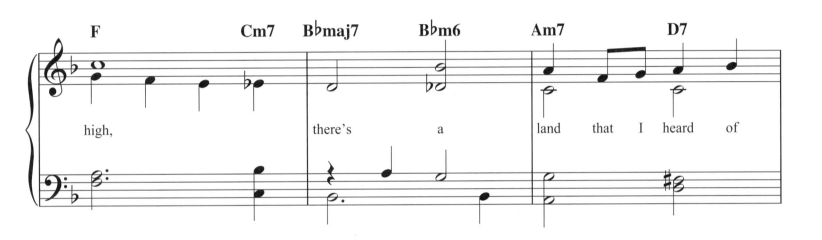

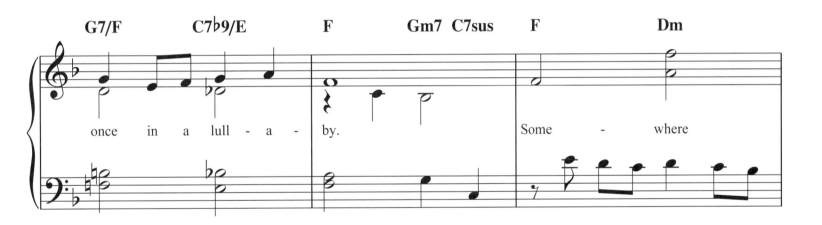

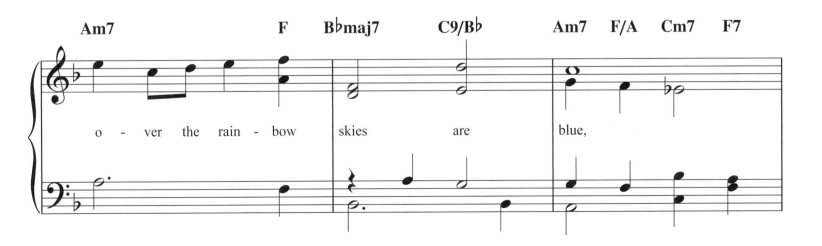

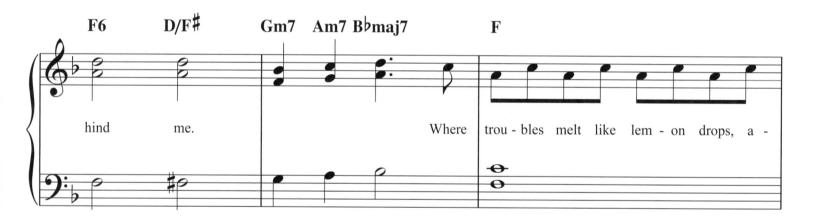

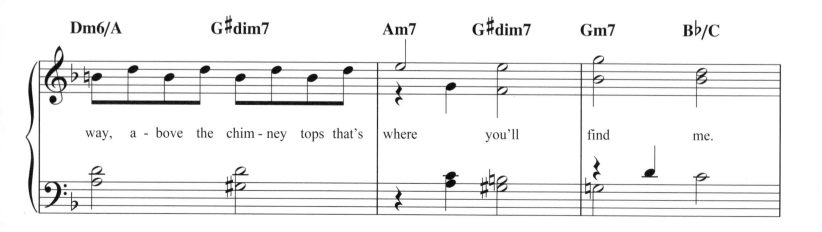

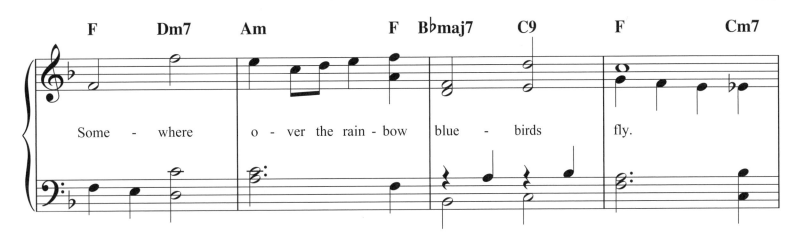

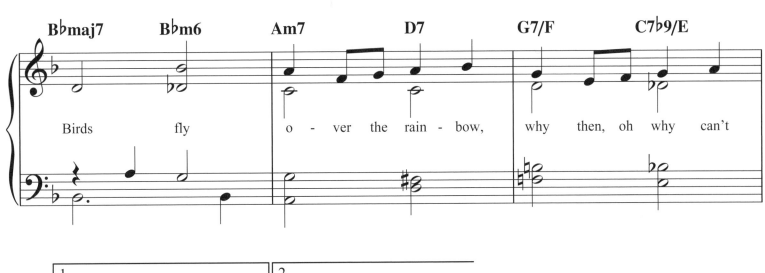

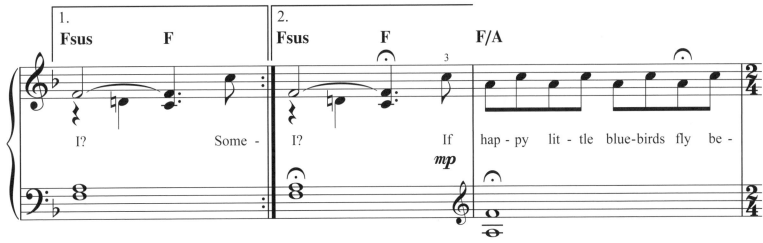

OVER THE RIVER AND THROUGH THE WOODS

Traditional

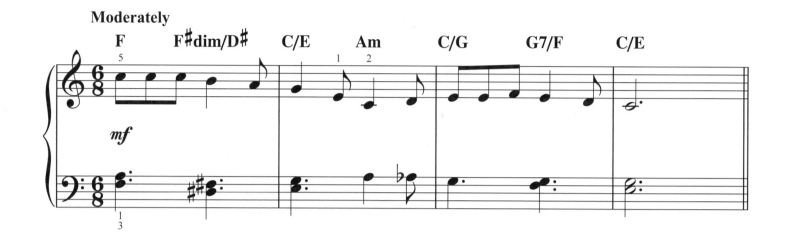

O - ver the riv - er and through the woods, to Grand - fa - ther's house we
O - ver the riv - er and through the woods, to have _____ a first - rate
O - ver the riv - er and through the woods, and straight through the barn - yard

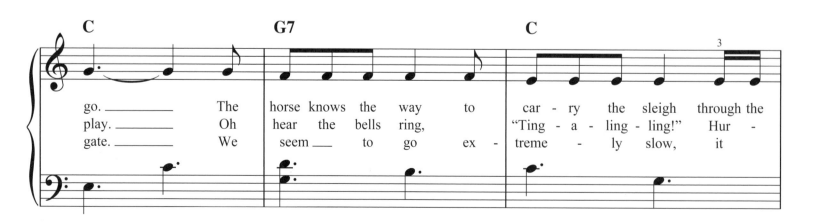

go. _____ The horse knows the way to car - ry the sleigh through the
play. _____ Oh hear the bells ring, "Ting - a - ling - ling!" Hur -
gate. _____ We seem _____ to go ex - treme - ly slow, it

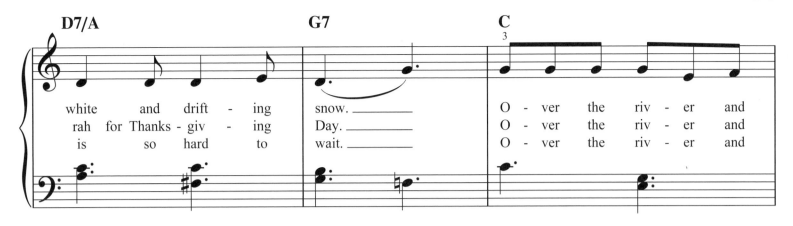

white and drift - ing snow. _____ O - ver the riv - er and
rah for Thanks - giv - ing Day. _____ O - ver the riv - er and
is so hard to wait. _____ O - ver the riv - er and

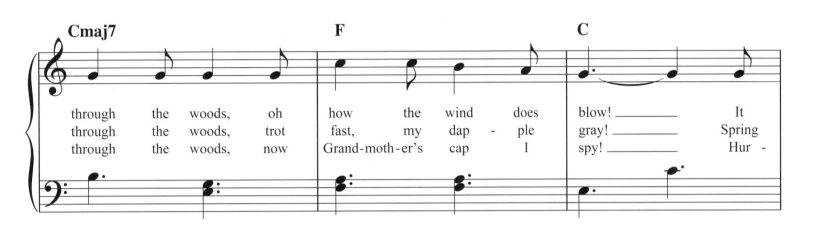

through the woods, oh how the wind does blow! _____ It
through the woods, trot fast, my dap - ple gray! _____ Spring
through the woods, now Grand-moth-er's cap I spy! _____ Hur -

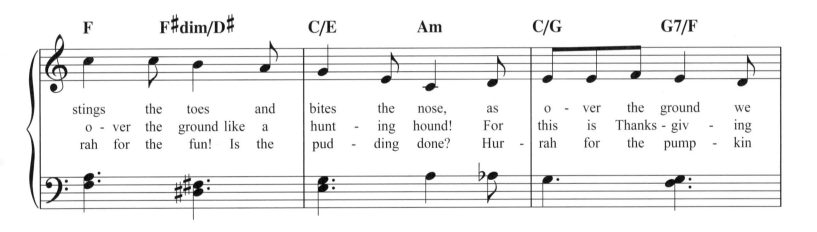

stings the toes and bites the nose, as o - ver the ground we
o - ver the ground like a hunt - ing hound! For this is Thanks-giv - ing
rah for the fun! Is the pud - ding done? Hur - rah for the pump - kin

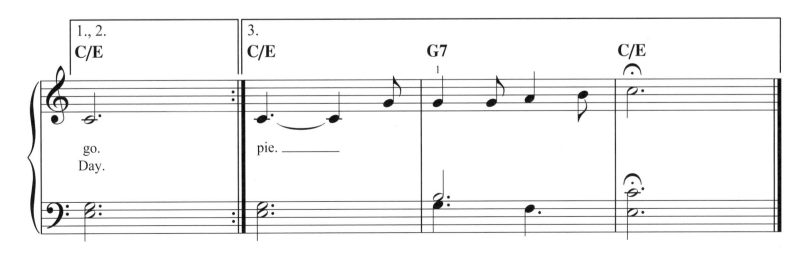

go.
Day.

pie. _____

PETER COTTONTAIL

Words and Music by STEVE NELSON
and JACK ROLLINS

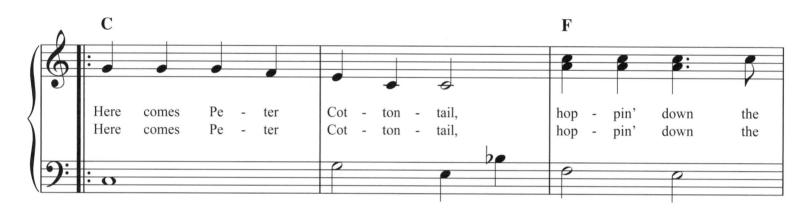

Here comes Pe - ter Cot - ton - tail, hop - pin' down the
Here comes Pe - ter Cot - ton - tail, hop - pin' down the

bun - ny trail, hip - pi - ty hop - pin' Eas - ter's on its
bun - ny trail, look at him stop, and lis - ten to him

way. Bring - ing ev - 'ry
say: "Try to do the

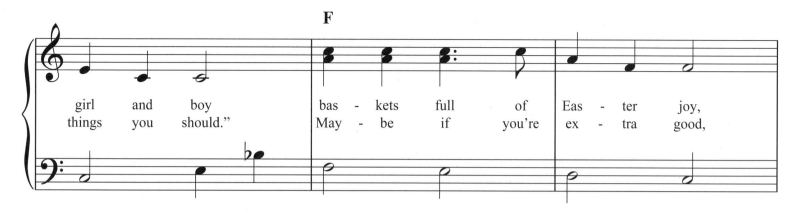

girl and boy / things you should." bas- kets full of Eas - ter joy, / May - be if you're ex - tra good,

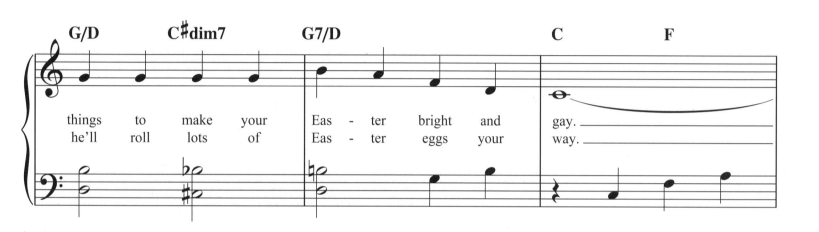

things to make your / he'll roll lots of Eas - ter bright and / Eas - ter eggs your gay. ___ / way. ___

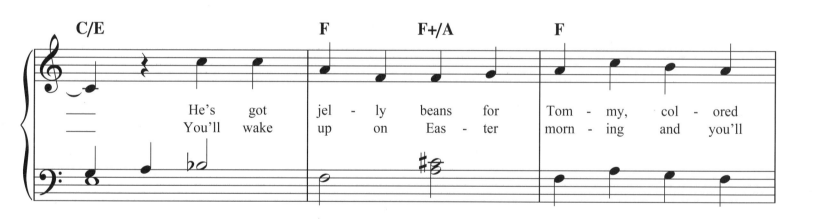

___ He's got / ___ You'll wake jel - ly beans for / up on Eas - ter Tom - my, col - ored / morn - ing and you'll

eggs for sis - ter / know that he was Sue, / there. there's an / When you find or - chid for your / those choc - 'late

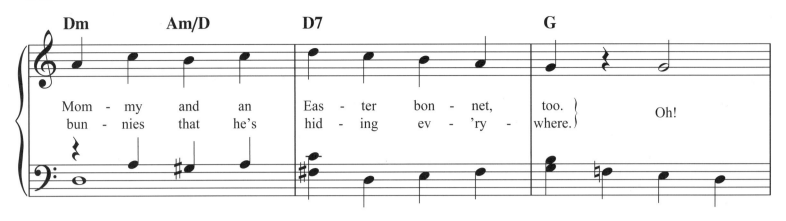

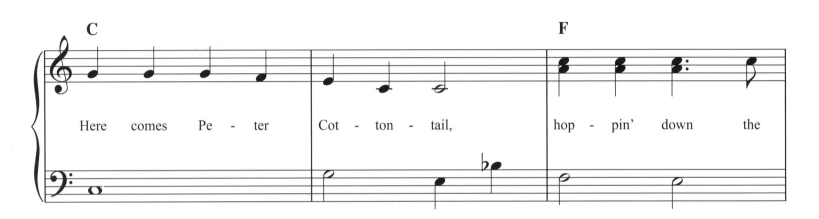

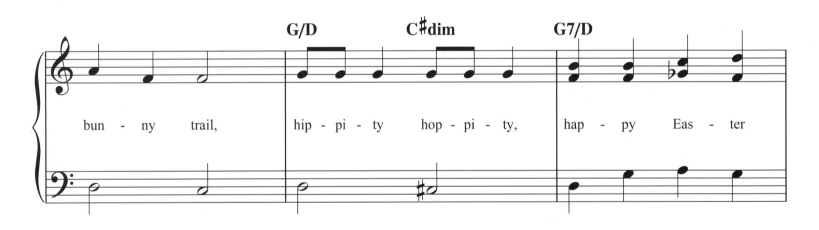

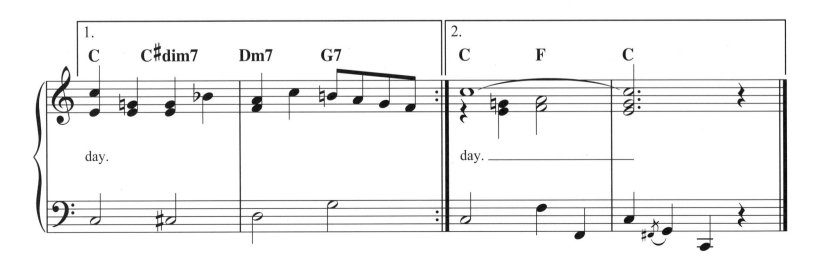

POP GOES THE WEASEL

Traditional

PUFF THE MAGIC DRAGON

Words and Music by LENNY LIPTON
and PETER YARROW

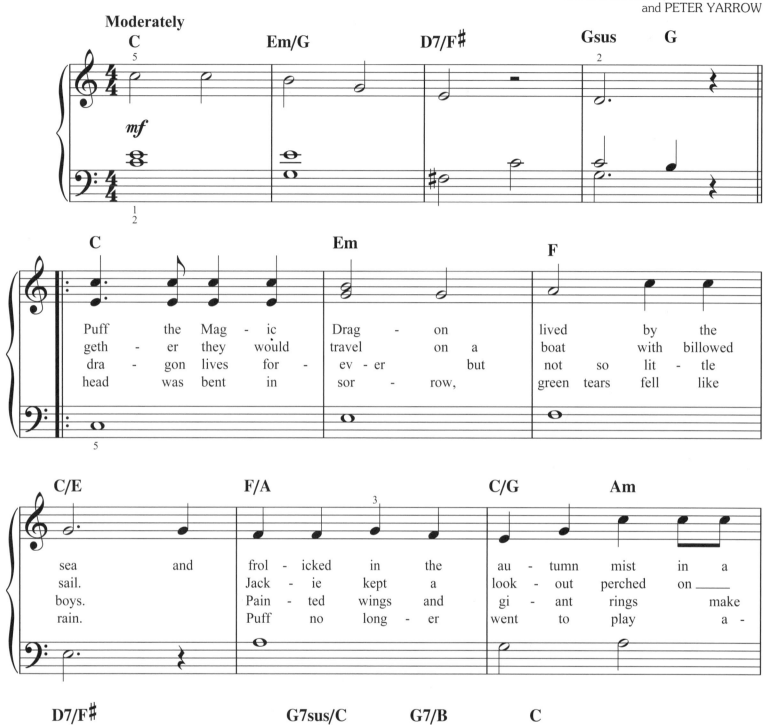

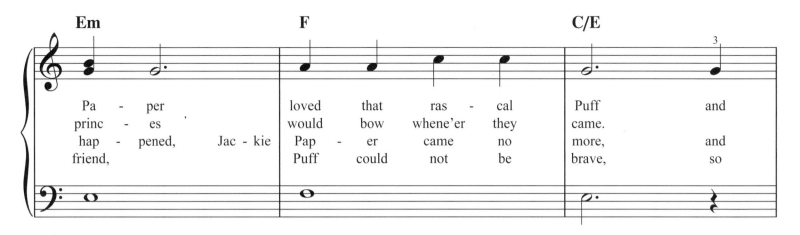

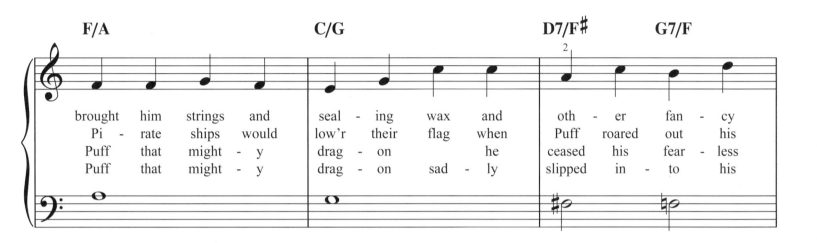

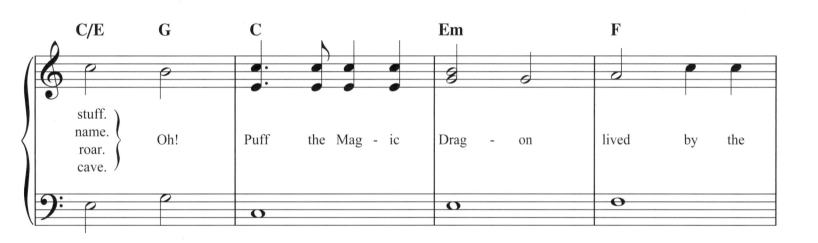

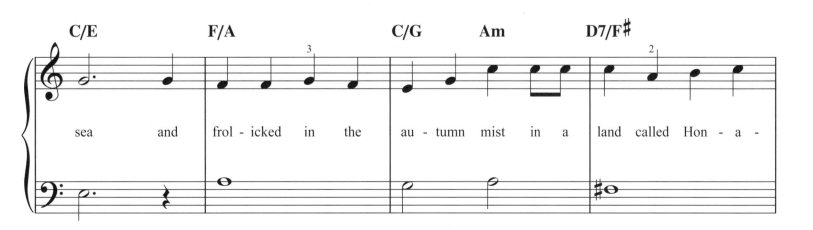

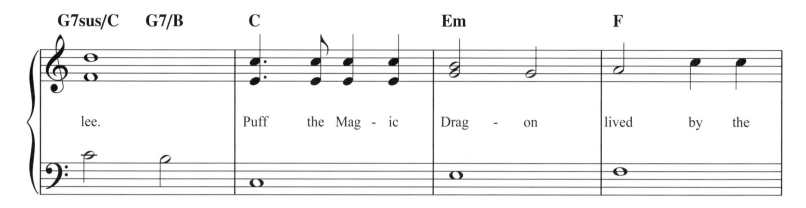

G7sus/C **G7/B** **C** **Em** **F**

lee.   Puff   the   Mag - ic   Drag - on   lived   by   the

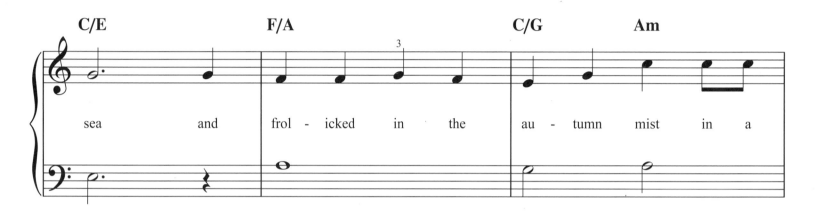

C/E **F/A** **C/G** **Am**

sea   and   frol - icked   in   the   au - tumn   mist   in   a

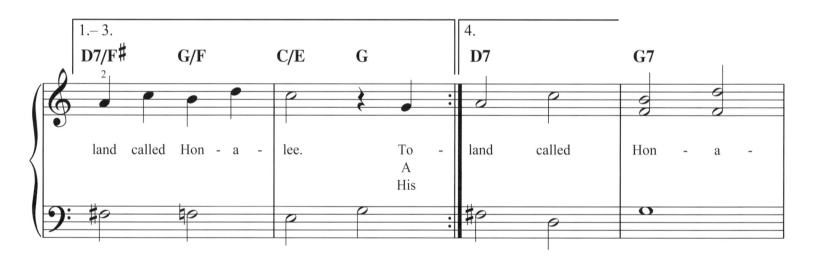

1.– 3.
D7/F# **G/F** **C/E** **G**   **4.** **D7** **G7**

land called Hon - a - lee.   To - land called Hon - a -
                         A
                         His

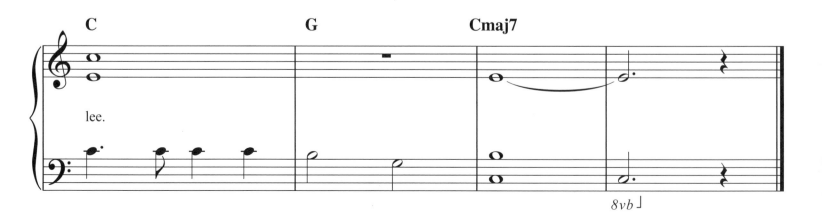

C **G** **Cmaj7**

lee.

8vb

QUE SERA, SERA
(Whatever Will Be, Will Be)
from THE MAN WHO KNEW TOO MUCH

Words and Music by JAY LIVINGSTON
and RAYMOND B. EVANS

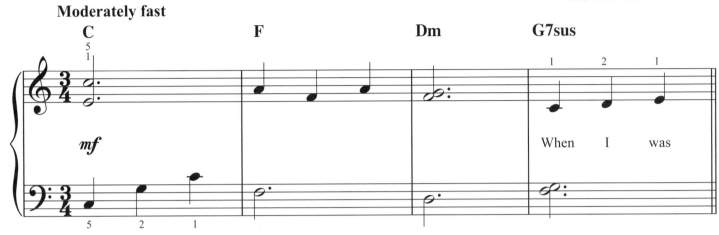

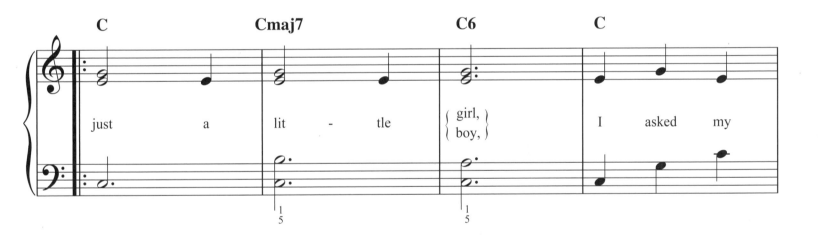

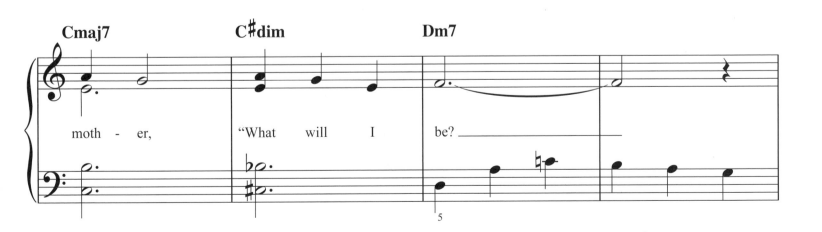

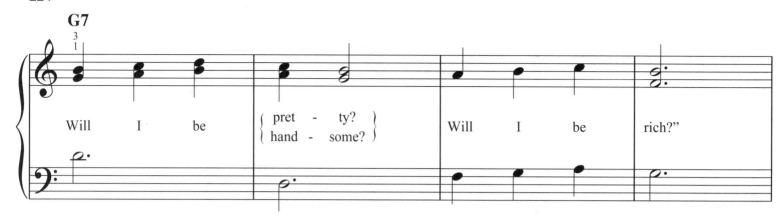

G7

Will I be { pret - ty? / hand - some? } Will I be rich?"

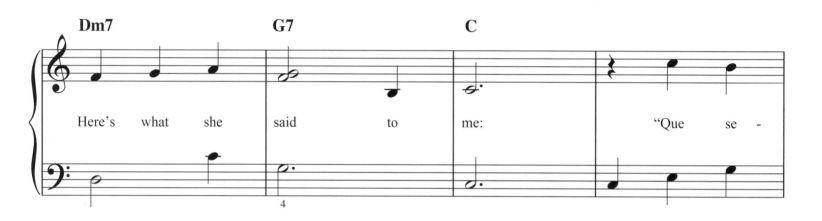

Dm7   **G7**   **C**

Here's what she said to me: "Que se -

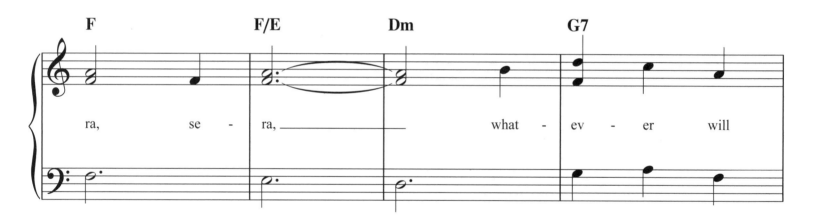

F   **F/E**   **Dm**   **G7**

ra, se - ra, _____ what - ev - er will

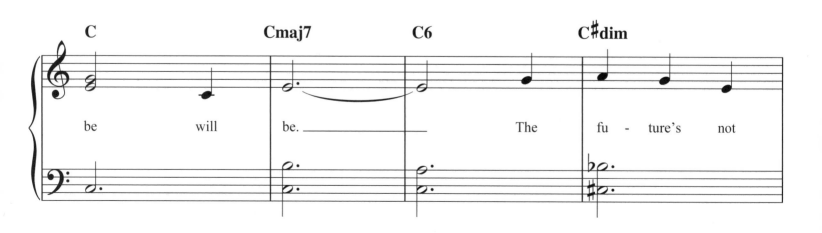

C   **Cmaj7**   **C6**   **C#dim**

be will be. _____ The fu - ture's not

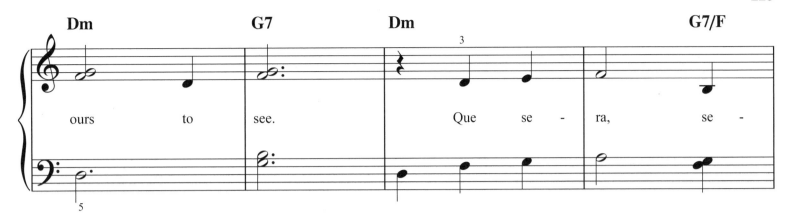

ours to see. Que se - ra, se -

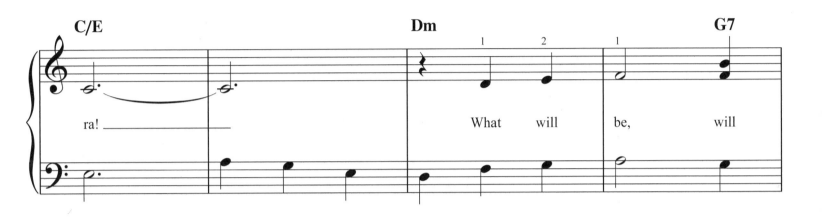

ra! _____ What will be, will

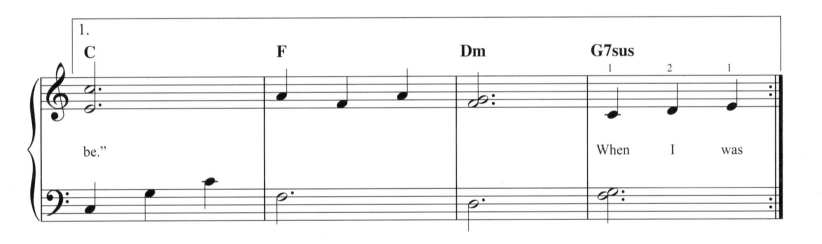

be." When I was

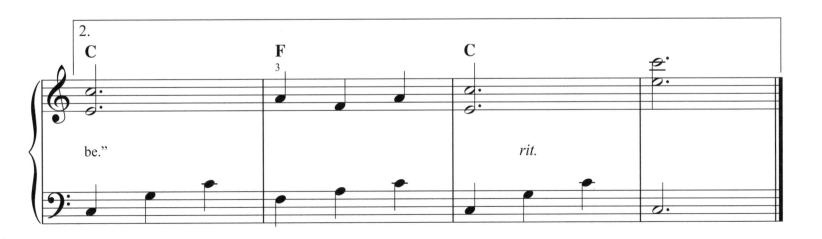

be." *rit.*

THE RAINBOW CONNECTION

from THE MUPPET MOVIE

Words and Music by PAUL WILLIAMS
and KENNETH L. ASCHER

Flowing Waltz

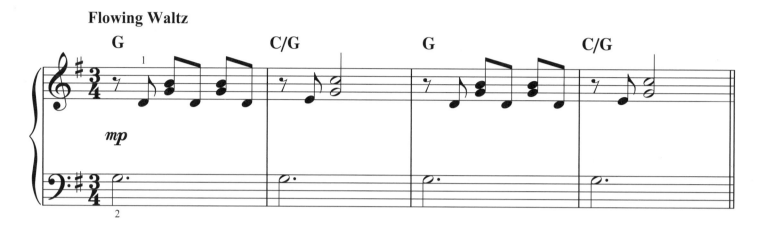

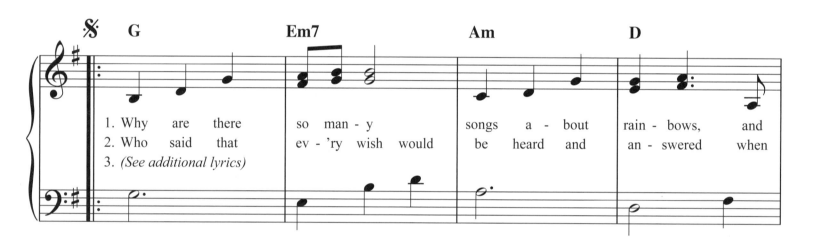

1. Why are there so man-y songs a-bout rain-bows, and
2. Who said that ev-'ry wish would be heard and an-swered when
3. *(See additional lyrics)*

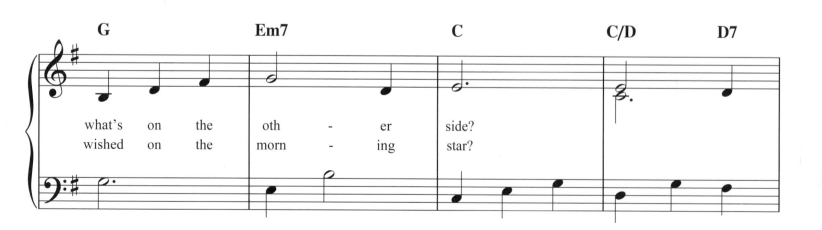

what's on the oth - er side?
wished on the morn - ing star?

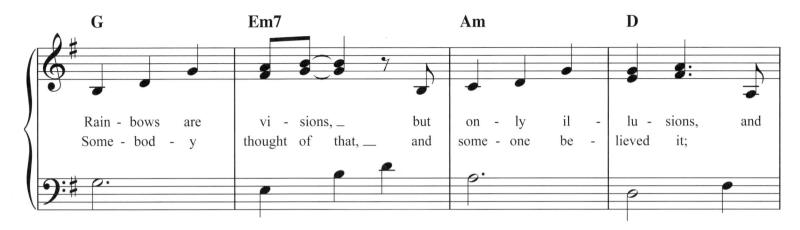

Rain - bows are vi - sions, __ but on - ly il - lu - sions, and
Some - bod - y thought of that, __ and some - one be - lieved it;

rain - bows have noth - ing to hide.
look what it's done ____ so far.

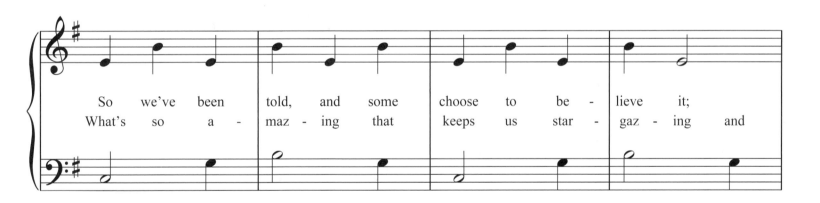

So we've been told, and some choose to be - lieve it;
What's so a - maz - ing some that keeps us star - gaz - ing and

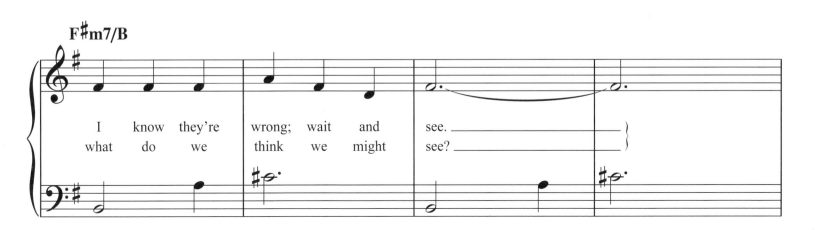

I know they're wrong; wait and see. ____
what do we think we might see? ____

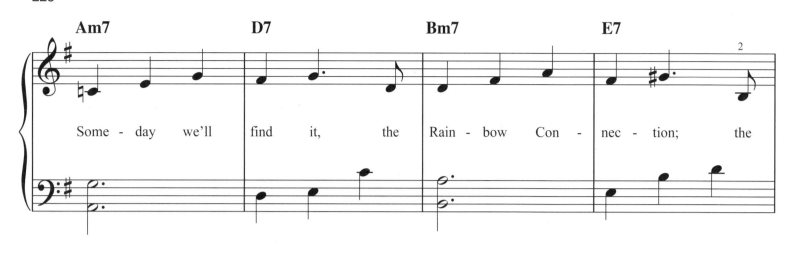

Am7 — **D7** — **Bm7** — **E7**

Some-day we'll find it, the Rain - bow Con - nec - tion; the

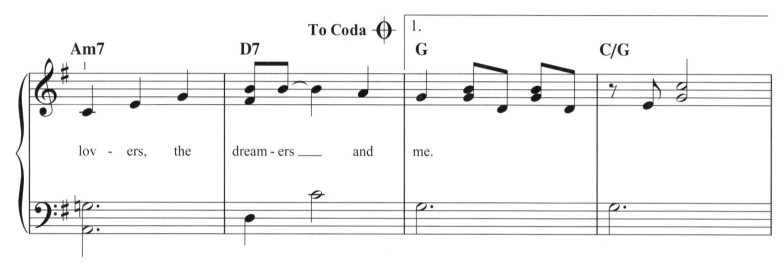

Am7 — **D7** — **To Coda** — **1.** **G** — **C/G**

lov - ers, the dream-ers ___ and me.

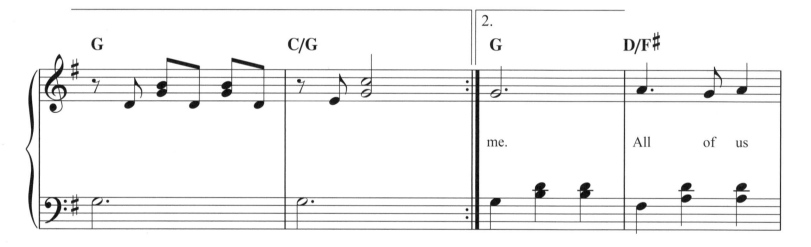

G — **C/G** — **2.** **G** — **D/F#**

me. All of us

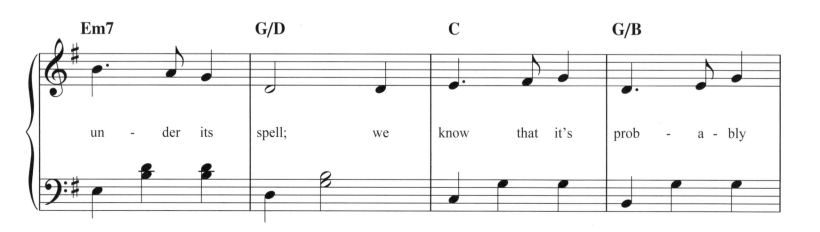

Em7 — **G/D** — **C** — **G/B**

un - der its spell; we know that it's prob - a - bly

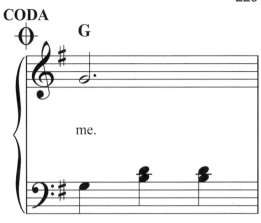

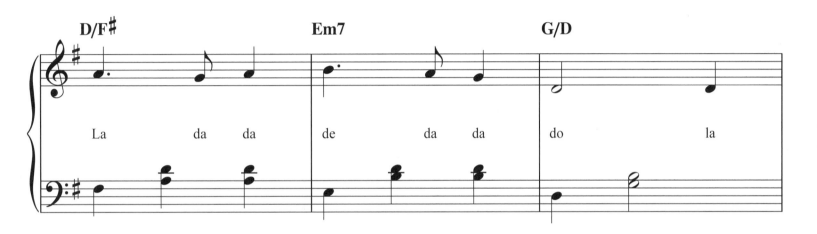

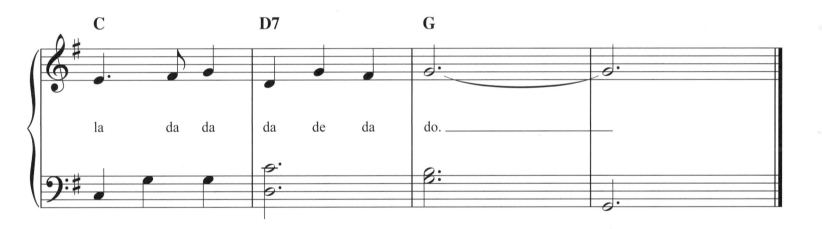

Additional Lyrics

3. Have you been half asleep and have you heard voices?
   I've heard them calling my name.
   Is this the sweet sound that calls the young sailors?
   The voice might be one and the same.
   I've heard it too many times to ignore it.
   It's something that I'm s'posed to be.
   Someday we'll find it,
   The Rainbow Connection;
   The lovers, the dreamers and me.

ROW, ROW, ROW YOUR BOAT

Traditional

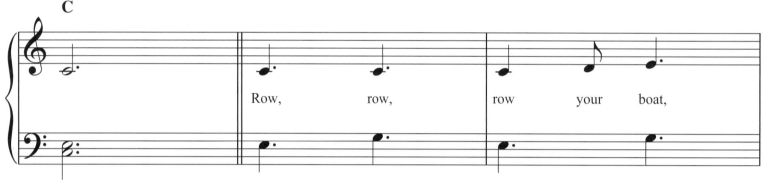

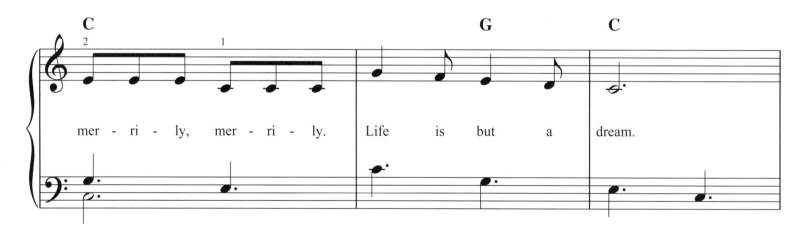

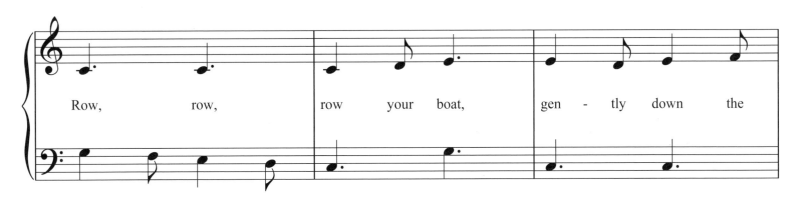

Row, row, row your boat, gen - tly down the

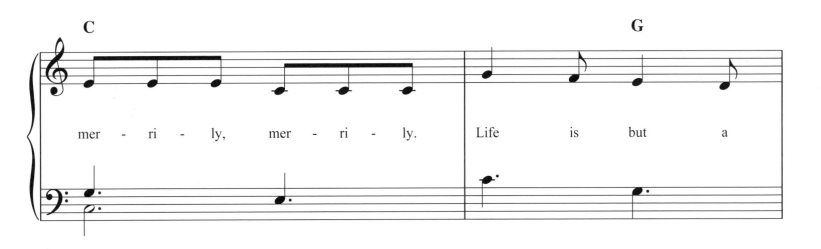

stream. Mer - ri - ly, mer - ri - ly,

G7

C

mer - ri - ly, mer - ri - ly. Life is but a

G

C

dream.

G

RUBBER DUCKIE

from the Television Series SESAME STREET

Words and Music by
JEFF MOSS

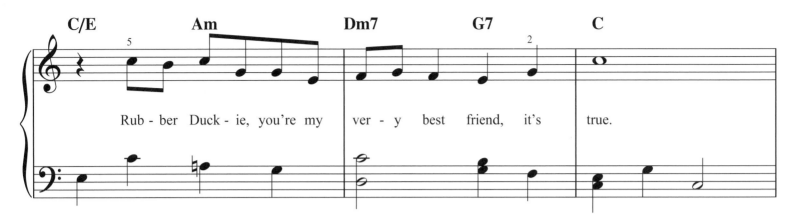

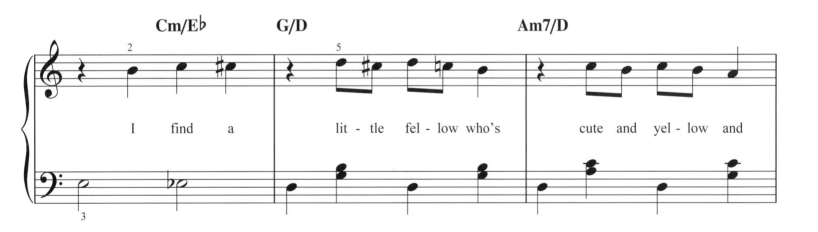

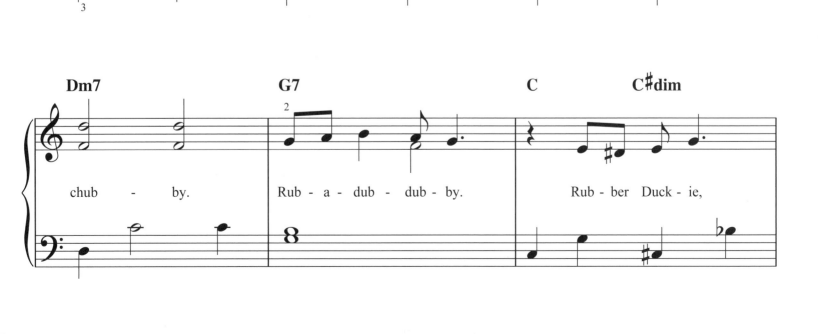

you're so fine,   and I'm luck - y   that you're mine.

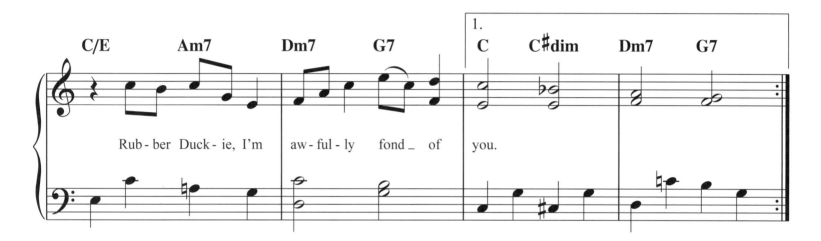

Rub - ber Duck - ie, I'm   aw - ful - ly   fond _ of   you.

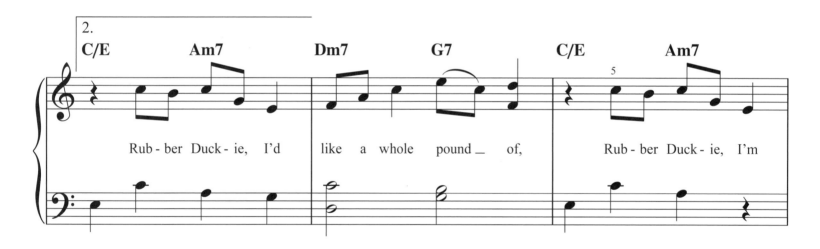

Rub - ber Duck - ie, I'd   like a whole pound _ of,   Rub - ber Duck - ie, I'm

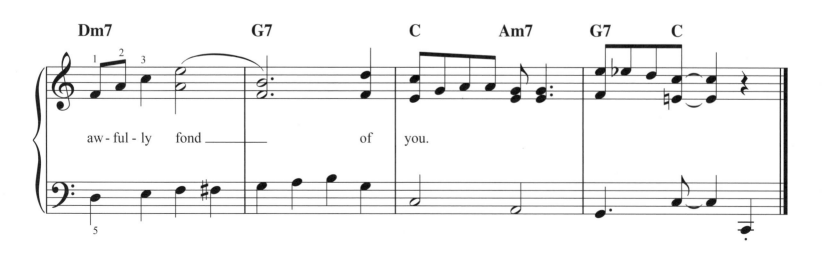

aw - ful - ly   fond _____   of   you.

SING
from SESAME STREET

Words and Music by
JOE RAPOSO

Medium Swing

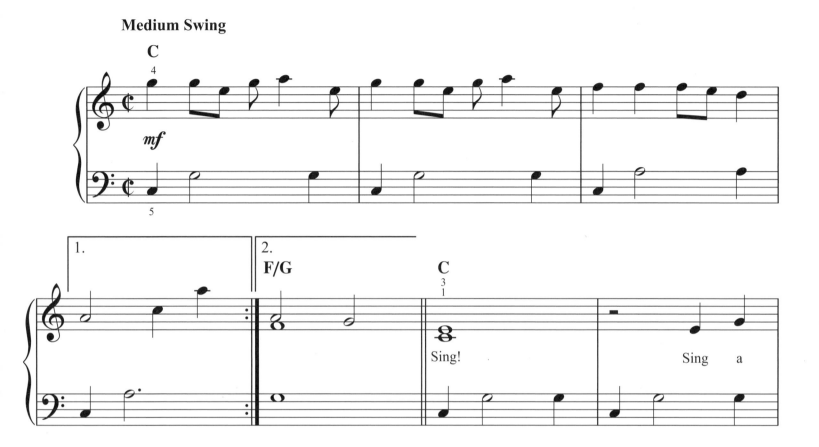

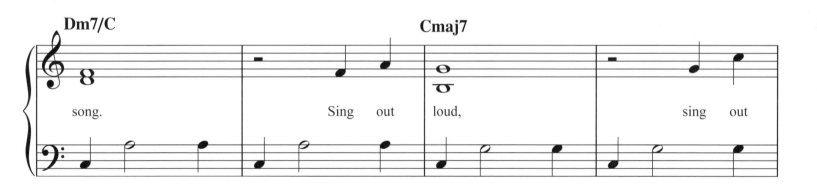

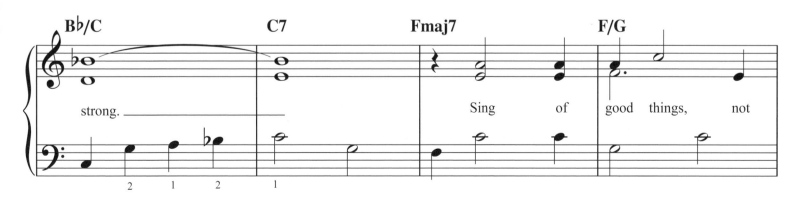

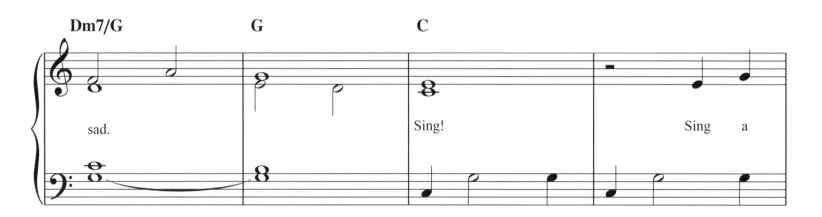

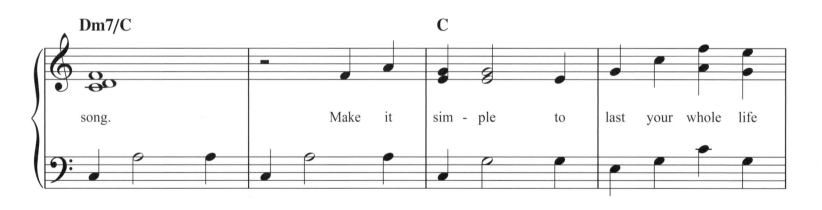

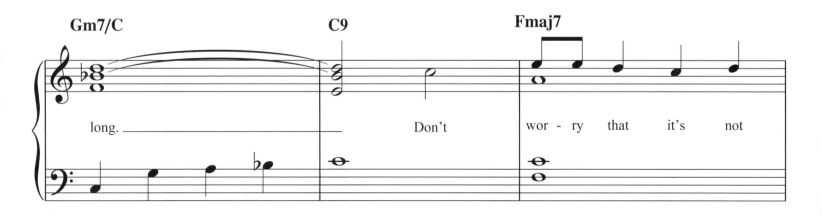

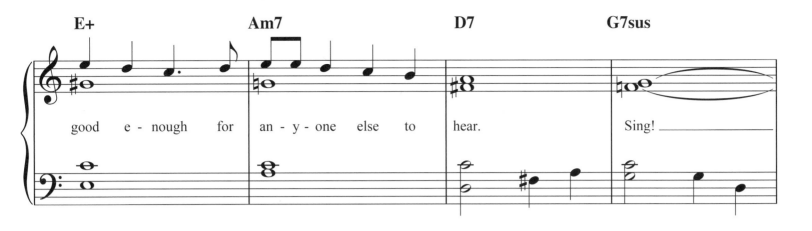

good e-nough for an-y-one else to hear. Sing! _____

____ Sing a song. La la do la da, la

da la do la da, la da da la do la da. La la do la da, la

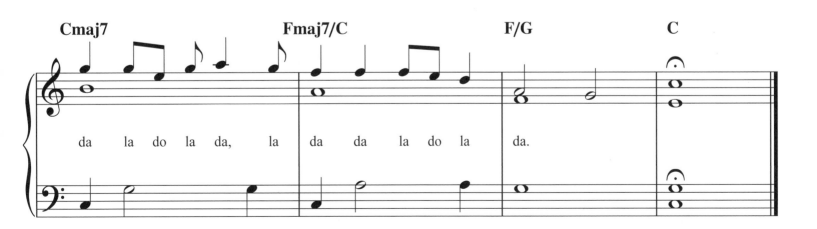

da la do la da, la da da la do la da.

THE SIAMESE CAT SONG

from Walt Disney's LADY AND THE TRAMP

Words and Music by PEGGY LEE
and SONNY BURKE

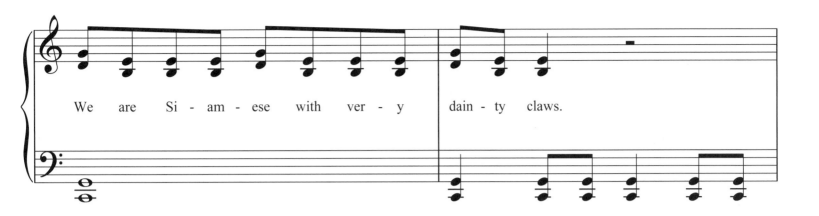

We are Si - am - ese with ver - y dain - ty claws.

G7

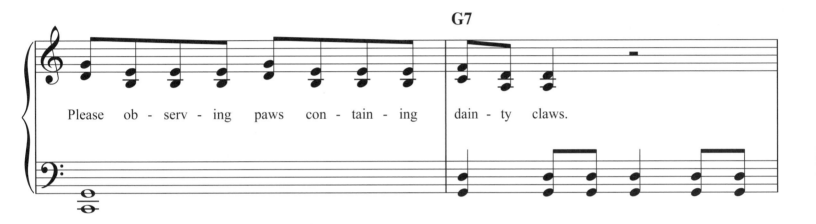

Please ob - serv - ing paws con - tain - ing dain - ty claws.

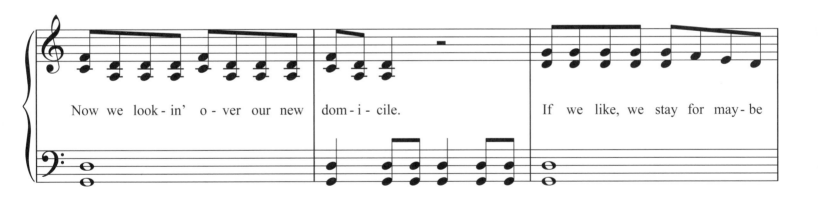

Now we look - in' o - ver our new dom - i - cile. If we like, we stay for may - be

C   **G7**   **C**

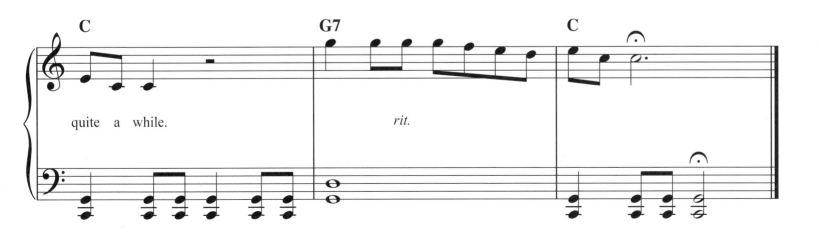

quite a while.   *rit.*

SPLISH SPLASH

Words and Music by BOBBY DARIN
and MURRAY KAUFMAN

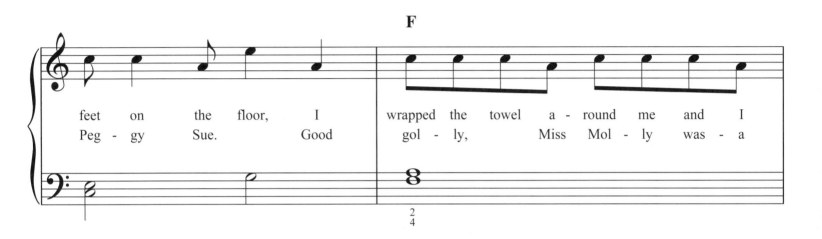

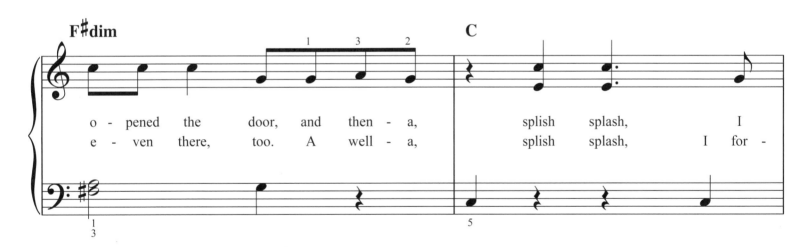

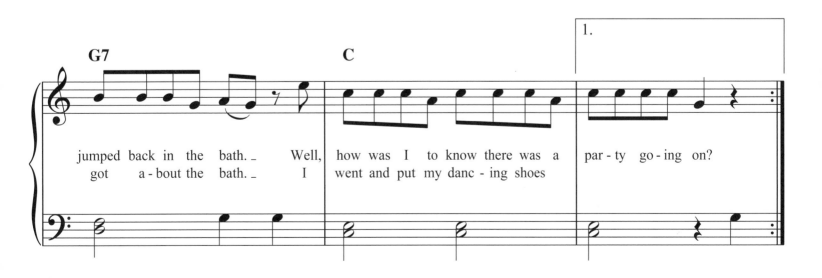

SO LONG, FAREWELL

from THE SOUND OF MUSIC

Lyrics by OSCAR HAMMERSTEIN II
Music by RICHARD RODGERS

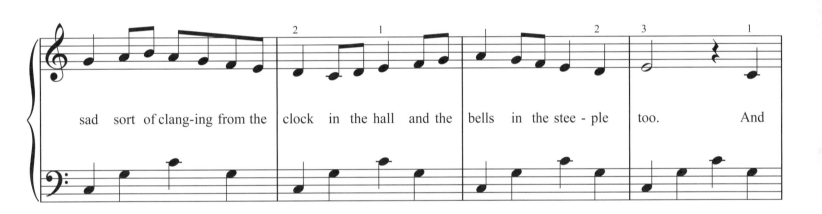

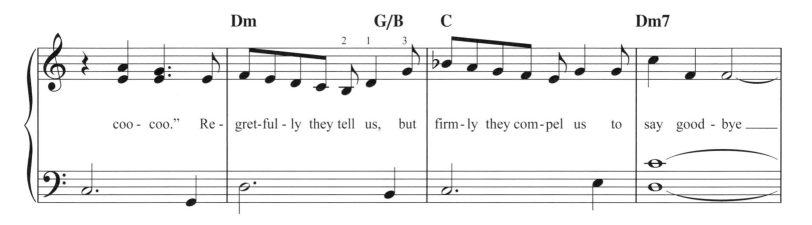

coo - coo." Re - gret-ful - ly they tell us, but firm-ly they com-pel us to say good-bye

to you.

MARTA:

So long, fare-well, auf wie-der-sehn, good-night. _ I hate to go and

leave this pret - ty sight. _

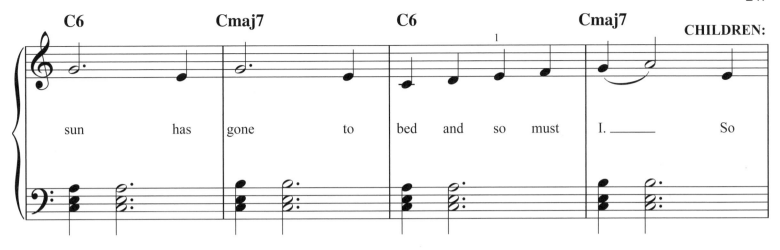

sun has gone to bed and so must I. _____ So

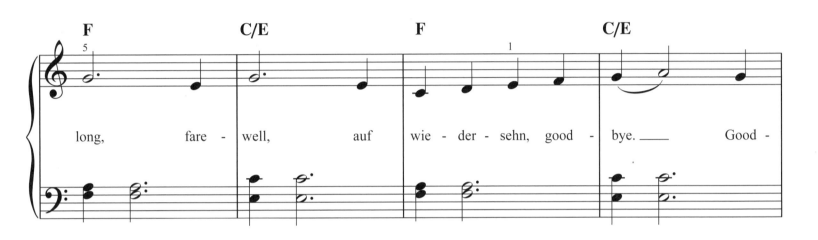

long, fare - well, auf wie - der - sehn, good - bye. _____ Good -

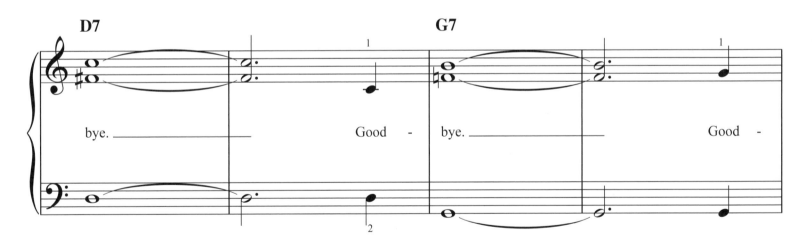

bye. _____ Good - bye. _____ Good -

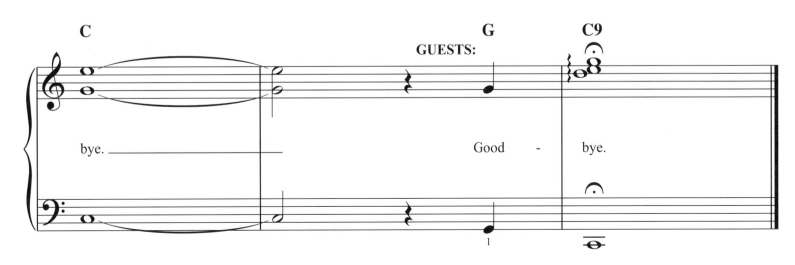

bye. _____ Good - bye.

A SPOONFUL OF SUGAR

from Walt Disney's MARY POPPINS

Words and Music by RICHARD M. SHERMAN
and ROBERT B. SHERMAN

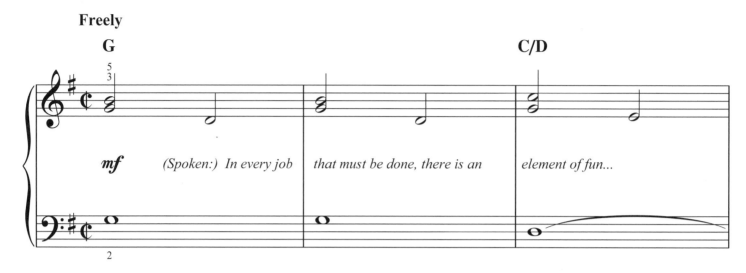

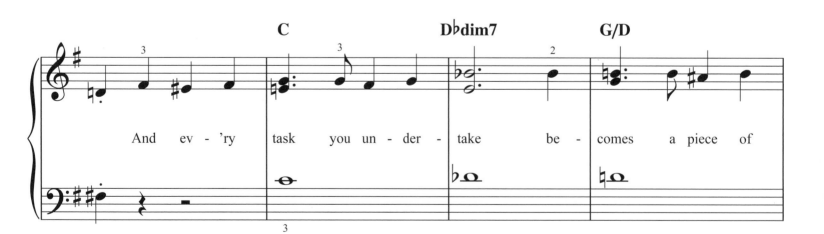

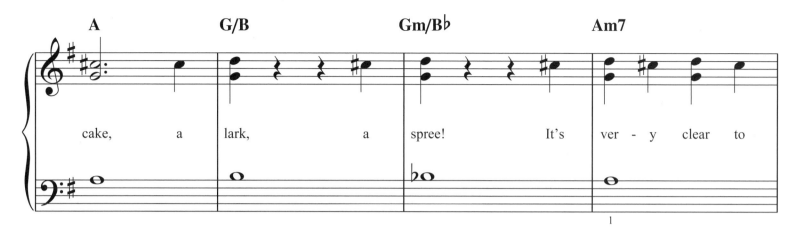

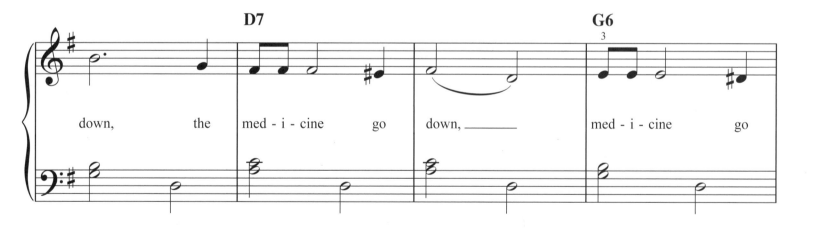

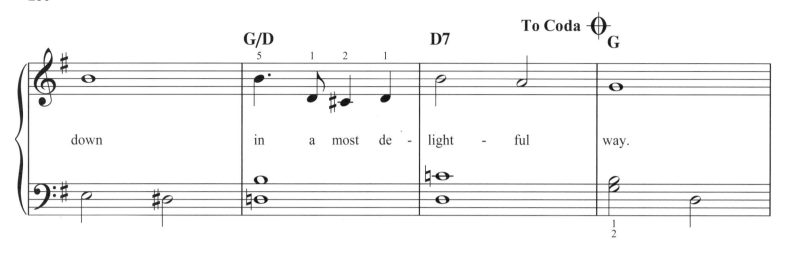

down in a most de - light - ful way.

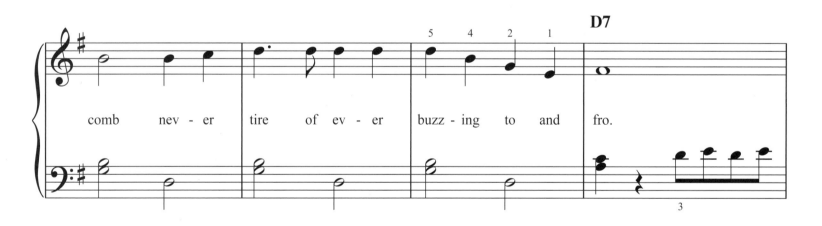

The hon - ey bees that fetch the nec - tar from the flow - ers to the

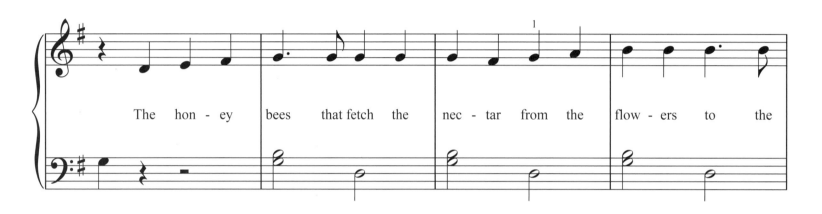

comb nev - er tire of ev - er buzz - ing to and fro.

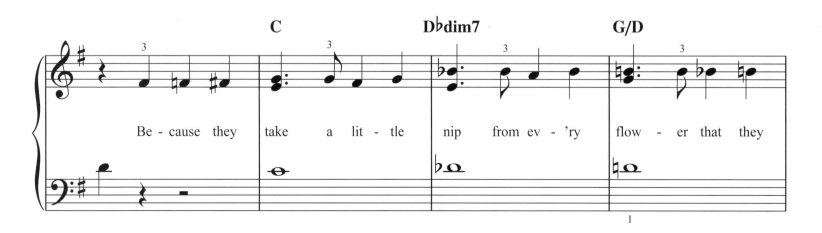

Be - cause they take a lit - tle nip from ev - 'ry flow - er that they

A7   G/B   Gm/B♭   Am7

sip,   and   hence   they   find   their   task   is   not   a

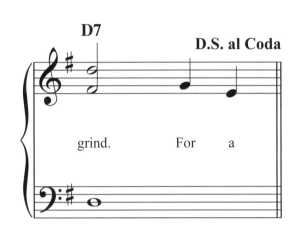

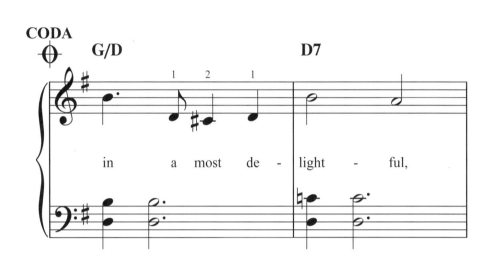

D7   D.S. al Coda

grind.   For   a

CODA   G/D   D7

in   a   most   de - light - ful,

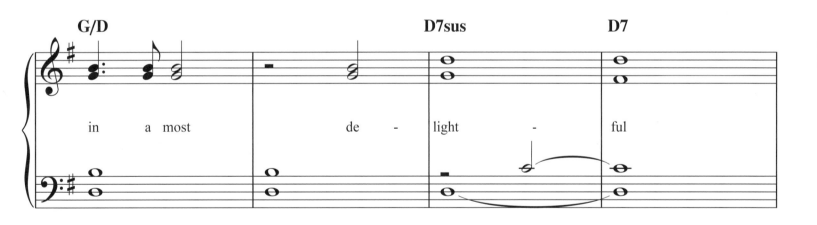

G/D   D7sus   D7

in   a   most   de - light - ful

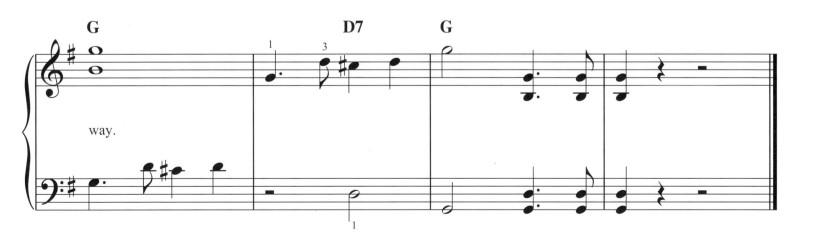

G   D7   G

way.

SUPERCALIFRAGILISTICEXPIALIDOCIOUS
from Walt Disney's MARY POPPINS

Words and Music by RICHARD M. SHERMAN
and ROBERT B. SHERMAN

G7   **C**

Um did - dle did - dle did - dle, um did - dle ay! Um did - dle did - dle did - dle,

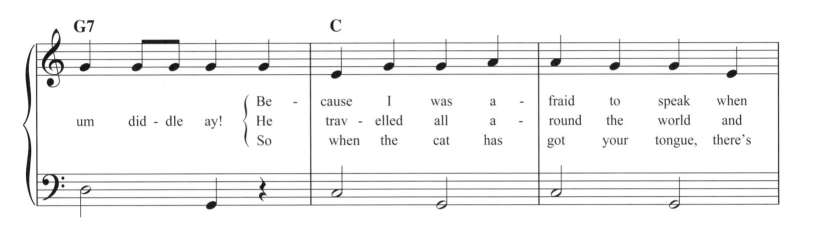

G7   **C**

um did - dle ay!

Be - cause I was a - fraid to speak when
He trav - elled all a - round the world and
So when the cat has got your tongue, there's

C♯dim   **G7**

I was just a lad, me fa - ther gave me nose a tweak and
ev - 'ry - where he went, he'd use his word and all would say, "there
no need to dis - may. Just sum - mon up this word and then you've

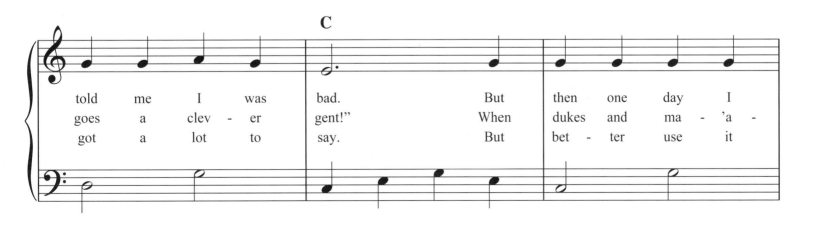

C

told me I was bad. But then one day I
goes a clev - er gent!" When dukes and ma - 'a -
got a lot to say. But bet - ter use it

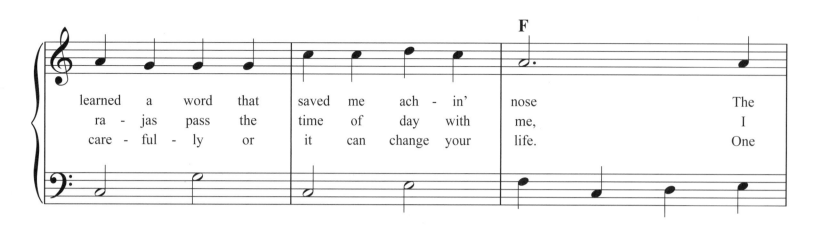

F

learned a word that saved me ach - in' nose me, The
ra - jas pass the time of day with me, I
care - ful - ly or it can change your life. One

D

big - gest word you ev - er 'eard and this is 'ow it
say me spe - cial word and then they ask me out to
night I said it to me girl and now me girl's me

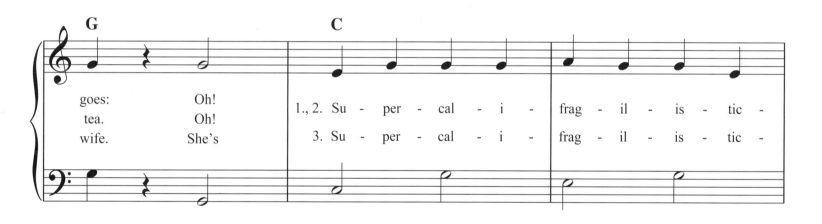

G **C**

goes: Oh! 1., 2. Su - per - cal - i - frag - il - is - tic -
tea. Oh! 3. Su - per - cal - i - frag - il - is - tic -
wife. She's

C#dim **G7**

ex - pi - al - i - do - cious! E - ven though the
ex - pi - al - i - do - cious! Su - per - cal - i -

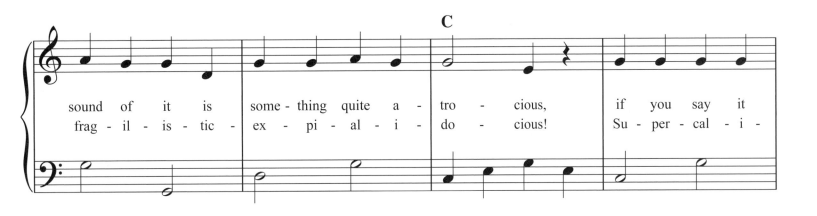

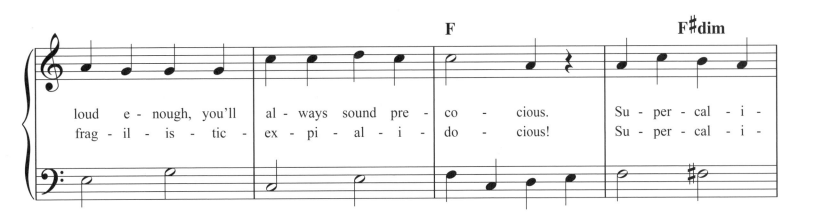

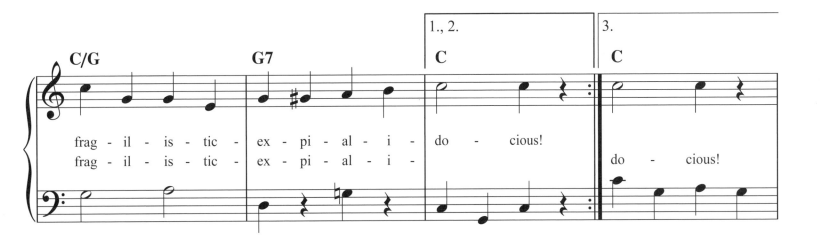

TAKE ME OUT TO THE BALL GAME

Words by JACK NORWORTH
Music by ALBERT VON TILZER

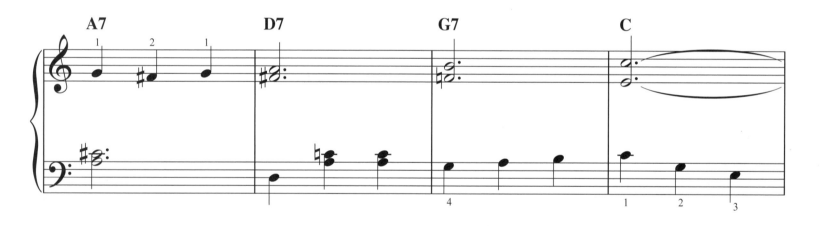

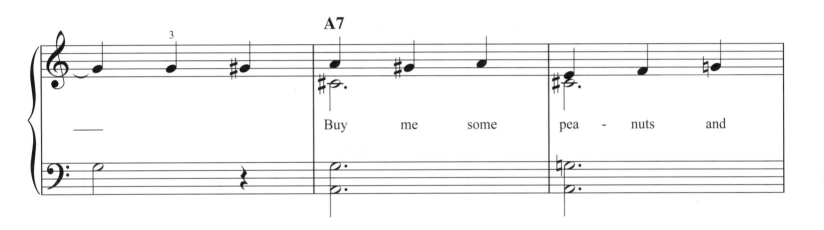

root   for   the   home   team,   if   they   don't

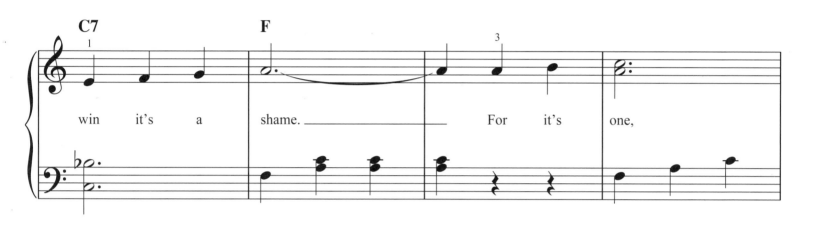

win   it's   a   shame. _____   For   it's   one,

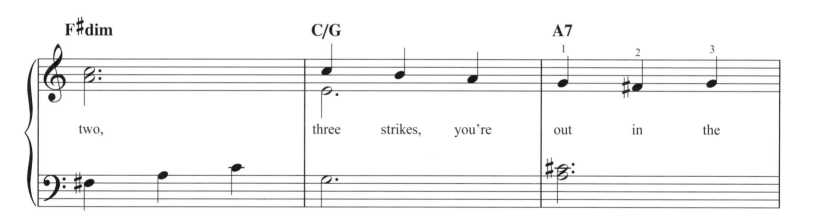

two,   three   strikes,   you're   out   in   the

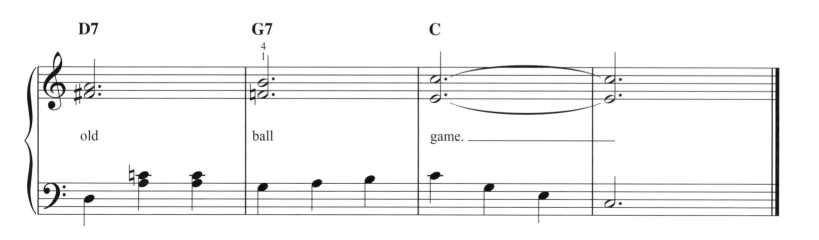

old   ball   game. _____

THERE'S A HOLE IN THE BUCKET

Traditional

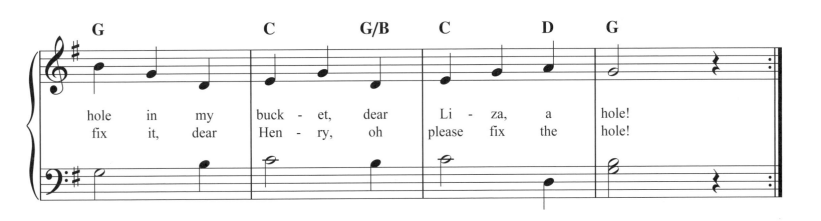

THIS LAND IS YOUR LAND

Words and Music by
WOODY GUTHRIE

With gusto

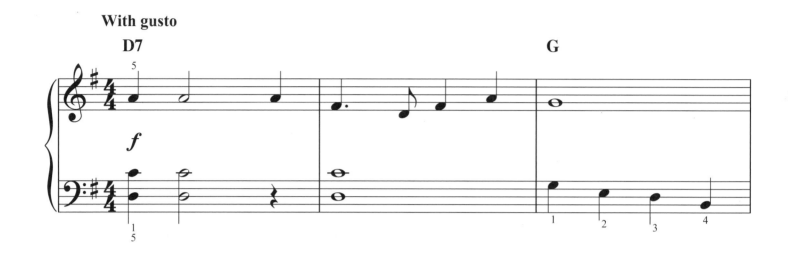

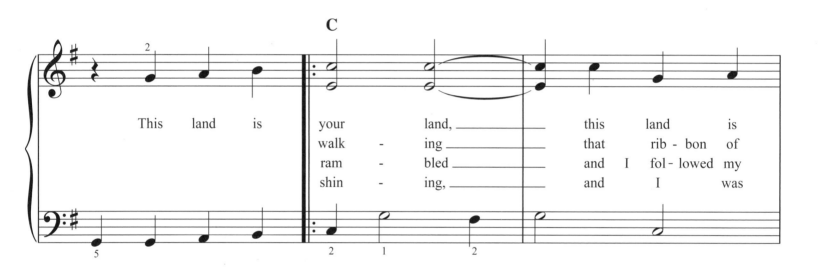

This land is your land, this land is
walk - ing that rib - bon of
ram - bled and I fol - lowed my
shin - ing, and I was

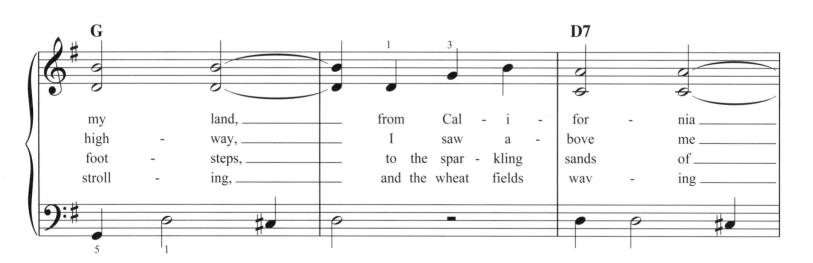

my land, from Cal - i - for - nia
high - way, I saw a - bove me
foot - steps, to the spar - kling sands of
stroll - ing, and the wheat fields wav - ing

THIS OLD MAN

Traditional

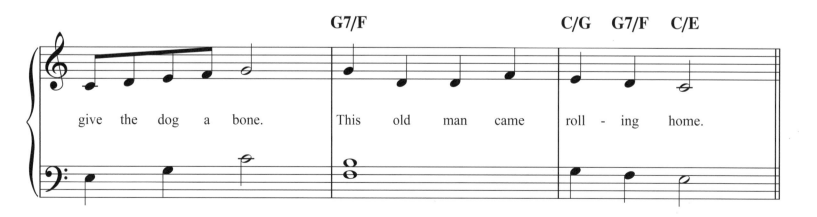

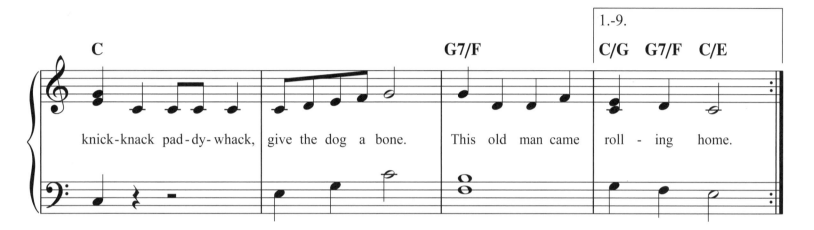

Additional Lyrics

3. This old man, he played three.
   He played knick-knack on my knee,
   Chorus

4. This old man, he played four.
   He played knick-knack on my door,
   Chorus

5. This old man, he played five.
   He played knick-knack on my hive,
   Chorus

6. This old man, he played six.
   He played knick-knack on my sticks,
   Chorus

7. This old man, he played seven.
   He played knick-knack up to heaven,
   Chorus

8. This old man, he played eight.
   He played knick-knack at the gate,
   Chorus

9. This old man, he played nine.
   He played knick-knack on my line,
   Chorus

10. This old man, he played ten.
    He played knick-knack over again,
    Chorus

TOMORROW
from the Musical Production ANNIE

Lyric by MARTIN CHARNIN
Music by CHARLES STROUSE

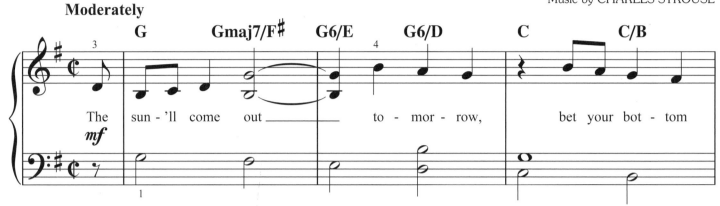

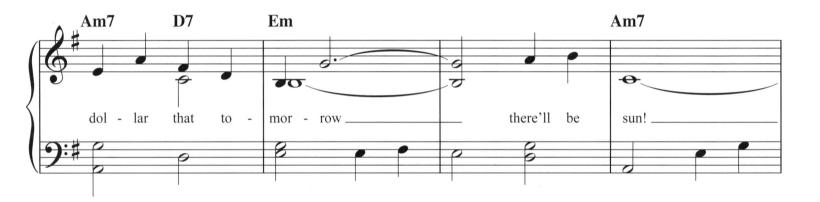

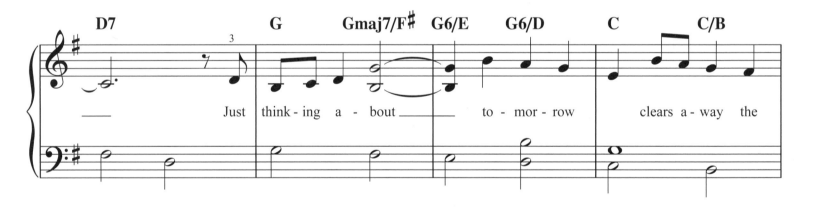

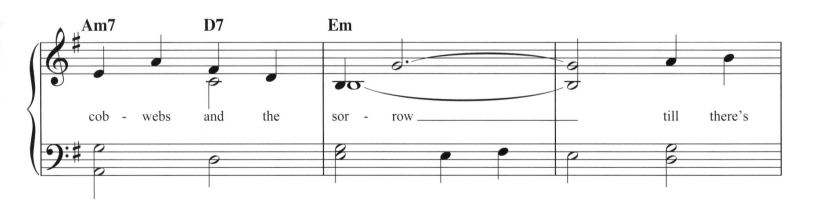

none._____ When I'm stuck with a day that's

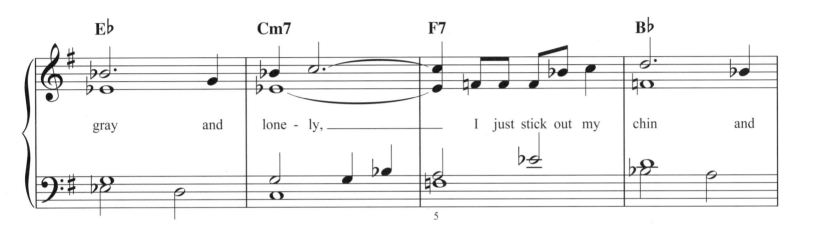

gray and lone - ly,_____ I just stick out my chin and

grin and say:

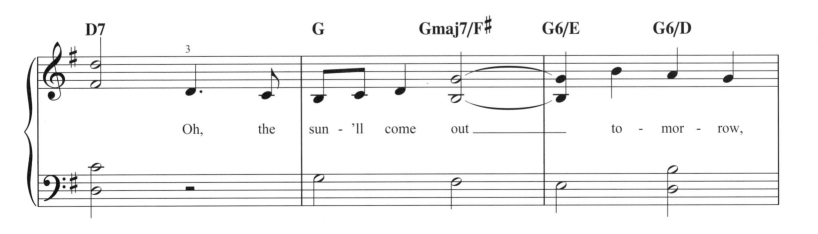

Oh, the sun - 'll come out_____ to - mor - row,

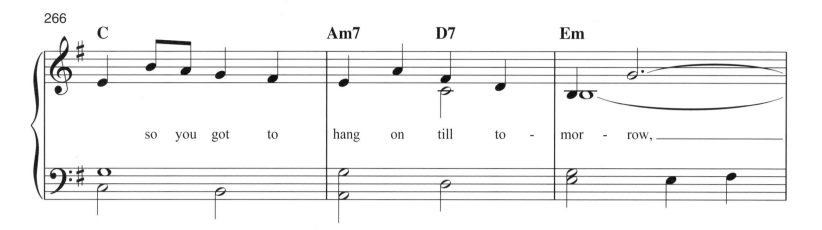

so you got to hang on till to - mor - row, ____

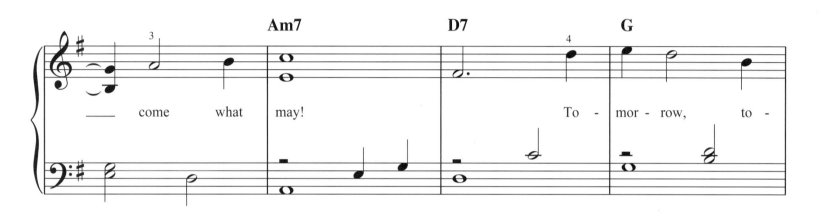

____ come what may! To - mor - row, to -

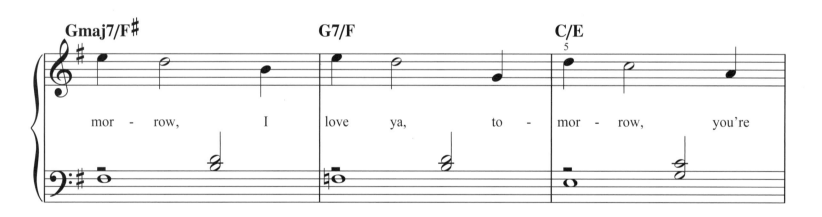

mor - row, I love ya, to - mor - row, you're

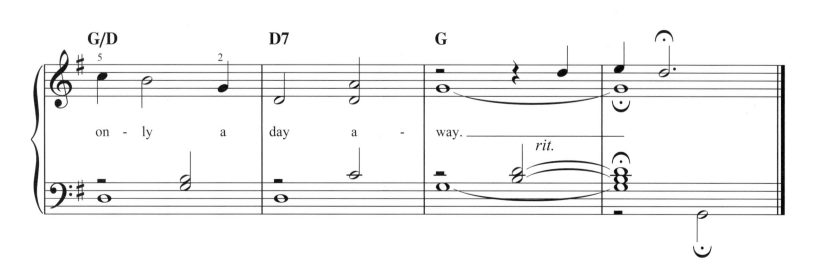

on - ly a day a - way. ____ *rit.*

THE UNBIRTHDAY SONG
from Walt Disney's ALICE IN WONDERLAND

Words and Music by MACK DAVID,
AL HOFFMAN and JERRY LIVINGSTON

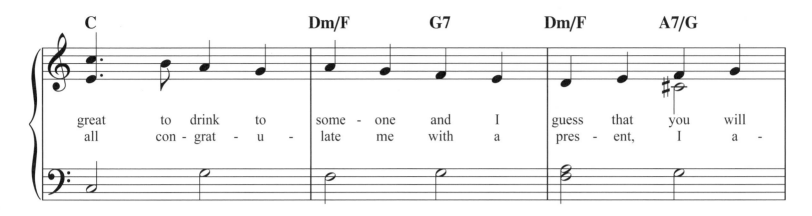

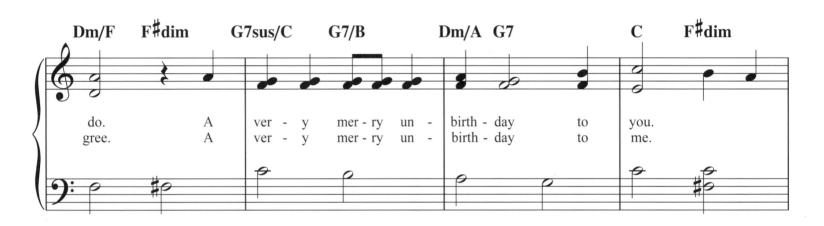

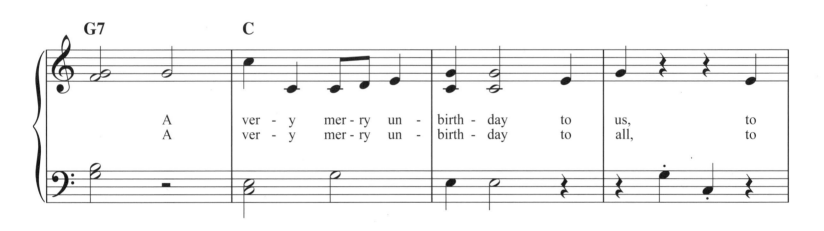

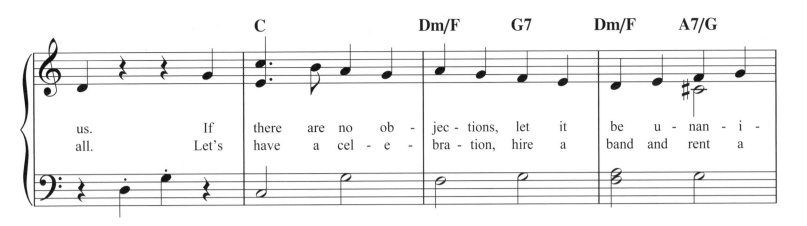

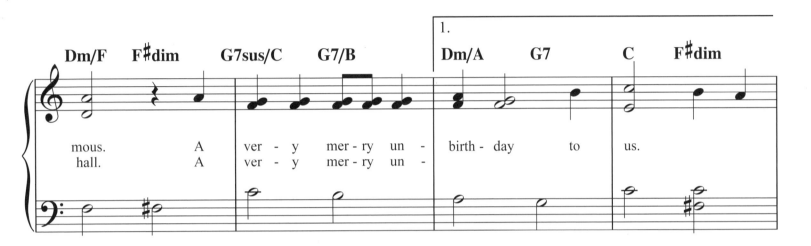

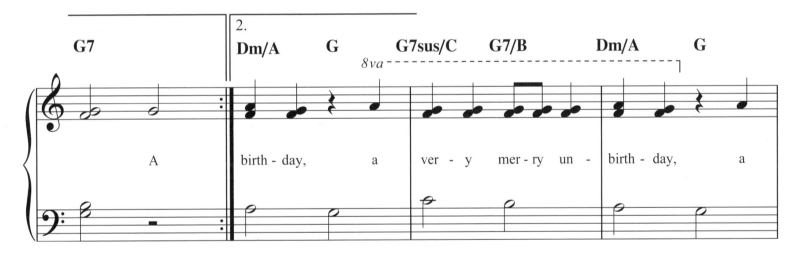

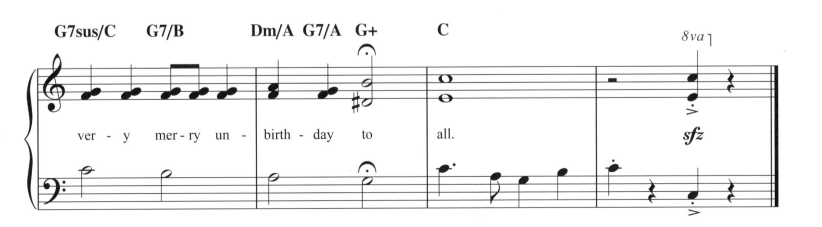

WE'RE OFF TO SEE THE WIZARD

from THE WIZARD OF OZ

Lyric by E.Y. "YIP" HARBURG
Music by HAROLD ARLEN

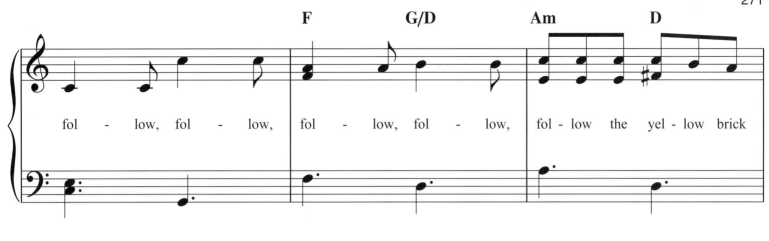

fol - low, fol - low, fol - low, fol - low, fol - low the yel - low brick

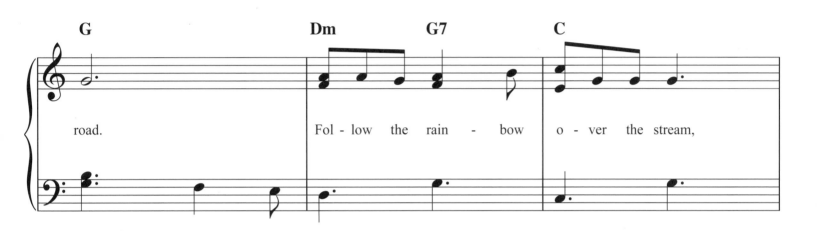

road. Fol - low the rain - bow o - ver the stream,

fol - low the fel - low who fol - lows a dream, fol - low, fol - low,

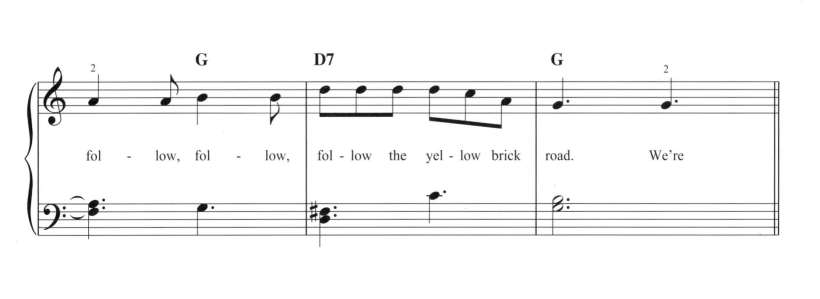

fol - low, fol - low, fol - low the yel - low brick road. We're

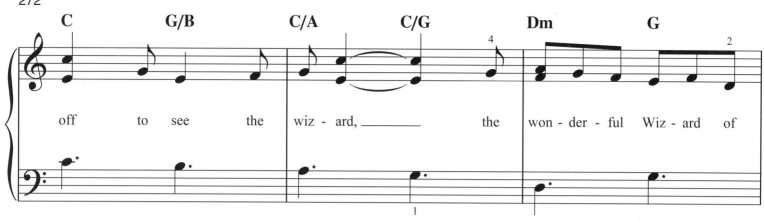

off   to see   the   wiz - ard, _____   the   won - der - ful Wiz - ard of

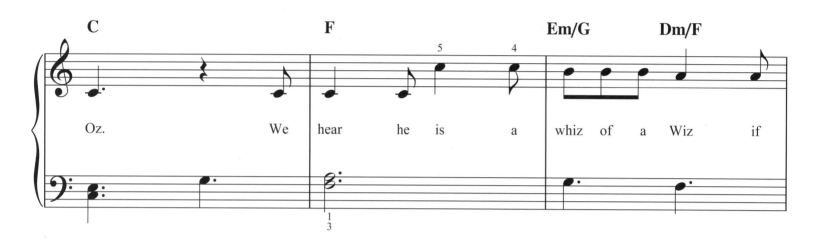

Oz.   We hear   he   is   a   whiz of   a Wiz   if

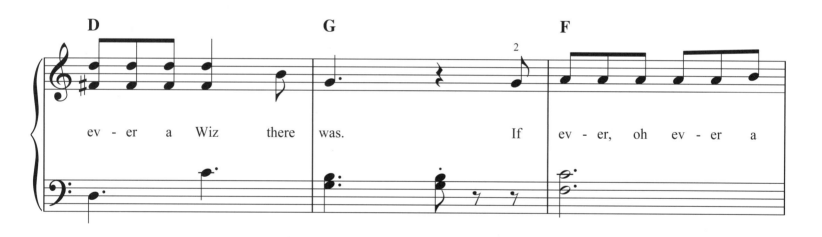

ev - er a Wiz there   was.   If   ev - er, oh ev - er a

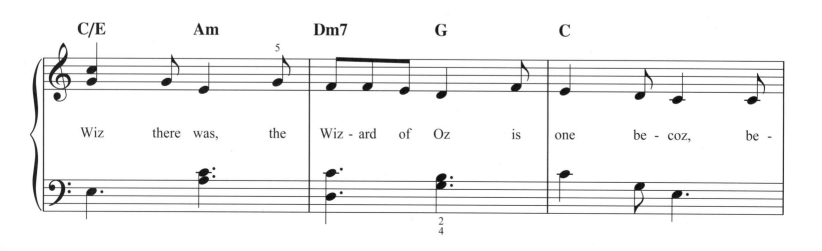

Wiz   there was,   the   Wiz - ard of Oz   is   one   be - coz, be -

coz, be - coz, be - coz, be - coz, be - coz,

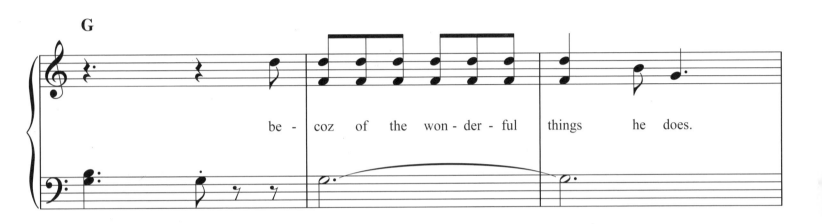

be - coz of the won - der - ful things he does.

We're off to see the

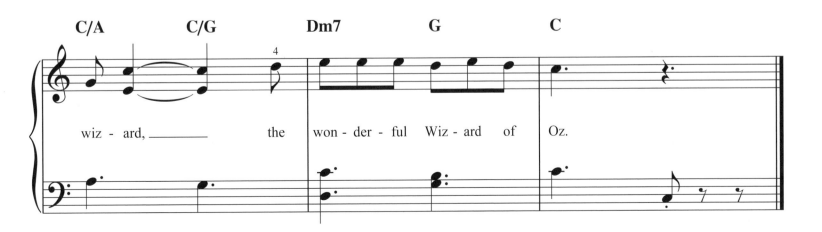

wiz - ard, _____ the won - der - ful Wiz - ard of Oz.

WHEN I GROW TOO OLD TO DREAM

Lyrics by OSCAR HAMMERSTEIN II
Music by SIGMUND ROMBERG

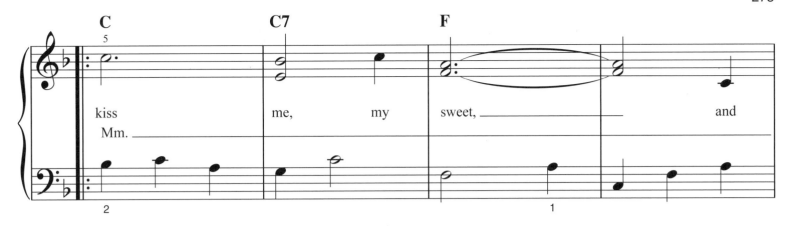

C   C7   F

kiss   me,   my   sweet, _____   and
Mm. _____

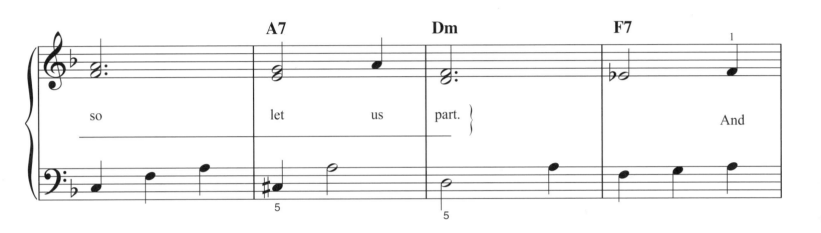

A7   Dm   F7

so   let   us   part.   And

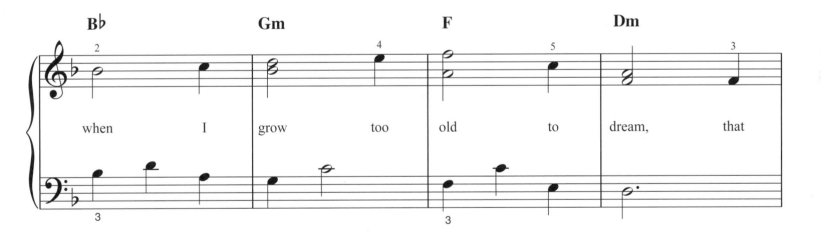

B♭   Gm   F   Dm

when   I   grow   too   old   to   dream,   that

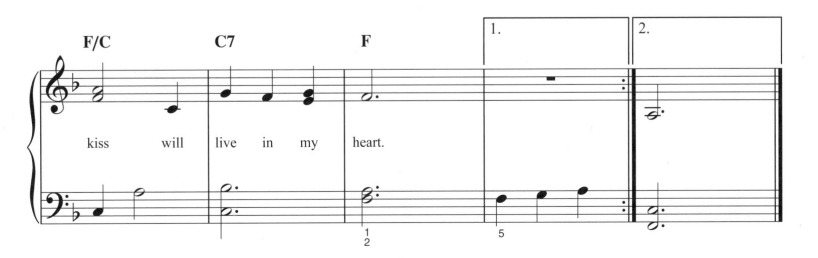

F/C   C7   F

kiss   will   live   in   my   heart.

1.   2.

WHEN I'M SIXTY-FOUR

Words and Music by JOHN LENNON
and PAUL McCARTNEY

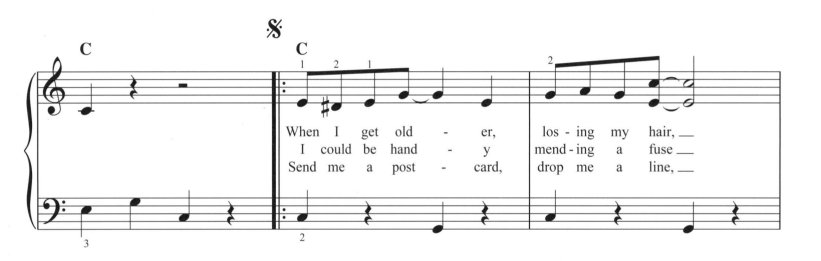

When I get old - er, los - ing my hair, ___
I could be hand - y mend - ing a fuse ___
Send me a post - card, drop me a line, ___

man - y years from now,
when your lights have gone.
stat - ing points of view.

will you still be send - ing me a
You can knit a sweat - er by the
In - di - cate pre - cise - ly what you

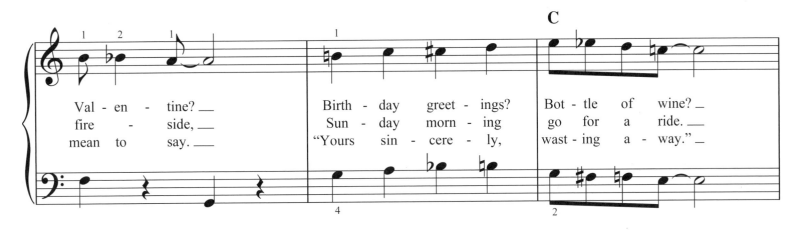

Val - en - tine? ___
fire - side, ___
mean to say. ___

Birth - day greet - ings?
Sun - day morn - ing
"Yours sin - cere - ly,

C

Bot - tle of wine? ___
go for a ride. ___
wast - ing a - way."

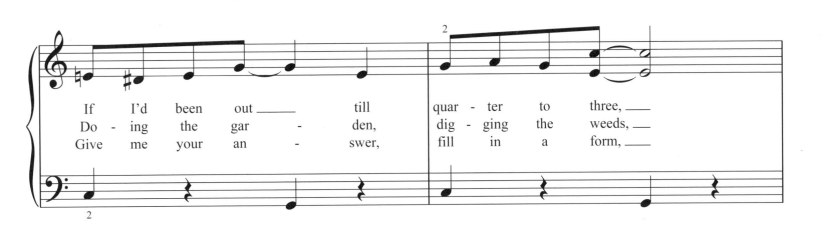

If I'd been out ___ till
Do - ing the gar - den,
Give me your an - swer,

quar - ter to three, ___
dig - ging the weeds, ___
fill in a form, ___

C7

would you lock the
who could ask for
mine for - ev - er -

F

door?
more?
more.

F♯dim7

Will you still need ___ me,
Will you still need ___ me,
Will you still need ___ me,

C/G

will you still feed ___ me
will you still feed ___ me
will you still feed ___ me

A7/G

D7/F♯

when I'm
when I'm
when I'm

G7/F

six - ty -
six - ty -
six - ty -

To Coda ⊕

C **Am**

four?
four?

(Instrumental)
Ev - 'ry sum - mer we can rent a cot - tage in the Isle of

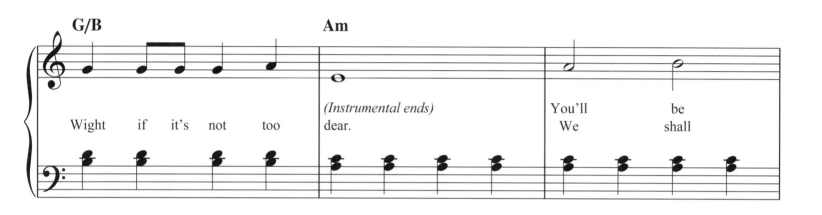

G/B **Am**

Wight if it's not too
(Instrumental ends) dear.

You'll be
We shall

E/G♯ Am **E/G♯ Am** **E/G♯ Am**

old - er,
scrimp and

too.
save.

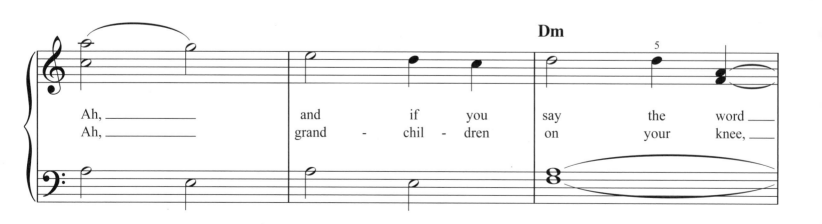

Dm

Ah,
Ah,

and if you
grand - chil - dren on

say the word
your knee,

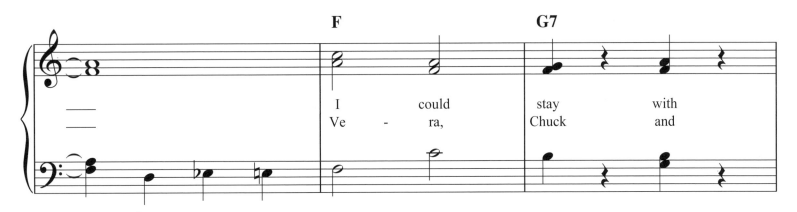

F   G7

I   could   stay   with
Ve   -   ra,   Chuck   and

C   N.C.   1.

you.
Dave.

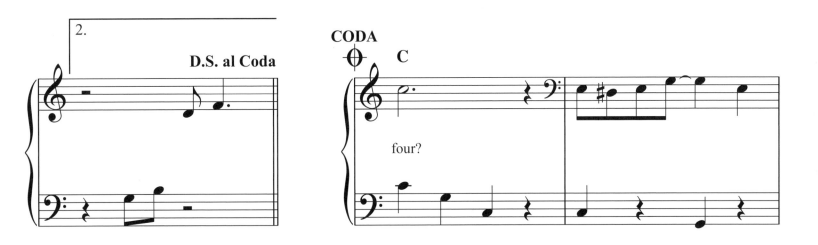

2.   D.S. al Coda   CODA   C

four?

Am   D7/F♯   G7/F   C

WHEN SHE LOVED ME

from Walt Disney Pictures' TOY STORY 2 – A Pixar Film

Music and Lyrics by
RANDY NEWMAN

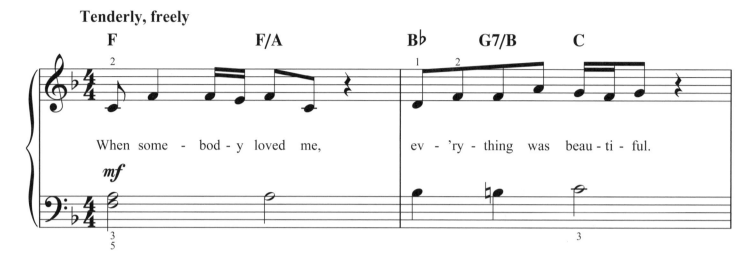

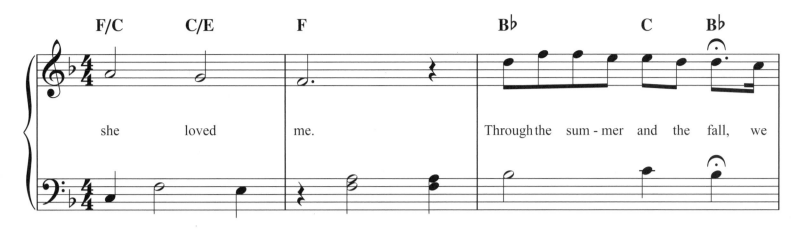

she loved me. Through the sum-mer and the fall, we

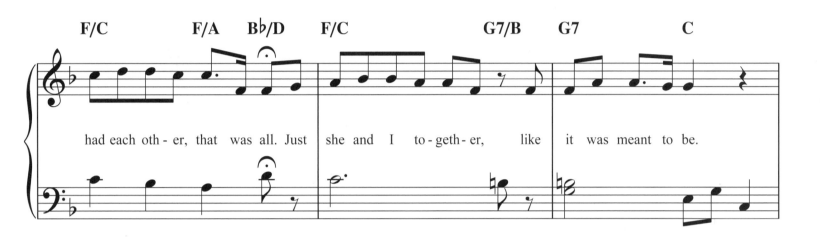

had each oth-er, that was all. Just she and I to-geth-er, like it was meant to be.

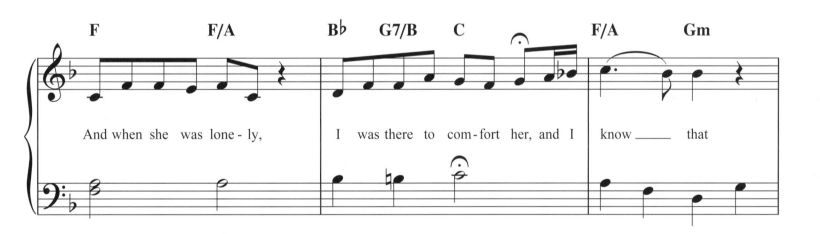

And when she was lone-ly, I was there to com-fort her, and I know _____ that

she loved me.

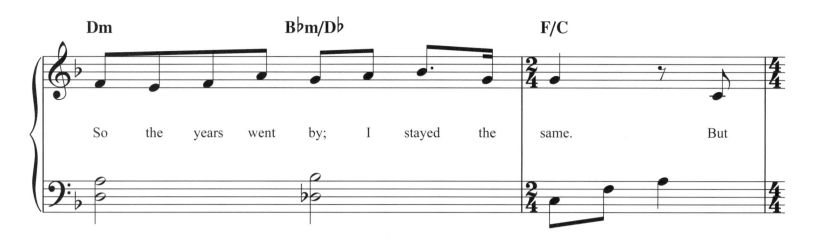

So the years went by; I stayed the same. But

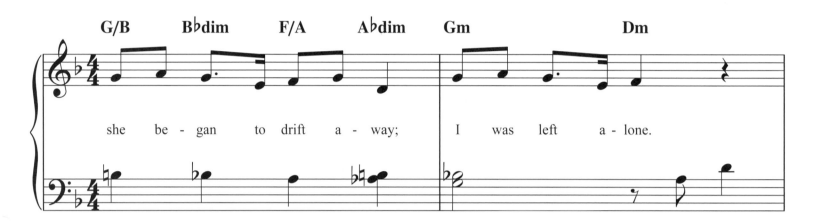

she be - gan to drift a - way; I was left a - lone.

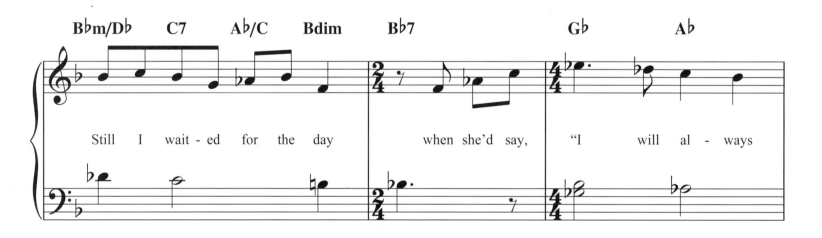

Still I wait - ed for the day when she'd say, "I will al - ways

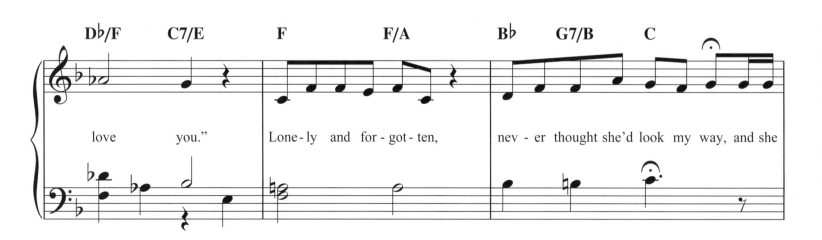

love you." Lone - ly and for - got - ten, nev - er thought she'd look my way, and she

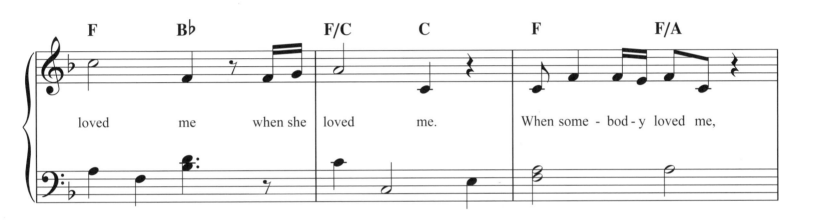

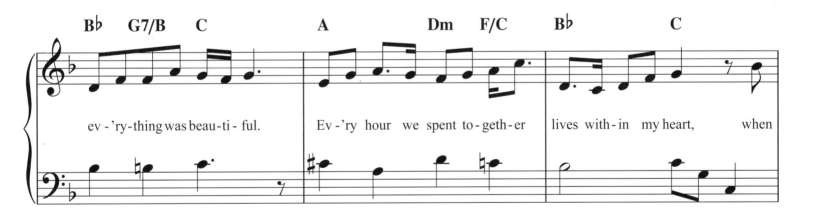

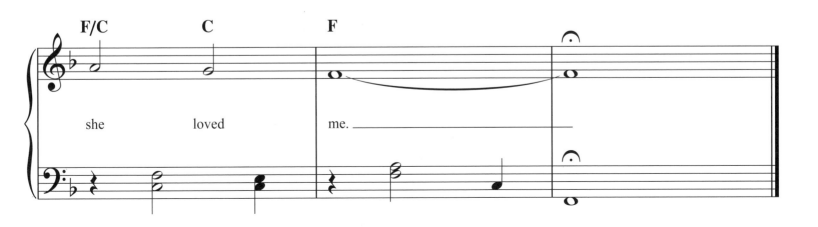

WHEN YOU WISH UPON A STAR

from Walt Disney's PINOCCHIO

Words by NED WASHINGTON
Music by LEIGH HARLINE

With expression

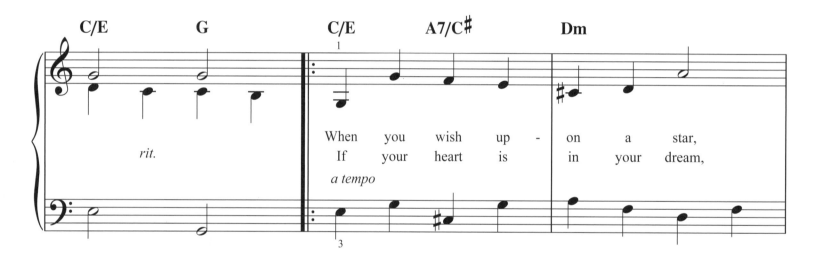

When you wish up - on a star,
If your heart is in your dream,

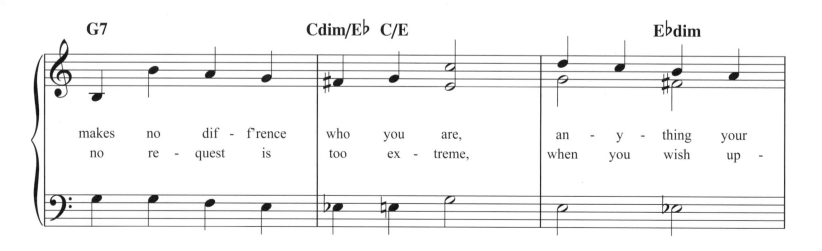

makes no dif - f'rence who you are, an - y - thing your
no re - quest is too ex - treme, when you wish up -

285

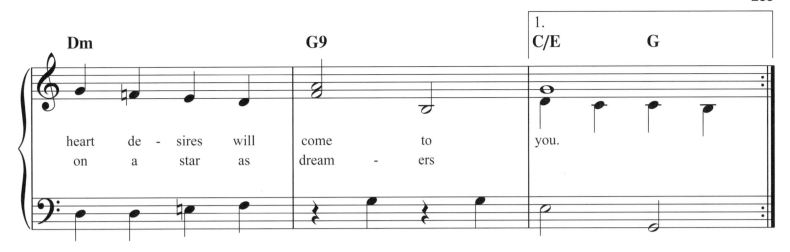

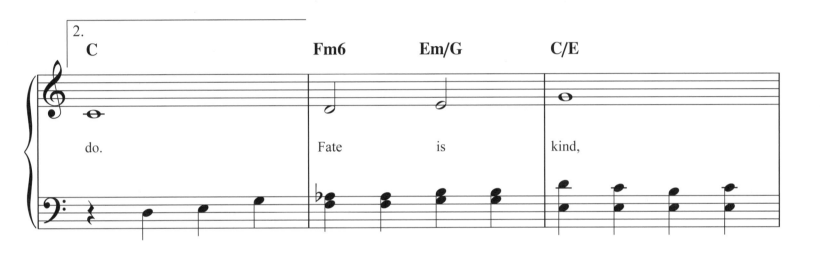

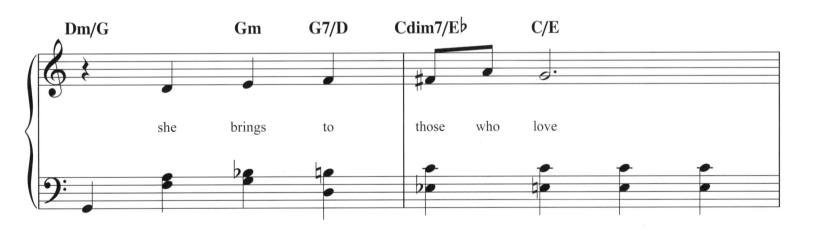

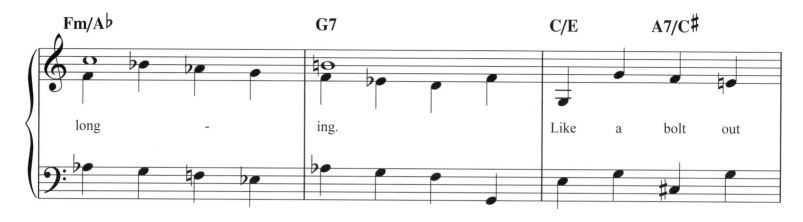

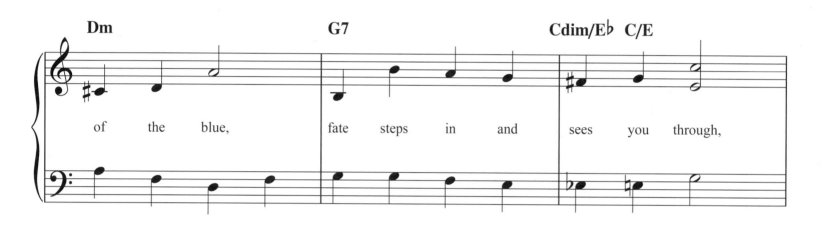

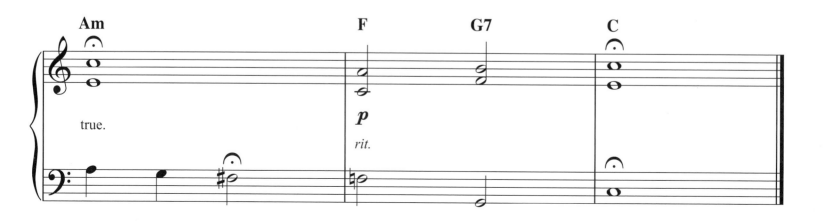

WHERE IS LOVE?

from the Broadway Musical OLIVER!

Words and Music by
LIONEL BART

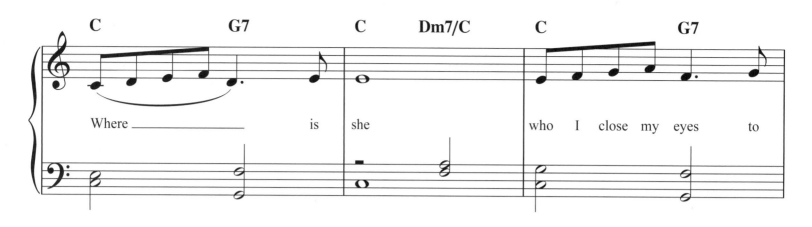

Where _____ is she who I close my eyes to

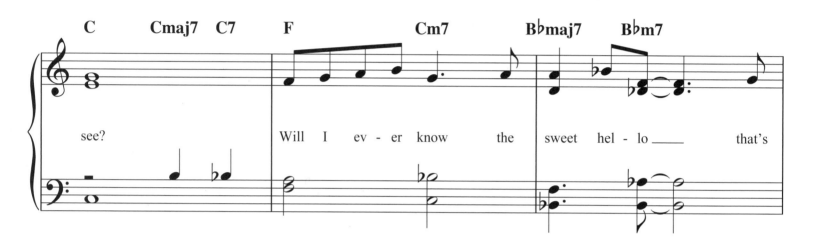

see? Will I ev - er know the sweet hel - lo _____ that's

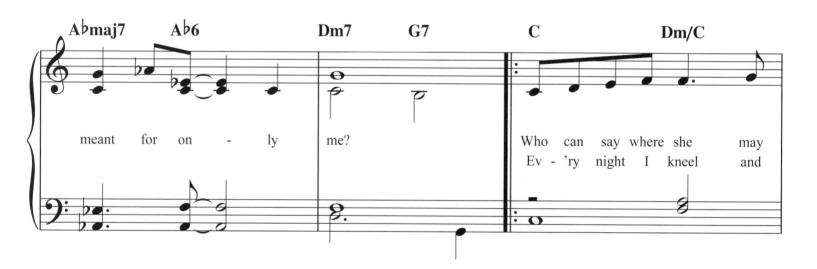

meant for on - ly me? Who can say where she may
Ev - 'ry night I kneel and

hide?
pray,
Must I trav - el far and wide
let to - mor - row be the day

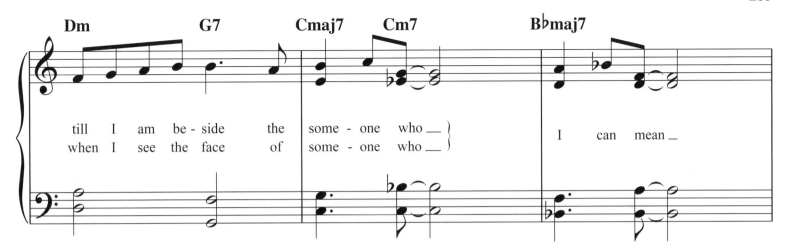

till I am be-side the some - one who —
when I see the face of some - one who —

I can mean —

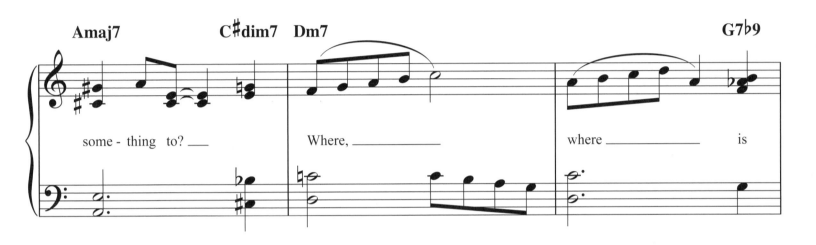

some - thing to? —

Where, _____

where _____ is

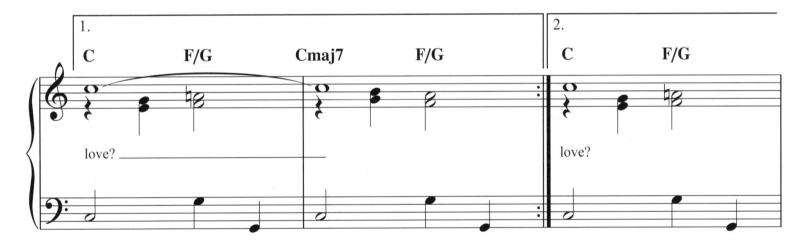

1.

love? _____

2.

love?

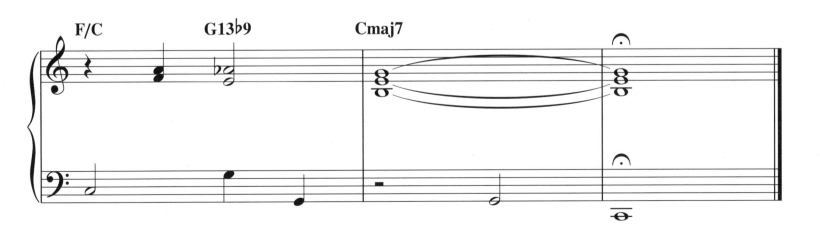

WHISTLE WHILE YOU WORK

from Walt Disney's SNOW WHITE AND THE SEVEN DWARFS

Words by LARRY MOREY
Music by FRANK CHURCHILL

there's too much to do, don't let it both - er you. For -

get your trou - bles, try to be just like a cheer - ful chick - a - dee. And

whis - tle while you work. *(Whistle)* _____ Come

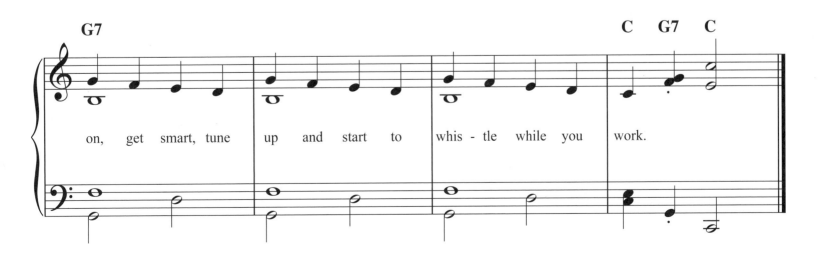

on, get smart, tune up and start to whis - tle while you work.

WHO'S AFRAID OF THE BIG BAD WOLF?

from Walt Disney's THREE LITTLE PIGS

Words and Music by FRANK CHURCHILL
Additional Lyric by ANN RONELL

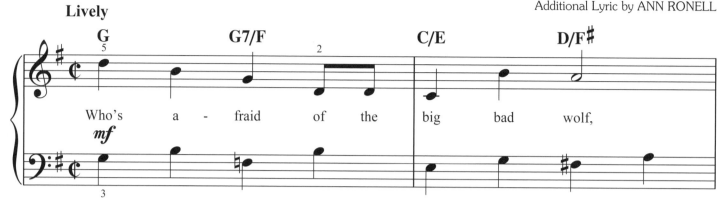

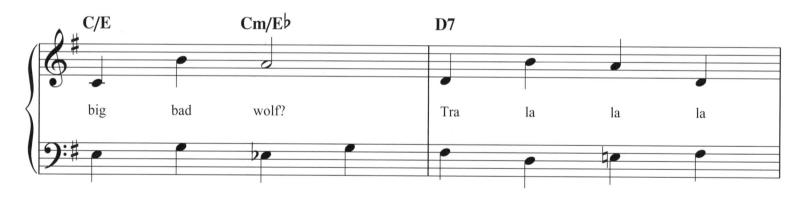

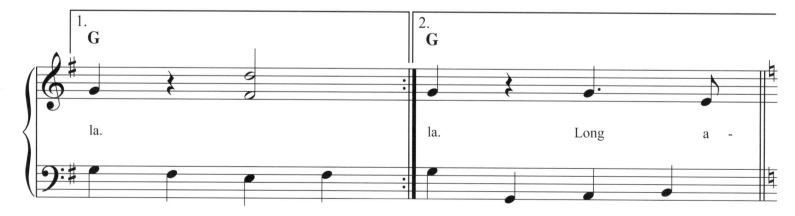

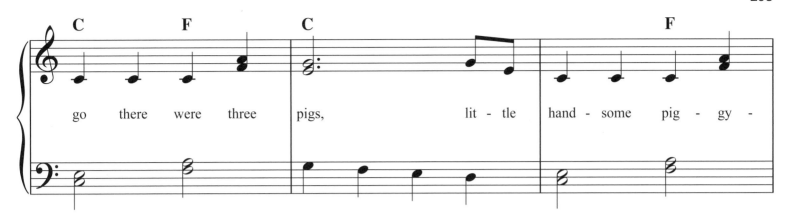

go there were three pigs, lit-tle hand-some pig-gy-

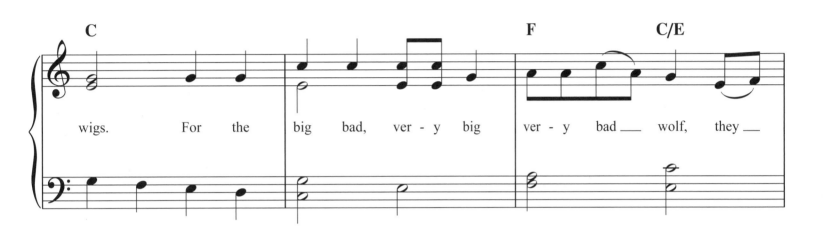

wigs. For the big bad, ver-y big ver-y bad __ wolf, they __

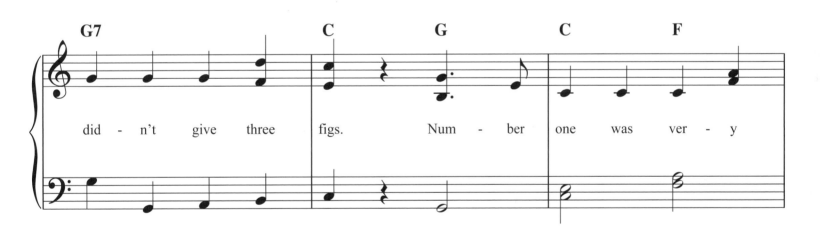

did-n't give three figs. Num-ber one was ver-y

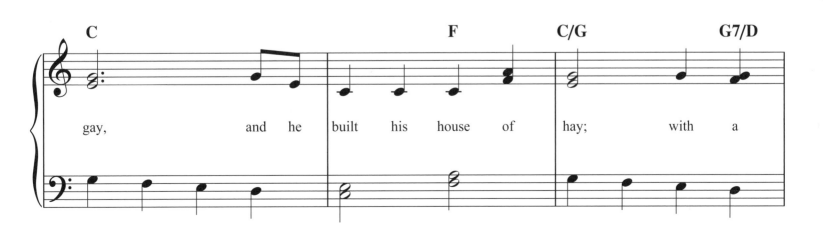

gay, and he built his house of hay; with a

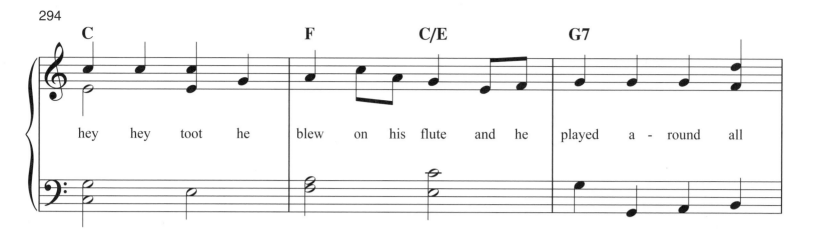

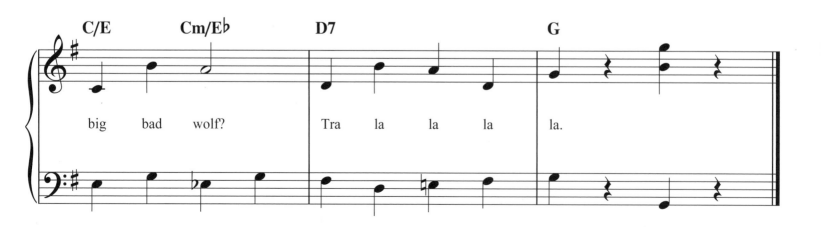

A WHOLE NEW WORLD

from Walt Disney's ALADDIN

Music by ALAN MENKEN
Lyrics by TIM RICE

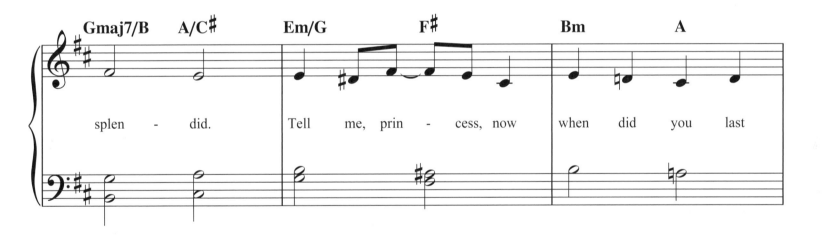

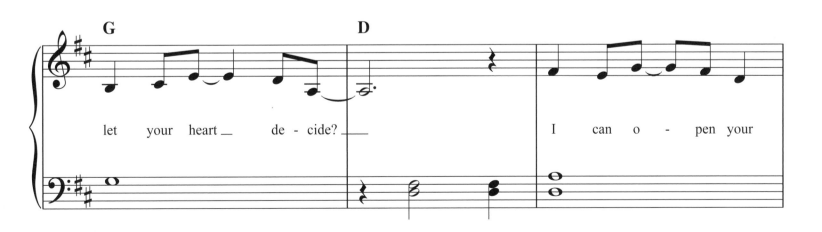

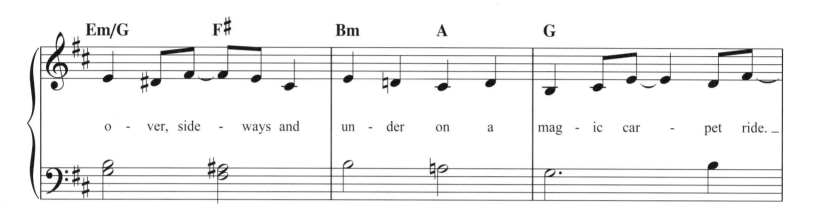

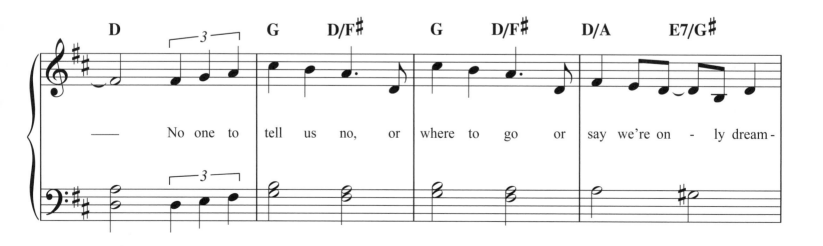

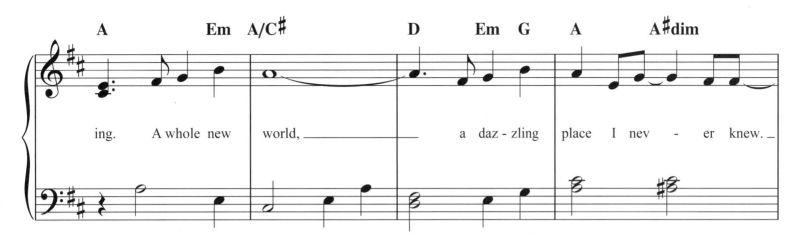

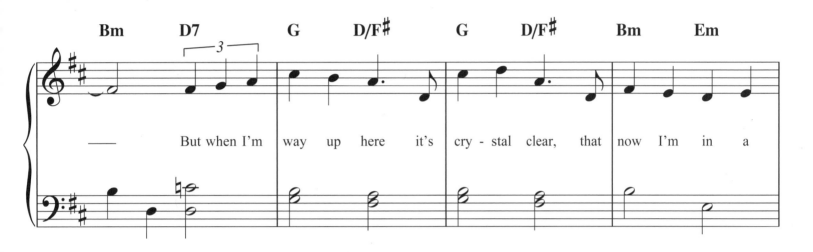

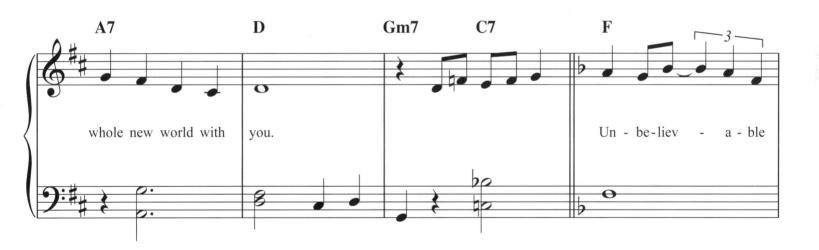

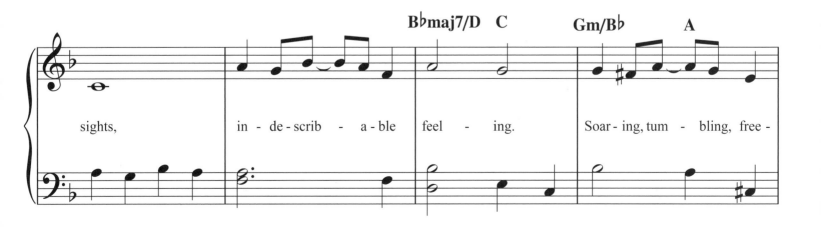

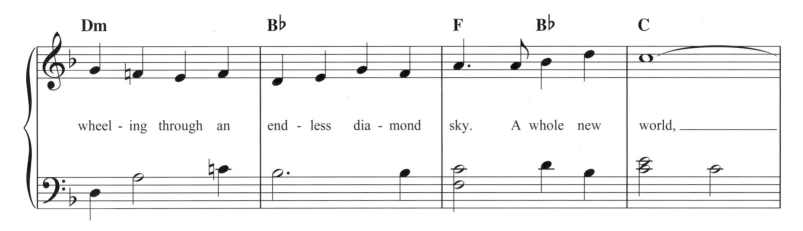

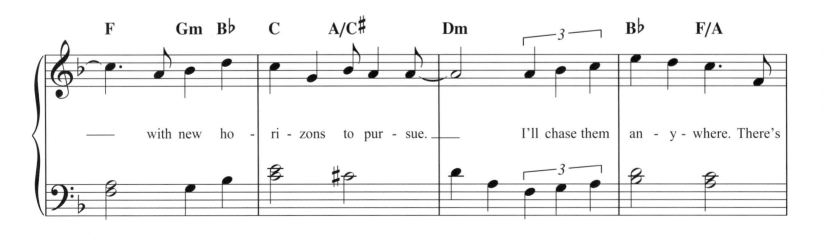

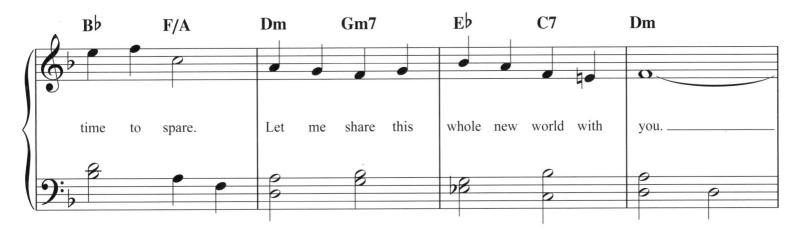

time to spare. Let me share this whole new world with you.

A whole new world, that's where we'll be.

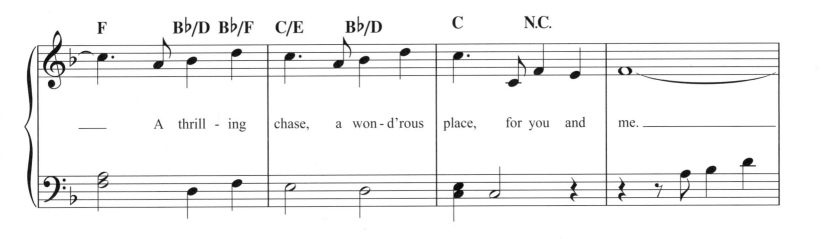

A thrill-ing chase, a won-d'rous place, for you and me.

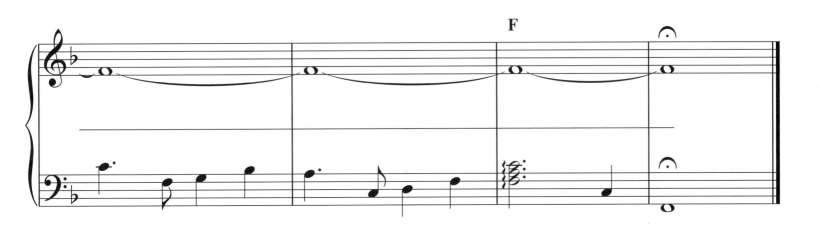

WINNIE THE POOH

from Walt Disney's THE MANY ADVENTURES OF WINNIE THE POOH

Words and Music by RICHARD M. SHERMAN
and ROBERT B. SHERMAN

a - cre wood where Chris - to - pher Ro - bin

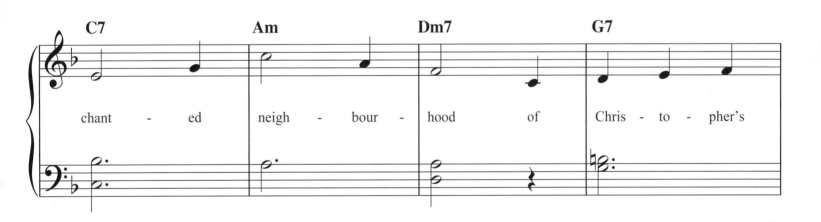

plays, _____ you will find the en -

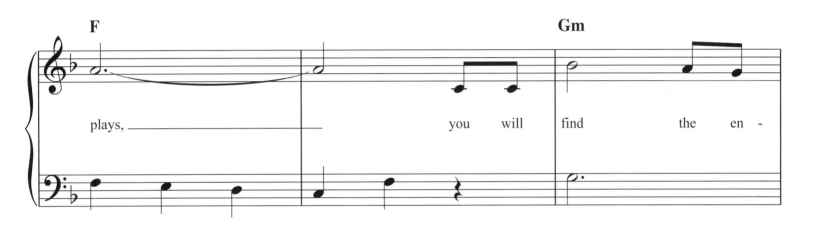

chant - ed neigh - bour - hood of Chris - to - pher's

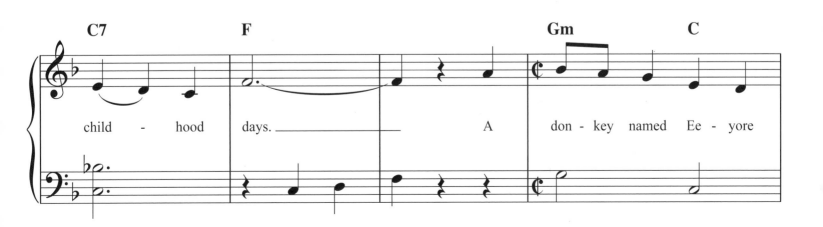

child - hood days. _____ A don - key named Ee - yore

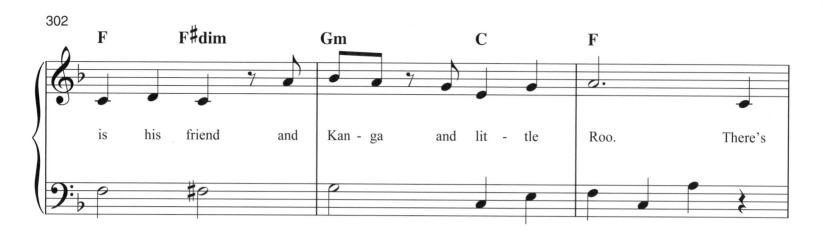

is his friend and Kan - ga and lit - tle Roo. There's

Rab - bit and Pig - let and there's Owl, but most of all Win - nie the

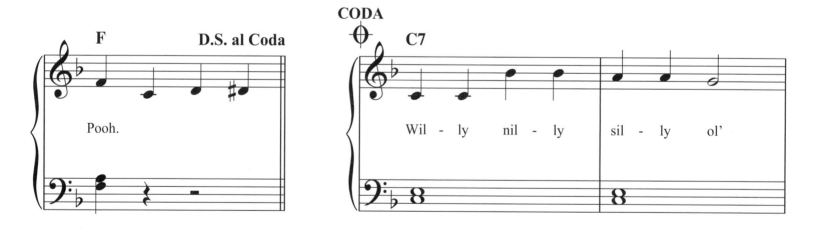

Pooh.

Wil - ly nil - ly sil - ly ol'

bear.

YELLOW SUBMARINE

Words and Music by JOHN LENNON
and PAUL McCARTNEY

March tempo

In the town _____ where I was born lived a

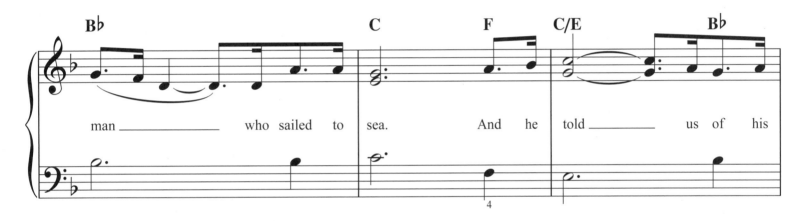

man _____ who sailed to sea. And he told _____ us of his

life in the land _____ of sub - ma - rines. So we

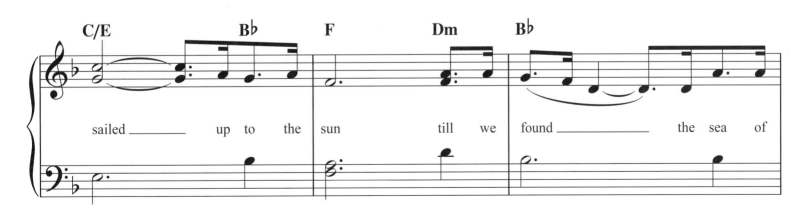

sailed _____ up to the sun till we found _____ the sea of

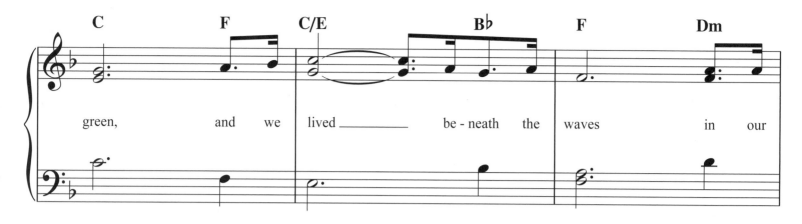

green, and we lived _____ be - neath the waves in our

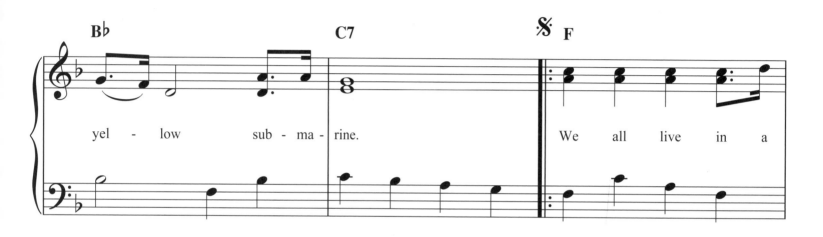

yel - low sub - ma - rine. We all live in a

yel - low sub - ma - rine, yel - low sub - ma - rine, yel - low sub - ma - rine.

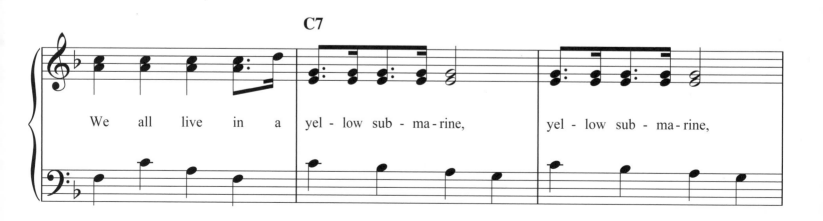

We all live in a yel - low sub - ma - rine, yel - low sub - ma - rine,

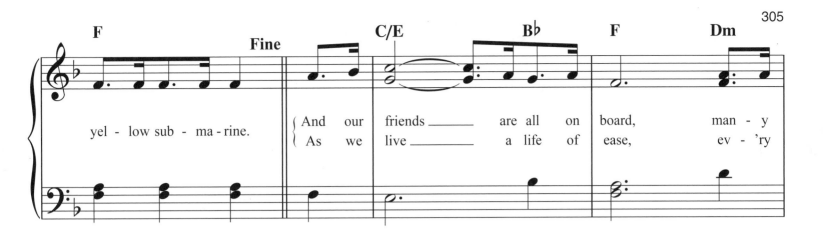

yel - low sub - ma - rine.
{ And our friends _____ are all on board, man - y
{ As we live _____ a life of ease, ev - 'ry

more of them _____ live next door. And the band _____ be - gins to
one of us _____ has all we need. Sky of blue _____ and sea of

1.

play:

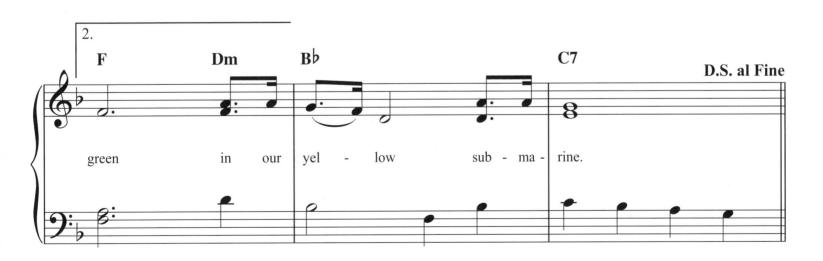

2.

green in our yel - low sub - ma - rine.

WON'T YOU BE MY NEIGHBOR?
(It's a Beautiful Day in the Neighborhood)
from MISTER ROGERS' NEIGHBORHOOD

Words and Music by
FRED ROGERS

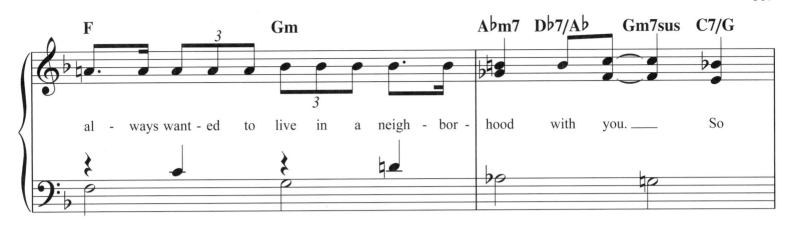

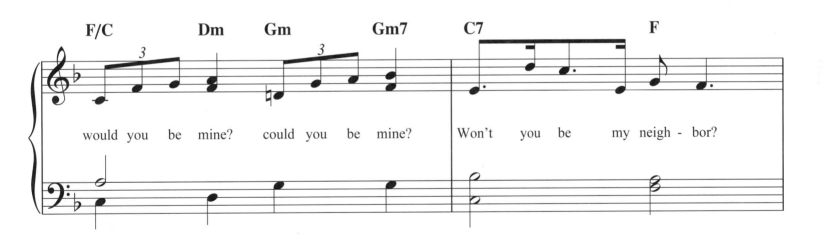

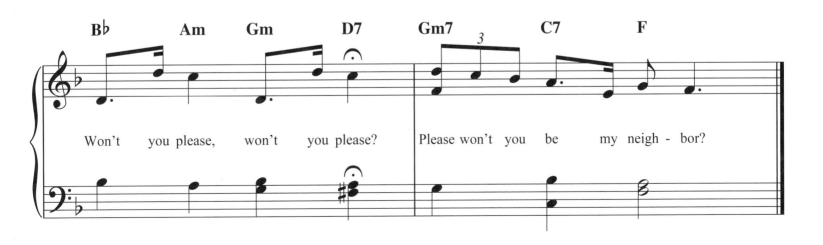

ZIP-A-DEE-DOO-DAH
from Walt Disney's SONG OF THE SOUTH

Words by RAY GILBERT
Music by ALLIE WRUBEL

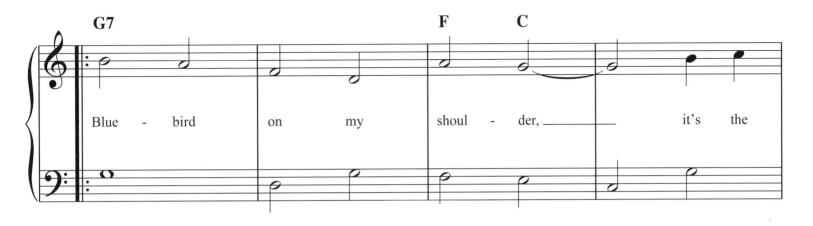

Blue - bird on my shoul - der, _____ it's the

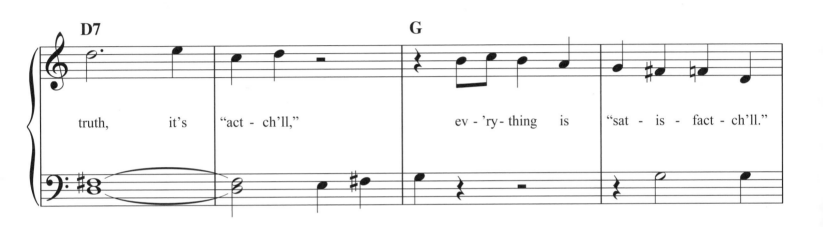

truth, it's "act - ch'll," ev - 'ry- thing is "sat - is - fact - ch'll."

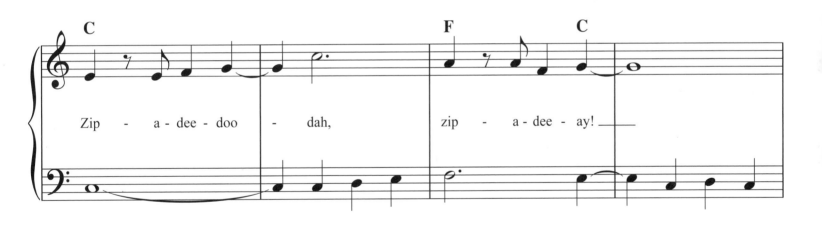

Zip - a - dee - doo - dah, zip - a - dee - ay! _____

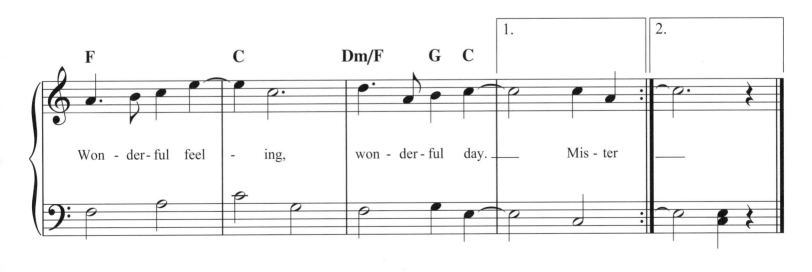

Won - der- ful feel - ing, won - der- ful day. _____ Mis - ter

YOU ARE MY SUNSHINE

Words and Music by
JIMMIE DAVIS

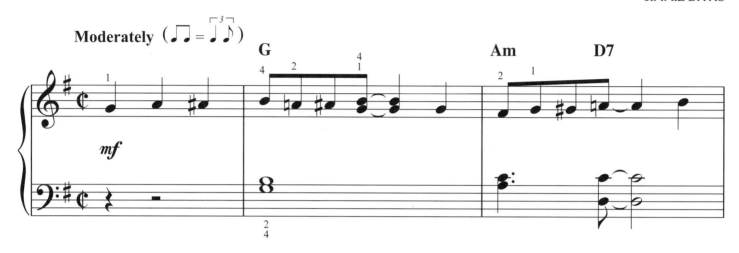

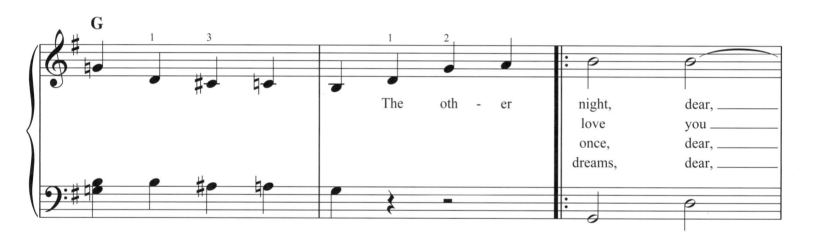

The oth - er   night,   dear, ____
            love   you ____
            once,   dear, ____
            dreams,   dear, ____

____ as I lay   sleep - ing ____   I dreamed I   held   you
____ and make you   hap - py ____   if you will   on - ly
____ you real - ly   loved   me ____   and no   one   could
____ you seem to   leave   me. ____   When I a - wake   my

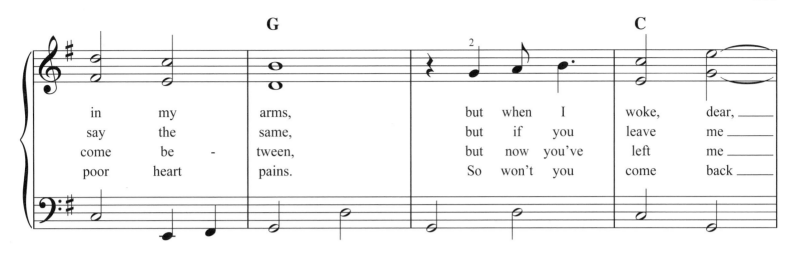

in my arms,
say the same,
come be - tween,
poor heart pains.

but when I woke, dear, _____
but if you leave me _____
but now you've left me _____
So won't you come back _____

_____ I was mis - tak - en, _____
_____ and love an - oth - er, _____
_____ to love an - oth - er. _____
_____ and make me hap - py? _____

and I hung my _____
you'll re - gret it _____
You have shat - tered _____
I'll for - give, dear, I'll

head and I cried.
all some - day.
all of my dreams.
take all the blame.

You are my sun - shine, _____

_____ my on - ly sun - shine. _____ You make _____ me hap - py when

skies   are   gray.   You'll nev - er   know,   dear, ___

___ how much I   love ___ you. ___   Please don't take my

1.-3.

4.

sun - shine a -   way.

I'll   al - ways
You told   me
In   all   my